LIFE and DEATH

IN THE CENTRAL HIGHLANDS

10 9 8 7 6 5 4 3 2

Permissions:
University of North Texas Press
1155 Union Circle #311336
Denton, TX 76203-5017

The paper used in this book meets the minimum requirements of the American National Standard
for Permanence of Paper for Printed Library Materials, z39.48.1984. Binding materials have been
chosen for durability.

Library of Congress Cataloging-in-Publication Data

Gillam, James T.
  Life and death in the Central Highlands : an American sergeant in the Vietnam War, 1968/1970 /
James T. Gillam ; foreword by Allan R. Millett.
     p. cm. -- (Number 5 in the North Texas military biography and memoir series)
  Previously published in 2006 by Edwin Mellen Press under the title: War in the Central
Highlands of Vietnam, 1968-1970.
  Includes bibliographical references and index.
ISBN 978-1-57441-292-5 (cloth : alk. paper)
ISBN 978-1-57441-951-1 (paper : alk. paper)
ISBN 978-1-57441-334-2 (ebook)

  1. Vietnam War, 1961-1975--Personal narratives, American. 2. Gillam, James T. 3. Vietnam War,
1961-1975--Campaigns--Vietnam--Central Highlands. 4. Central Highlands (Vietnam)--History.

5. Vietnam War, 1961-1975--Regimental histories. 6. United States. Army. Infantry Regiment, 22nd.
Battalion, 1st--History. I. Gillam, James T. War in the Central Highlands of Vietnam, 1968-1970. II.
Title. III. Series: North Texas military biography and memoir series ; no. 5

  DS559.5.G547 2010
  959.704'342092--dc22

2010015561

Life and Death in the Central Highlands: An American Sergeant in the Vietnam War, 1968–1970 is Number
5 in the North Texas Military Biography and Memoir Series

Previously published in 2006 by Edwin Mellen Press under the title *War in the Central Highlands of
Vietnam 1968–1970: An Historian's Experience.*

LIFE *and* DEATH
IN THE CENTRAL HIGHLANDS

An American Sergeant in the Vietnam War,
1968–1970

JAMES T. GILLAM

Number 5 in the North Texas Military Biography and Memoir Series

University of North Texas Press
Denton, Texas

Corporal Edward H. Gillam served in Vietnam with Company E, 2nd Battalion, 9th Marine Regiment, 3rd Marine Division. This book is dedicated to his memory.

This book is dedicated to many people. First among them are my family. My parents, James T. Gillam Sr., and Marie P. Gillam always encouraged my scholarship but they did not live to see it in hard copy from an academic press. Next are my wife Connie, my son Damon, and my daughters Jessica and Whitney. They all said to me for years, "you should write a book!" I thank you all for your encouragement and patience.

There are also some men I trained and served in Vietnam with who deserve special mention here. Among them are the four "G Men," Staff Sergeant Michael Mullen, and Specialist Fourth Class Robert Frost. Michael and Robert did not come home alive, but they are alive in memory.

Finally, there is my brother Corporal Edward H. Gillam (USMC Ret.). Ed "lost his life" in Vietnam, and he died in Ohio in January of 2005. Rest in peace, Ed, and thanks again for the advice that got me home alive.

Contents

Foreword

When Oliver Stone's movie *Platoon* sent us scurrying for a foxhole in our local theaters, I invited a faculty friend, Professor Robert Driscoll, to walk point with me on this cinematic stroll into Stone's Vietnam War. Bob had served in the Twenty-fifth Infantry Division at roughly the same time (1969–1970) and place (War Zones C and D in the III Corps area) as Stone. Both had been infantrymen. Jim Gillam's battalion (First of the 22d Infantry in Army-speak) belonged to the Fourth Infantry Division, which campaigned north of the Twenty-fifth's area of operations. Jim's tour, however, roughly matched Bob's in time, place, tactical environment, and "grunt" perspective. Bob and Jim had (and, I suspect, have) much in common, race excepted. They came from that part of our society, the demographic frontier between working and middle class, that furnishes the U.S. Army's best enlisted soldiers. They came from two-parent homes with siblings in northern Ohio where the work ethic and family security have been eroded by Rust Belt economic distress, but where attending college is still an ambivalent alternative to joining a union. College also remains a great family expense, which makes the Army college program very attractive. Bob and Jim both abandoned their indifferent early academic careers and their 2-S draft deferments to join the Army and become MOS 11B, basic infantryman, in an army fighting a war drifting toward disengagement. Unlike Jim, Bob did not complete a full tour since he was so severely wounded (twice) that our basketball-playing students thought he'd been in a bad motorcycle accident.

Bob liked *Platoon* despite some of its poetic license and the improbable death struggle of two veteran sergeants over the soul of one over-introspective PFC. It was too much *Billy Budd* meets *Heart of Darkness* with live ordnance. Bob's only mild complaint was to observe that all the nasty things that Stone portrayed probably happened to some unit in Vietnam while he was there, but not to one platoon in one company. My own objection, artistically speaking, was that *Platoon* was totally humorless. Many years ago the veteran Army tactical analyst and author S. L. A. Marshall made this point in his review of Norman Mailer's *The Naked and the Dead*. Although Mailer had been in combat in the Philippines, Marshall wondered if he had not been a pariah in his company for reasons cultural and behavioral because he never remembered the funny things— however macabre—that help soldiers cope with the insanity that lurks behind fear, pain, and exhaustion. Adolf Hitler had the same problem remembering anything funny in recalling his *frontsoldaten* services in World War I in *Mein Kampf*.

Jim Gillam experienced real combat in his Vietnam tour. His stunning accounts of killing and avoiding being killed ring true, in no small part because he still found some of his experiences humorous, then and now. Like Paul Fussell, Jim Gillam found irony in the infantry. He also served with more honor and skill than the literary lion of the ETO. Jim's memoir also adds further weight to some observations about the effect of ground combat in the Vietnam War upon the men who fought:

- They will always be self-conscious about their status as victims of a war that did not turn out well, but like the GIs of World War II, they know that winning alone does not relieve one of the guilt of killing and surviving. They know that surviving is seldom a matter of great fieldcraft and combat marksmanship and certainly not a moral judgment on one's future value to himself and society.

- For some human experiences there is no such thing as "closure." This mantra soothes only talk show hosts and passive non-participants.
- A wartime army creates its own absurdities that reflect the tension between those that fight and those that don't, complicated by issues of rank, job assignments, and access to privileged goods and facilities like clean uniforms and hot showers. As the social science pollsters that created the classic Samuel Stouffer, et al. *The American Soldier* learned, even World War II GIs, the "greatest generation," believed that the Army was often their greatest enemy. Bill Mauldin's "Willy" and "Joe" dissected that army of unequal danger and discomfort in the cartoons collected in *Up Front*.
- Comradeship in the field is a delicate association of individuals with a shared, common desire to be somewhere else not in harms' way. Other drives like revenge, fatalism, exhaustion, thirst, assertion of manliness, self-pity, and leadership responsibilities overwhelm sheer survivalism. Jim Gillam started and ended his tour as a leader, an infantry squad leader and platoon sergeant. Unless I missed an ambush or two in the reading, no one under Sergeant Gillam's direct command died in combat. [Gillam: Actually, I lost one.] His two Bronze Stars were well-earned along with his Combat Infantry Badge. Although wounded several times, Jim did not leave the field for treatment in a field hospital, so he never generated the paperwork for a Purple Heart or two or three. Although he would be appalled at the thought, his attention to duty was "lifer" behavior, a concern for the well-being of his squad that represents the best of NCO leadership in any army.

Jim Gillam may still suffer from post-traumatic stress disorder (PTSD), but when I worked with him during his graduate school days at The Ohio State University, he was focused, firm, and fearless in dealing with the whining freshmen in my American history survey class. He was a model teaching assistant. I'm sure our indulged, rudderless students frustrated him; in this operation he was still humping in the bush while I directed operations from afar or above in the best tradition of a full professor and Marine Corps Reserve colonel. Jim still cleaned his rifle first, metaphorically speaking, and kept his troops in hand.

In thinking about Jim's ability to write about his war experiences, I am drawn again and again to the writings of other enlisted men in other wars. Jim's story is not like Lester Atwell, *Private*, because Atwell remained the ultimate "Sad Sack," a GI who slid through his quixotic world of war without taking responsibility for anything but his own survival. Jim was no Audie Murphy or Ross Carter, warriors truly consumed by war and death, perhaps not "war lovers" in John Hersey's usage, but men who felt empowered by their ability to kill and ennobled in their grief. Jim's intelligence and sensitivity really made him the literary legatee of the soldiers of the Army Specialized Training Program who rapidly and reluctantly traded in their college books for M-1s in the winter of 1944–1945. Starved for infantry replacements in its European theater divisions, the Army cancelled the ASTP assignments of over 100,000 high-quality enlisted men and threw them into the war just in time for the Battle of the Bulge. The resulting literary output by the survivors included William P. McGivern, *The Soldiers of '44*; William Wharton, *A Midnight Clear*; and William Eastland, *Castle Keep*. These autobiographical novels provide the same mix of insight, honesty, descriptive power, and shock over the behavior of "normal" men caught in a madness of ground combat.

I am honored to be asked by Jim Gillam to write a foreword to his wartime memoir. He deserves a broad audience because he has written both as a professional historian and scarred "grunt." He is sharing his long emotional march to come to terms with the young GI he once was, not an unshared trip, but nevertheless lonely. The fact that Jim Gillam fought in a war the United States declined to win does not subtract one whit from the honorable and heroic nature of his own service. And Bob Driscoll will like this book, too.

Allan R. Millett
Maj. Gen. Raymond E. Mason, Jr.
Professor of Military History
The Ohio State University

Preface

This book is the product of all the pieces of the puzzle that I call my identity. I am a veteran of the Vietnam War, and I am also an Associate Professor of Chinese history. This book is the product of my military experiences, academic training, and the four decades I have lived as a veteran with a story to tell. It is essentially a memoir dedicated to the men I served with in Vietnam and Cambodia. It is also a description of the stages by which a politically naïve African-American college student evolved into a savage who hunted and killed people for almost a year.

I am a middle-aged baby boomer who has lived with the specter of Vietnam on the edge of my life, or dead center of it, since I was a child. I was seven years old when the French were defeated at Dienbienphu. As a second grader, I wrote a weekly current events report on Vice President Nixon's plans to send American paratroopers to help them. I was young enough and naïve enough to think soldiers, especially paratroopers, were pretty cool. After all, I had a father and several uncles who were veterans of World War II, and paratroopers were my favorite kind of soldier. So, as a child, I was all for sending American troops to Vietnam.

My brother Edward H. Gillam joined the Marines in 1964 and he got to Vietnam before I did. He served with the Second Battalion, 9th Marine Regiment, 3rd Marine Division, from June 1966 until he was brought home aboard the hospital ship *Repose* in March 1967. He was walking point for a patrol and got washed downstream during a river crossing. No one went to look for him. Instead, he was listed as missing in action. Ed wandered a week in the jungle, sick and unarmed until a unit of the First Cavalry (Airmobile) brought him to their base camp. My brother lost his life in Vietnam, but he didn't die until 2005.

My journey to Vietnam began in the fall of 1968. I was drafted into the Army as one of the replacements for the flood of casualties caused by the Tet Offensive in January of that year. I went to Fort Knox, Kentucky, for basic training. After that, I was assigned to the infantry. I learned the skills of an infantryman at Fort Polk, Louisiana, and from there I went on to the Non Commissioned Officers Academy at Fort Benning, Georgia. By the spring of 1969, I was a graduate of the NCO Academy and I then served a brief stint as a Training Sergeant at Fort McClellan, Alabama. In September of 1969, I joined the Vietnam Class of 1969–70.

When I arrived in Vietnam, I was assigned to B Company, First Battalion, 22nd Regiment, of the Fourth Infantry Division. I spent almost a year as a squad leader and sometime platoon sergeant in the Central Highlands of Vietnam. In May 1970 B Company and the rest of the battalion were attached to a composite unit called II FORCEV, and we participated in the brief invasion of Cambodia. The invasion was an integral part of President Richard Nixon's Vietnamization strategy. When II FORCEV was withdrawn to Vietnam, I went back to one last search-and-destroy mission in the Central Highlands, and then I was separated early from the Army to return to college at Ohio University in Athens, Ohio.

I earned a Bachelor's Degree in political science in the summer of 1971. In 1977, I earned an M.A. in Chinese History from Case Western Reserve University, and my Ph. D. in Chinese History was awarded in 1985. Clearly the academic journey was longer and more circuitous than normal, and there will be more about why in the epilogue.

The degrees are important because my training as a scholar is critical to the way I have perceived and described the events in this book. For example, as an academic, I describe myself a member of the Class of 1985 from The Ohio State University, and a tenured professor of nearly twenty-five years experience. When I consider my involvement with Vietnam over the course of my adult life, I have also found it convenient to continue the academic's practice of defining stages of development as classes, or stages of process designated by the year of occurrence. Thus, I also consider myself to be a member of the Draft Class of 1968, the Vietnam Class of 1969–1970, and the Vietnam Veteran's Class of 1970.

The Draft Class of 1968 includes the thousands of men who were conscripted and trained for military service that year. The Vietnam Class of 1969–1970 includes those men and women who finished their training and served in Vietnam. I finished my training in the late summer of 1969 and served ten and a half months as a sergeant with the Fourth Infantry Division in the Central Highlands of Vietnam. The Vietnam Veteran's Class of 1970 are the men and women who survived the experience and tried to get on with their lives. Some of us were better at that than others.

This is the second time I have written a book on my experiences in Vietnam. The first book was called *The War in the Central Highlands of Vietnam: An Historian's Experience*, and was published by the Edwin Mellen Press in 2006. In that book, I combined two of the basic formats of the historian: the monographic, or focused treatment on a specialized topic, and the memoir into a single work. I described that book as a "memograph." I chose to combine those styles in order to provide an historical context for the stages, or "classes" of my involvement with Vietnam.

The Mellen edition of my Vietnam experience contains four heavily documented, monographic sections. The first is a study of the Tet Offensive that created vacancies for the Draft Class of

1968. The next one was a study of the politics and social consequences of the draft and how it was used to create the institution known as the "Vietnam Only Army." The third part of the
monographic treatment focused on the Vietnamization process
that went into effect just before I went to Vietnam. The final
monographic section was an explanation of the regional politics,
diplomacy, and history attendant to the Cambodian invasion in
the spring of 1970.

The sources I relied on for the monographic sections of the
Mellen Press edition as well as the current edition of this book,
are the standard tools of the historian: primary sources from the
National Archives and various on-line sources, periodicals, and
even other monographs and edited volumes of scholarly essays.
In all those sources, especially the archival ones, there has been a
reliance on the impersonal reporting and statistical focus characteristic of an army conducting a war of attrition. So, operational
names and the description of the actions of what the army calls
"maneuver units," like brigades and battalions, figured prominently in both editions. Also, both editions have statistics aplenty
about things like tonnage of supplies, captured weapons, and the
numbers of killed and wounded on both sides.

One of the major consequences of relying on those kinds of
sources is that the reader is rarely cognizant of the reality behind
the formal reports and statistics. Monographs by definition do
not say, for example, what it was like to finally get to Vietnam,
or to hear about or witness the death of friends. Neither do they
explain the daily anxiety of walking point, being the first man
on the trail when there is the likelihood of an ambush, or the
stark terror of beating someone to death in a pitch-black tunnel inside a mountain. Furthermore, primary sources like After
Action Reports and Duty Officer's Logs fail to address the details
of things like the long period of recovery and adjustment that all
veterans of Vietnam have faced: social awkwardness, the lack of
an appropriate civilian frame of social references, post traumatic

stress, and the search for that overused term called closure. It is for those reasons that I have made some subtle, but what I hope are important changes from my last attempt to describe what happened during the year after the Tet Offensive in the Central Highlands of Vietnam.

The first of those changes was the significant reduction of the monographic foci of the story. The Tet Offensive started with the Battle of Kontum. This book uses that battle as an example of the offensive and the detailed description of other major battles of Tet throughout the Central Highlands have been omitted. The lengthy discussion of the politics, structure, and social consequences of the draft were also largely curtailed in this volume. They were replaced with a more personal account of how that system felt from the inside when I found my "Greetings from Uncle Sam" in my mailbox. The political motives and deceptive chicanery of the Vietnamization process was also reduced in this volume. This time I focused on describing the naïve hope Vietnamization created for me and other members of the Vietnam Class of 1969–70. Many of us actually thought that at best, we might not even go to Vietnam, or at worst, that we might arrive in September and be home for the holidays. Almost all the regional politics and diplomatic history before the Cambodian invasion are gone too. They were replaced by a personalized account of the military preparations for invasion, the fighting at the landing zone on the far edge of the invasion, and the fatalistic attitude I developed about dying there during my last month in the war.

I also added a few things to this book in order to supplement its personal, memoir style. I added maps of areas where I served and diagrams of a few specific incidents I was involved in. The purpose was to give a visual reference and background to the life and death struggles that happened in those places. Since memoirs are personal, this book also has photographs of the people and places that were important parts of the story in this book. As a memoirist, I have described events as they actually occurred, and relied when possible on primary sources to support my recall and descriptions. I have altered the record in only one regard. Two names, Carl Dover and Johnny Wolf, have been used to replace the names of two men in B Company, First Battalion, 22nd Infantry Regiment. All other names and facts described here are real, accurate, and described as they happened.

1. ✹

The Tet Offensive: Making Space for the Draft Class of 1968

Major Attacks in the Tet Offensive of 1968
Source: *Commons.wikimedia.org/wik/File:Tet-Offensive.*

THE TET OFFENSIVE

In every war, there are critical offensives and battles that redirect the course of the conflict. The Tet Mau Than, or Tet Offensive was one of those kinds of events during the Vietnam War. I learned a lot about Tet in January of 1991. At that time, I was back in Vietnam as a guest of the Vietnamese Ministry of Education. I was part of a delegation of Fulbright Scholars who were invited to attend seminars in Ho Chi Minh City and Hanoi on post-colonial Vietnamese history. An important part of that history is what the Vietnamese call the Second Indochina War. We call it the Vietnam War. So, as expected, there was a significant focus on the Tet Offensive and its effect on the war.

Retired Gen. Tran Van Tra was the lead seminarian for our sessions on Tet, and I had the opportunity to meet him the evening before the seminar at his home. He sent his eldest daughter with a car to pick up me and Professor Keith Taylor, a faculty member at Princeton University, for dinner. Taylor and Tran knew each other personally during the war, and each man had tried to kill the other. In 1989, Tran visited Princeton on a speaking engagement and spent a week in Professor Taylor's home. The general matched Professor Taylor's hospitality with an open invitation to his home if Taylor ever came back to Vietnam. Taylor and I were two of the combat veterans among our delegation and we got on well. So, he invited me to go with him for dinner with the general. That evening, General Tran and I only spent a little time talking about the war. The most memorable thing he said to me about Tet was that its basic purpose was "to break your will to war."[1] Then, the conversation shifted and Tran and I did what old men often do. We bragged about our children. We both have three: a son and two daughters for each of us.

The next day, our entire group met at the Ministry of Education and the history lesson began. Tran was especially qualified for the task of seminar leader. He was not only one of the planners of the offensive, he also commanded the troops who carried it out. In a concise briefing, translated into French and English, Tran set out for us the strategic, political, and diplomatic objectives of Tet. He said that he and the Politburo of the Party Central Committee in Hanoi had three goals that combined strategy and politics when they planned the Tet Mao Than. The first objective was to attack and destroy the bulk of the Army of the Republic of Vietnam (ARVN) troops, cripple the South Vietnamese government at all levels, and incite a popular uprising to replace Saigon's administration. It was for this reason that Tran and most Vietnamese call the event the Tet Mau Than, which means "General Offensive and Uprising of the Tet Holiday."

Tran and the Politburo also planned to destroy major portions of American forces and their materiel to prevent them from fulfilling their political and military support for Saigon. Finally, they planned to force America to accept defeat in South Vietnam, and end all aggression against North Vietnam. In a near repetition of his statement the night before, he summed up this objective by saying emphatically, "we were determined to break America's will to war."[2]

Next, Tran set us straight about the duration of Tet. Most Americans who know anything at all about the Tet Offensive work from the misperception that it began at the start of the Lunar New Year celebration on January 31, 1968, and ended with the defeat of the combined North Vietnamese Army (NVA)-Viet Cong contingent that held the ancient city of Hue on February 24, 1968. That period, according to Tran, was only the first of three phases of the offensive. The next one ran from May 4 to June 18. The third phase was from August 17 to September 23.[3]

Phase two of Tet was a focused attack on the ARVN command structure in and around Saigon. Tran's forces scored some big hits. Nine field-grade officers (colonels and generals) were killed, and Gen. Nguyen Ngoc Loan, who achieved instant fame for his on-camera execution of a Viet Cong prisoner, was wounded in both legs.[4] Tet's third phase shifted the first phase's attacks against large bases and cities to heavy fighting against maneuver-size units of battalions and brigades in the area Tran called the Bulwark B2 area. That was the region north and west of Saigon. In that six-week period, Tran's forces destroyed twelve American mechanized infantry battalions, one battalion of ARVN troops, and most of several companies. They also took control of over 200 villages and hamlets with a population of about 1.5 million people.[5]

After a midmorning break, General Tran began a summary of the consequences of Tet from the Vietnamese perspective. The opinions he offered that day in Ho Chi Minh City have also appeared elsewhere by him in print, and I think he has remained remarkably consistent in all those versions. His shortest written version appeared in an essay he wrote for the edited volume called *The Vietnam War: Vietnamese and American Perspectives*. In those pages, Tran said there were two primary political consequences of Tet. The first was the replacement of Gen. William Westmoreland, the MACV Commander, with Gen. Creighton Abrams. The second was Lyndon Johnson's virtual resignation from the presidency on March 31, 1968.

Tran also talked to us about what he felt were important strategic and diplomatic consequences of Tet, and he has written about them, too. In his opinion, the biggest strategic change was the shift of American efforts from "search-and-destroy" missions to "clear-and-hold" missions. The former type is an aggressive attempt to locate an enemy and his materiel and destroy both. Then, the units move on to do the same thing in another area of operations. In clear-and-hold missions, the idea is to destroy the enemy in a limited area, then remain in that area. The change, he said, was consistent with a policy of "Vietnamizing" the responsibility for the war and "de-escalation" of America's role. Finally, Tran pointed out that Lyndon Johnson's decision to speed up talks at the Paris Peace Conference was also an important diplomatic consequence of Tet and another clear signal that America had lost its "will to war." [6]

As an American historian I find myself in agreement with many of General Tran's opinions about the Tet Offensive, especially its political, diplomatic, and strategic consequences. The differences I see in our evaluation I think, are the result of nationality, culture, and of course, personal circumstances when the Tet Offensive happened. Tran was a long-serving warrior in a national war of liberation. I was a college student observing the war through the lenses of the American news media and college debates. Years later, I did begin what I hope has been an organized and scholarly study of Tet and its effects, but still, a critical difference remains between Tran's view and mine. He lived the experience and I did not.

When General Tran started the Tet Offensive, I was a junior political science major at Ohio University in Athens, Ohio. Like most Americans, my experience of Tet was limited to the daily dinner-time ritual of scanning the major print media, and watching either the *Huntley-Brinkley Report* on NBC, or Walter Cronkite's *CBS Evening News* report. What struck us then, and even years later, was the astounding surge in casualties. The year after I talked with General Tran, Ronald Spector, a Vietnam Veteran and historian, published a monograph called *After Tet: The Bloodiest Year in Vietnam*. Spector's book quantified General Tran's claim of success in causing American casualties and put them into a stunning historical context. Spector's figures are here, with some analysis, as a reminder of the cost in blood that Americans paid that year.

In the first week of the offensive, 203 Americans were killed, and that was the lowest number of deaths for the six months covered in the report. The death rate peaked in the second week of May 1968 when 616 Americans died, and on four occasions, there were weeks when more than 500 Americans died. After reviewing six months of casualty reports compiled by the White

U.S. CASUALTIES FEB.–MAY 1968 AS COMPILED BY THE WHITE HOUSE SITUATION ROOM			
WEEK	KILLED	WOUNDED-NOT HOSPITALIZED	HOSPITALIZED
27 Jan–3 Feb	203	499	543
4–10 Feb	421	666	720
11–17 Feb	No Report		
18–24 Feb	584	775	839
25 Feb–2 March	536	989	1070
3–9 March	520	1262	1398
10–16 March	356	913	991
17–23 March	371	948	1026
24–30 March	335	1800	2000
31 March–6 April	290	1500	1600
7–13 April	369	1251	1356
14–20 April	287	694	752
21–27 April	324	No Report	No Report
28 April–4 May	374	No Report	No Report
5–11 May	616	1139	1235
12–18 May	552	1149	1244
19–25 May	443	1360	1475
26 May–1 June	459	No Report	No Report[7]

House Situation Room for President Johnson, Spector wrote that "From January to July 1968 the overall rate of men killed in action in Vietnam would reach an all time high and would *exceed* the rate for the Korean War and the Mediterranean and Pacific theaters during World War II."[8]

The Situation Room also recorded two categories of wounded: those who were not hospitalized and those who were. Men in the former category could have had minor wounds or, they could not be taken to a hospital. During the time I spent in Vietnam, I experienced this situation often due to the triple canopy jungle or the lack of transportation. Also, a commander could decide to keep what were called walking wounded in the field if he was short handed. After I got to Vietnam, I was one of the walking wounded on several occasions. I was struck by grenade shrapnel twice and shot twice. Sending me to a hospital was never mentioned.

The intense media coverage of the Tet Offensive allowed Americans to see the war as it happened. We also watched historic political events caused by the war. We read about and saw the attack on the American Embassy in Saigon; we saw Ambassador Ellsworth Bunker's evacuation from his official residence by heavily armed soldiers. [9] We were daily observers of the dramatic battle for control of the Marine base at Khe Sanh, and, of course, we argued interminably about whether Khe Sanh, was another Dienbienphu.

The day after the attack on the American Embassy, American Tet watchers also saw what was, up to that time, the most memorable and controversial incident of the war. A Viet Cong, the last of his unit, was captured and delivered with bound hands to Gen. Nguyen Ngoc Loan, commander of the South Vietnamese Police. General Loan shot the man in the head with a .38 Special revolver. Associated Press photographer Eddie Adams recorded the killing, and a Vietnamese cameraman working for NBC videotaped the incident.[10] The execution was shown on the evening newscasts across the nation, and the photo was used as the front cover on the next edition of *Newsweek* magazine. Walter Cronkite, the leading news anchor of the era, broadcast his nightly anchor spot from the CBS studio in New York or Saigon. At the end of his broadcast in late February, Cronkite responded to the murder witnessed by most of America. He said, "We have been too often disappointed by the optimism of the American leaders, both in Vietnam and Washington, to have faith any longer in the silver linings they find in the darkest clouds . . . The bloody experience of Vietnam is to end in a stalemate."[11] Lyndon Johnson, who was watching the show, said, "If I have lost Walter Cronkite, I have lost Mr. Average Citizen."[12]

The massive casualty count, the daily observance of the war in real time, and the political reactions to the war led President Lyndon Johnson to important strategic and political decisions. Gen. William Westmoreland, the MACV Commander in Vietnam, had requested an additional 206,000 troops. Secretary of Defense Clark Clifford, speaking for a presidential advisory committee, recommended against the increase, and President Johnson agreed with him.[13] Clifford's rationale appeared later in an essay for *Foreign Affairs* magazine. He wrote that "a further substantial increase in American forces could only increase the devastation and the Americanization of the war, and thus leave us even further from our goal of . . . peace."[14]

Clifford's committee recommendation was made public by the press on March 24, 1968. It was part of Charles Mohr's *New York Times* article called "Departure of Westmoreland May Spur Shift in Strategy." Mohr's piece also told the American people that President Johnson had recalled Westmoreland to Washington for reassignment to the Pentagon where he would serve as Chief of Staff of the Army.[15]

If there were doubts that kicking Westmoreland upstairs from the command of MACV to the Pentagon was a sign of strategic change, they were cleared away decisively by President Johnson's historic speech on the evening of March 31, 1968. I watched that too, on the television in the lounge of Gamerstsfelder Hall, the dormitory where I lived. That dormitory, like many others that spring, was often the scene of heated debates about the war, Tet, and the draft. That last topic—the draft—was a really hot one for me because I was on academic probation and in danger of losing my category 2-S deferment from the draft. That meant I was potential "draft bait" and "cannon fodder" for the war machine.

As we sat around waiting for the broadcast, there was also much discussion of the news in the 6:00 p.m. *Huntley-Brinkley Report* that Marine Capt. Charles Robb, Lyndon Johnson's son-in-law, was landing on Okinawa, en route to Vietnam that day. Many of us, especially those of us in academic trouble, felt that if the president's in-laws were being thrown into the fight, anyone without a precious 2-S deferment for student status really had no chance of avoiding the draft, and eventual combat in Vietnam.

At 9:00 p.m. sharp, a haggard and depressed-looking President Johnson appeared at his desk in the Oval Office. He announced three important policy changes. First, he said there was to be an immediate, unilaterally initiated halt of the bombing campaign against targets in North Vietnam. The only exceptions were to be in cases where enemy troop concentrations directly threatened our men in forward positions. It was the president's hope that this concession would expedite negotiations in Paris to end the war. Johnson went on to say that he had named Averell Harriman, a diplomat of long standing, to be his personal representative in Paris. It was Johnson's last announcement, though, that was a real shocker for viewers in the dorm, and the rest of America, too. Lyndon Johnson announced that he would not seek or accept the nomination for another term as president.[16] In effect, a sitting president of the United States had announced his virtual resignation.

I didn't know it then, in March 1968, but the plan of Tran Van Tra to "break the American will to war" had just been realized. Twenty-three years later, when Tran and I discussed the war in his home, I finally got it. On March 31, 1968, Tran's Tet Offensive had achieved two of its most important objectives. Tran's stated goals were to end America's willingness to fight, speed the negotiations at the Paris Peace Talks, cause a popular uprising against the South Vietnamese government by attacking it at home, and bring the war to the cities and other areas that had been considered relatively safe during the war. [17] It had also set in motion the series of events that drew me into the Army and eventually to Vietnam.

CONCLUSION: VACANCIES TO BE FILLED

Judging from the reports filed by American units, the American ambassador's office, and MACV, the Tet Mau Than spent itself in the Central Highlands by the end of July 1968. It did continue, however, in other parts of Vietnam, particularly the region adjacent to Saigon, until late September. Yet, the tactical and even the strategic stages were both set in the Central Highlands for most of the next year. More importantly for me, the personnel picture was set. Most of the 14,589 men who would die in the Tet Offensive in 1968 were already in their body bags, and the Draft Boards across America had begun steps to fill those vacancies. Of the Draft Class of 1968, 475,200 would become the Vietnam Class of 1969.[18] I was a member of both classes.

2.

Training the Draft Class of 1968

MOVING TOWARD THE DRAFT CLASS OF 1968

In the winter and spring when the Tet Offensive unfolded, I was closing a very poor performance as a student at Ohio University in Athens, Ohio. My poor performance was caused in part by a personal dilemma that reached all the way from Vietnam and struck me in Athens, Ohio. In December 1967, my brother Edward was serving in Vietnam with the 3rd Marine Division, and his name appeared in the obituary list of the Marine Corps monthly magazine, *Leatherneck*. He was walking point when he was swept away crossing a river. His company commander never went to look for him. He wandered in the jungle, alone, unarmed, and delirious from malaria and dysentery. A week later, a unit from the 1st Cavalry (Airmobile) found him and delivered him to the hospital ship USS *Repose*. It was February 1968 before we found out he was alive.

In March 1968, Ed arrived at the Naval Health Clinic at the Great Lakes Naval Station in Chicago. He had gone to Vietnam as a wiry 165-pound Marine with the stamina of a horse. I barely recognized him as the man I had shared a bedroom with for most of my life. He weighed 116 pounds and was bedridden.

He had malaria and amoebic dysentery from the river water he had swallowed. At the time, I was in the Reserve Officers Training Corps (ROTC). ROTC gave me a small scholarship and expected me to enter the Army as a lieutenant when I graduated from college. Initially, I accepted those conditions because I was certain to be drafted, and I felt being an officer rather than an enlisted man would be better. But my brother's experience soured me on all things military, and I resigned from ROTC at the end of the semester.

My life and that of many other African-Americans was also deeply touched by the assassination of Martin Luther King, Jr., on April 4, 1968, at the Lorraine Motel in Memphis, Tennessee. There were riots on many college campuses, and mine was no exception. I had not yet resigned from the ROTC program and, therefore, I had access to some of the antiquated World War II weapons and ammunition we trained with. My refusal to get the keys to the armory and pass them to angry African-American students made my life difficult. Twice that semester, the college closed for several days because of violence. My indifferent performance in classes when the campus was open put me right on the borderline for dismissal. I appealed a couple of grades and went home to work for the summer.

As I expected, the appeals were turned down, and I was dismissed from the university. Within a month, I was notified that I had lost my draft deferment. My draft notice came on August 14, 1968. It was the day my first niece Schauna was born. My brother and I had gone to see her and his wife, and then we went to dinner and a movie. When I got home, I thought to bring the mail in for my parents, and my notice to report for a physical in two weeks was there. My only surprise was that it took them three months to get around to sending it.

JOINING THE DRAFT CLASS OF 1968

I almost failed my physical. They said I had a chronic inflammation of the lower back and spinal column called myoficitis. At day's end, another man and I anxiously waited for a panel of doctors to decide our fate. He had been hit by a garbage truck and his hip healed badly, causing a limp. When they came out and told him he was leaving for Fort Knox, Kentucky, in the morning, I called home on the pay phone and told my mother I would be about two years late for dinner.

The medical panel's deliberations made us miss the plane to Kentucky, so they put several of us in a cheap hotel room and told us to stay there. I went AWOL my first night in the Army. I went back to see my fiancée. We called some friends and I had a second going away party. The next day, I got on a plane with a hangover and two hundred other men in the Draft Class of 1968 and we flew to Fort Knox, Kentucky.

BASIC TRAINING

The average draftee spent about six months in the Army before he got to Vietnam. The first six weeks were spent on basic training. This was when you got your haircut, learned to march in straight lines, and learned to salute everything and everyone that outranked you. It was also a time when the Army stripped away our civilian identities and replaced them with the physical and psychological pieces that make soldiers. I imagine the process of "seasoning" for slaves must have been somewhat similar. In both cases, the subject starts out with a certain physique, culture, and behavior. Then, gradually a new version of all those things is created.

They started with the physique by emphasizing two things: cardiovascular endurance and upper body strength. So, from day one, there was a lot of double timing, which is just basically jogging, to build endurance. We were never allowed to walk if we were outside a building. The distances we ran gradually increased until most of us could comfortably cover a five-mile run through the hills of Kentucky. The upper body development was built almost exclusively on pushups. We did hundreds of them every day. Every mistake in training required at least twenty, and drill sergeants believed in group responsibility. So, if anyone made a mistake, everyone did pushups.

For sedentary civilians, the physical side of basic training was the worst part. It wasn't that way for me. I played football, wrestled, and ran track in high school. In college, I joined intramural teams for football and wrestling, and worked out with the gymnastic team. I also worked construction jobs in the summer with my dad, so the physical side of basic wasn't all that bad. It was like being locked in gym class with a crew of slightly demented phys-ed instructors.

On the psychological side, I also had some advantages, but, still I could feel myself changing. Three years in the ROTC program gave me a leg up because I usually knew what was expected of me and how to do it before I was told. Getting things right the first time kept the drill sergeants off my back, and soon I began coaching my platoon mates on what to expect, especially the guys who were having a hard time. Staff Sergeant Tony Short, our drill instructor, made me a trainee squad leader. All things considered, there were only two big adjustments I had to make in basic training: having forty people in my bedroom and no door to shut when I sat on the toilet. My biggest disappointment was that I never got to see the gold at Fort Knox.

Despite the advantages I took into basic training, I did experience some stresses and my personality did change. Over time, the laid-back easy-going Jim Gillam faded away. He morphed into Private Gillam, serial number US 514684921, a man with a shrunken sense of humor, a quick temper, an aggressive personality, and a foul-mouthed vocabulary that only comes from living with drill sergeants. Some of the change was also due to the tension of knowing that, in a few months, I would be in Vietnam and possibly wounded or dead. But also, I was tired of the petty harassment from some of the demented phys-ed instructors who made things worse than they had to be. That harassment usually came from the people with the lowest rank: privates first class, specialists fourth class, and corporals. Our nemesis was a corporal. Behind his back, we called him Corporal Numbnuts. To his face, we had to call him "Corporal, Sir."

Corporal Numbnuts was our company clerk, but he occasionally abandoned his typewriter to scream at someone for not saluting the flag rank on an officer's car or not running when he was alone outside a building. He did that to me once, and the confrontation got physical. A man in my squad named Gary was an emotional wreck over the pregnancy of his wife. I had asked to see the company commander to ask if Gary could get a compassionate leave to visit her when she went into labor. Corporal Numbnuts came to the barracks to tell me the C.O. (commanding officer) wanted me. I left Numbnuts as he was kicking over bunks he thought were improperly made and making everyone do pushups.

I walked slowly across the street while I rehearsed my best pitch to get Gary home for a few days. Before I knew it, Corporal Numbnuts was behind me screaming for me to run all the way across the street. I ignored him. He ran up behind me and kicked me in the Achilles tendon. I went to one knee from the pain. He bent over to get in my face, and I slammed a forearm into his jaw and knocked him down. Staff Sergeant Short broke up the fight. He surprised me by not reporting either of us. Instead, he promised we would get to "work things out" in a day or so.

We "worked things out" quite satisfactorily the next day at bayonet practice. This is practice for the kind of fighting that is about as intense as it gets, and the drill sergeants did all they could to give us the physical skills and psychological aggressiveness to survive it. Part of that aggressiveness was developed through the use of the call-and-response system that slaves used.

The drill sergeant would call, "What is the sprit of the bayonet?" Two hundred trainees would scream out the answer: "To kill without mercy!"

On the physical skill side, they taught us to stab for the throat first. Second choice was the chest, and we were told to kick the bottom of the blade with the toe of a boot before withdrawing it. That causes more damage and gets the blade free of the rib cage. Some days we practiced precise moves with rifles and bayonets on straw-filled dummies. Some days we fought mechanical contraptions designed to offer resistance as we learned to parry an enemy's bayonet and stab him with ours. Other days, we used pugil sticks on each other. Pugil sticks are the padded version of a rifle and bayonet. They are used along with football helmets with face guards and hockey gloves to prevent concussions and broken hands and fingers. Once you suited up, you got to practice stabbing and beating people to death.

Staff Sergeant Short paired me up with Corporal Numbnuts. When the fight started, he charged right in, seeking to use his weight advantage to batter my stick down and set me up for a "butt stroke." A butt stroke has nothing to do with touching someone's rear end. It is what you do after a thrust to the throat misses and you find yourself face to face with your opponent. Then you swing the butt end of the rifle around and smash your opponent in the side of the head.

In pugil stick fights, butt strokes are also more satisfying than poking someone with the padded end of your stick. They are also dramatic because you can literally knock someone off his feet. I parried Numbnuts' thrust, let him get close, and then I grabbed his shirt and sat down as hard as I could. That started him headfirst over my shoulder, and I used my feet to boost the rest of him in an arc that landed him hard on the small of his back. He had the wind knocked out of him, and when I got on my feet, he was on his hands and knees reaching for his pugil stick. I screamed "No Mercy" and started kicking him in the head. The first one turned his helmet sideways and broke his nose. The next one knocked him unconscious. I kept at it until Sergeant Short pulled me away.

Numbnuts stayed in his office after he recovered from his concussion. While he was there, the company commander had him type orders for Gary to visit his wife. I graduated from basic training as the outstanding trainee of the training cycle, but Gary got recycled. That meant he had to start all over again after he got back from seeing his wife. I never heard from him again. I moved on to Advanced Individual Training (AIT), at Fort Polk, Louisiana.

INFANTRY TRAINING: FORT POLK, LOUISIANA

In1968, a draftee received a battery of tests called the Armed Forces Qualification Test, or AFQT, during the first week in the Army. It was a standardized test to determine academic knowledge, physical skills, and psychological makeup. Based on your scores and, of course, the personnel needs of the Army, you were assigned an MOS, or Military Occupational Specialty. Your MOS was the job you would have for the rest of the time you were a soldier, and they had codes to represent them. AIT is when you learn how to do that job.

The MOS code for the infantry is 11B. When I found out what my MOS was, I joked with Robert "Bobby" Johnson, a fellow draftee from Cleveland, Ohio, that I should never have checked "yes" on the AFQT when it asked if I had ever been camping. Bobby was really surprised he ended up in the infantry, especially since he checked "no" to the questions about owning or using firearms. I think he thought he would get a safe and civilized job as a clerk or mechanic. Actually, given the historical time and circumstances, neither one of us should have been surprised by what happened. It was the fall of 1968, and Gen. Tran Van Tra's men had spent most of the year creating vacancies in all five of the combat branches of the Army, but they specialized in infantry vacancies. They succeeded well beyond the expectations of General Westmoreland, so there was a place for me and several thousand other men that month in the infantry. Looking back, I think it would have been a bigger surprise if things had turned out differently.

As I conducted research for this book, I checked a couple websites and did a little reading on the subject of how the MOS of 11B was assigned. Actually, it didn't take much at all to qualify for the job. I found a website article called "Army Enlisted Job Descriptions and Qualifications." Under the category 11B, I found there were "Special Qualifications for the Initial Award of MOS: color discrimination of red/green, a minimum correctable vision of 20/20 in one eye, 20/100 in the other eye, and a minimum score in aptitude area CO." There was no explanation of what aptitude area CO was.[1] I finished my reading on the subject of draftees and infantry assignments by checking the observations of Ronald Spector, a Marine Corps historian and author of *After Tet: The Bloodiest Year in Vietnam*. On the subject of draftees and infantry assignments, Spector wrote that by 1969, draftees accounted for 88 percent of the infantrymen in Vietnam.[2] So, I guess Bobby and I shouldn't have been surprised. We could breathe, stand upright, and we had been drafted.

In early November 1968, I boarded a plane from the now defunct Trans Texas Airlines, (TTA) bound for Fort Polk, Louisiana. A drill sergeant on the plane joked that TTA also stood for Tree Top Airlines because that was as high as they flew. Sure enough, we flew low and at night over one end of the machine-gun ranges. Looking down, we saw thousands of red tracers flying around in a night fire exercise. I think every one of us must have had sobering thoughts about what was in store for us. We knew for sure things would be different because in basic training, we were seldom outside our barracks after dark. As it turned out, we had pretty awful barracks at Fort Polk, but it didn't really matter.

We rarely slept in them. You see, war is an outdoor activity after all, and we were there to learn to make war.

Learning to make war meant most of the time was spent hardening our bodies and learning the practical side of our MOS. There was hardly a day when we didn't learn another way to kill someone. Actually, I was surprised at the results of the hardening process, not to mention the speed of it. In the third week of training, I was on a five-mile run with my platoon to the firing range, and I saw a grubby soldier in the mirror on the side of Company Headquarters. I was some distance past it when I realized it was me in the mirror.

THE SERGEANTS AT POLK

For the entire time we were at Fort Polk, we rarely saw or had any contact with officers of any rank. It was a school for enlisted men, and a cadre of sergeants primarily ran it. Our contacts with the training cadre started with two men: our platoon sergeant and the company first sergeant. We got to the company area about 1:00 a.m. and we were handed over to them. Through these two men, we met a series of other NCOs who were all Vietnam combat veterans and specialists in one or more of the requisite skills for surviving Vietnam. They began teaching us what we had to know at "O Dark-Thirty," also known as 4:30 a.m. to civilians.

The elder of the two sergeants we saw every day was our stern-looking company first sergeant. His manner was calm and aloof, and he started every day with us at roll call. Everyone called him the Preacher behind his back because he looked like one. He met us at 1:00 a.m. that first morning in his Class A uniform with all his awards and decorations on it. To the professional soldier, those awards are a resumé and, even though I was new to the Army, I knew enough to be impressed by how many decorations he had and the unusual Combat Infantry Badge (CIB) that he wore above them.

The CIB is only awarded to men who have faced a minimum of sixty consecutive days in combat. It is a blue badge, about three inches long and one inch high. In the center is a silver flintlock rifle and a silver wreath surrounds the badge. If you earned the CIB in two wars, you got a silver star between the two ends of the wreath. First Sergeant Preacher had two stars. That meant he had survived three wars as an infantryman: Vietnam, Korea, and World War II. There is also an award known as the Purple Heart. You get it if you are wounded in combat. I knew what it looked like, and it was not to be found among the four rows of ribbons on First Sergeant Preacher's uniform.

The other sergeant we saw every day was Sergeant Terry. He was our platoon sergeant, and he had served with a Long Range Reconnaissance Patrol (LRRP) unit in Vietnam's Central Highlands. His one-year tour of duty included the first phase of the Tet Offensive. I asked him about the first sergeant's CIB. He confirmed the fact that the man had been in three wars, but there was much more to the story. The first sergeant had been at the Anzio landing in World War II. Later, he was transferred to the 4th Infantry Division in time for the Normandy landing on D-Day. He survived the last year of World War II and then went to Korea. He fought in Korea for three years. Besides the Koreans, he had fought Mao Zedong's Red Army at the Yalu River. He also fought at Inchon and the Pusan perimeters. The Preacher left Korea with frostbitten toes but no wounds. When I met him in November 1968, First Sergeant Preacher had done three years' combat duty in Vietnam. In total, he had spent eight years in combat and never been wounded. He was not only good but lucky too. Sergeant Terry never said much directly about what he did in Vietnam. However, he always seemed to be able to describe a number of "situations" that might come up when we got to Vietnam and advise us about how we should handle them.

TOOLS OF THE TRADE

In AIT, you learn to use the basic tools of your military trade. For the infantry, there were a lot of those tools, but the two most important ones were the M-16 rifle and the M-60 machinegun. Of all the weapons we learned to use at Fort Polk, I disliked and mistrusted the M-16 the most. The earliest version was called an Armalite, or AR-16, and it was developed by Eugene Stoner, an aircraft engineer at Fairchild Aircraft Corporation. Colt Arms Manufacturers bought the patent and production rights for the Armalite and got an initial order from the Army for a million rifles in 1964. Secretary of Defense Robert McNamara made the decision to equip the U.S. Army and later our allies, especially ARVN, with them in 1966.[3]

The M-16 had problems in two areas: production/quality control and technical issues of function. The production/quality control issues started in 1967 when Colt took on additional customers. Colt stretched itself thin to make 25,000 weapons a month for America. Then, it took a contract for 28,985 more to be sold, mostly in Singapore.[4] Subcontracts were let to Harrison & Richardson of Worcester, Massachusetts, and General Motor's Hydrodynamic Division. Harrison & Richardson fell behind by 12,895 units in June 1968, then had 5,000 more rejected for poor quality. Maj. Gen. Walter Woolwine of the Army Materiel Command cancelled their contract despite assuring the House Armed Services Committee that the M-16 was "a fine weapon."[5] One wonders why he was saying it was a fine weapon even though he couldn't get good ones produced on a timely basis.

The list of functional problems with the M-16 is long and varied, but the main ones were that it overheated and frequently jammed because of poor quality powder, and the barrel and chamber pitted with frequent use. In January 1968, the Department of the Army told the House Armed Services Committee that a stiffer operating spring to slow the rate of fire solved the overheating issue.[6] Nothing was said about the heat-conducting properties of a plastic and aluminum weapon compared to one made of wood and steel.

The issues with powder and pitting were not effectively solved until 1983, eight years after the Vietnam War ended. Those problems were originally the result of a cost-saving decision by Secretary of Defense Robert McNamara. He replaced DuPont Corporation's reliable IMR powder in the shells with Army Ball brand to save money and standardize production.[7] Ball brand's ignition was unpredictable and dirty. The weapon operates on the gas pressure generated by the explosion of powder in the chamber when the trigger is pulled. The explosion sends the bullet to the target and drives the bolt back to extract the spent shell casing. The buffer spring pushes the bolt forward again, stripping a new round from the top of the magazine, and closes the chamber.

Poor quality powder forces the bolt back only about half as far as it should go. Then, the spent casing and the new round from the magazine both end up in the chamber. That actually happened to me in a close-range firefight in the jungle. Maj. Thomas Johnson, a marksmanship instructor at the Fort Benning School of Infantry and veteran of the Tet Offensive in Saigon, also had that experience. In an essay he wrote for *Army* magazine, he said that the first time he fired the M-16 in combat was at the fight for the U.S. Embassy. He said he fired once and the weapon jammed.[8] I temporarily solved my jamming problem by shooting one man seven times with a .45-caliber automatic and killing the other with his own AK-74. Major Johnson's article never said what he did.

Ball powder also made pits in the barrel and chamber. Pits in the barrel destroyed accuracy. During rapid fire with an over-heated pitted chamber, the brass cartridge expanded into the pits. They were locked so firmly that the extraction ridge at the back end of the cartridge broke off when the bolt was pushed back during the firing cycle. Then, on the return stroke of the bolt, a new round from the magazine jammed into the chamber behind the spent cartridge. Chrome or stainless steel coating for barrels and chambers was the recommended answer, but Secretary McNamara rejected that idea as another production cost-saving measure.[9]

In short, the M-16 had a lot of problems, and everybody, even the enemy, knew it. An article in the *Quan Doi Nhan Dan*, a Vietnamese paper published in Hanoi, said, in part, "The U.S. troops in the South dislike it; many troops have lost their lives because of the M-16 . . . The M-16 has many weaknesses . . . The main objection is that its structure is too complicated. It collects dirt, and because of this, it often jams . . . The bullet is too small and rapidly loses velocity. When the rifle is shot rapidly, much heat is produced. Because of the expansion caused by the heat, the rifle is only accurate up to a range of 100 meters."[10]

I suppose General Westmoreland made the really telling comment about the M-16 after he was recalled as MACV Commander for reassignment as Army Chief of Staff. He ordered all men training for combat in Vietnam to learn to use the AK-47. He did not say the AK-47 was better. He said the training was for realism.[11] But, again, given the history of the M-16, one could well wonder about what was between the lines of that order.

The other basic tool of the infantryman's trade in Vietnam was the M-60 machinegun. It was the workhorse of firepower. The uninitiated think a machinegun is used like a hose to spray bullets at the enemy. Not true. The M-60 was most effectively fired in spaced bursts of six to nine rounds each. In capable hands, the M-60 could fire 600–800 rounds per minute into the "beaten zone" without overheating and damaging the barrel. The "beaten zone" is the place on a person that gets battered with bursts of half a dozen heavy-caliber bullets. It was the prospect of knowing you could get shot half a dozen times every time you moved that made the M-60 effective, not the fact that you could fire it like a water hose.

In Vietnam, the M-60 gunner carried a belt of five hundred rounds. The rest of the men in the machinegun squad carried a thousand rounds each for the M-60 in addition to the basic load of 500 rounds for their M-16. For a ten-man squad, this basic load of ammunition meant the enemy could face 10,500 rounds of heavy caliber bullets. So, superior, reliable firepower was another benefit of the M-60. The downside of the M-60 was its weight. It weighed about eighteen pounds empty, but no one carried an empty one. A big gunner carried a hundred-round belt of ammunition in the gun and another 400 wrapped around his waist or looped on his shoulders. That was another twenty pounds or so in addition to the heavy packs we carried.

In AIT, the hardest part of using the M-60 was carrying it and getting accurate bursts into the beaten zone on live-fire exercises. Running and crawling with my field pack and the machinegun in those swamps was hard. I only weighed about 120 pounds, and the pack and weapon together weighed about half that. But for some reason, using the M-60 just seemed easier in actual combat. Go figure. Maybe it was the adrenaline or the fact that I was climbing hills and mountains instead of wading through mud. Still, whether I was in Louisiana or Vietnam, a day spent carrying the M-60 always made me wonder what idiot made up the term "light infantry."

The M-79 grenade launcher, the M1911A1 automatic and the combat knife were also tools of the trade. The M-79 fired an explosive 40-millimeter round and was used to cover the theoretical midrange of fire between the point where the rifle stopped and the mortars began. Basically, the M-79 enabled you to throw a grenade accurately anywhere from 40 to 400 meters. The M-79 also fired flares and shotgun shells. The powder charge in its shells and the large bore made a loud thump rather than a big bang, so it was nicknamed a "thumper." The 40-millimeter shotgun shell held about a dozen .32-caliber pellets. Its effect on a person was not impressive. It was ghastly.

The M1911A1 automatic, another Colt weapon, was a .45-caliber pistol that was adopted by the Army in 1911, two years before the end of the Philippine Insurrection. It fired a heavy, slow-moving projectile that was a 90 percent knockdown on any man you hit. I preferred it to a revolver because the clip made it a faster reload. The two-handed "Weaver Stance" with a pistol was not recommended during the Vietnam War, and marksmanship instructors taught the "Classic" one-handed grip. I have small hands, so I was never able to cock the .45 or aim well with one hand. I took a lot of teasing about that. Sergeant Terry also taught me to ignore the standard sighting technique. It required you to line up the front sight post in the notch of the rear sight, and then place both of them on the target. Combat allowed no time for such finesse. Instead, Sergeant Terry taught me to focus "front sight, front sight, front sight." I hit my targets' center mass all nine times I tried it for real.

The combat knife was the last basic tool. Since its effective range was arm's length, I didn't want to even think about using it. Sergeant Terry told me there might be some "situations" when I would need to, and it was with a grudging stubbornness that I took his lessons to heart. He taught me the first two psychological rules you needed in a knife fight. The first was the mind-set of cold-blooded, heartless rage that would allow you to rip someone apart while he screamed in your face. The second one was about determination. "You should never consider losing," Sergeant Terry said. "Second place in this kind of fight is a body bag, so make up your mind to do whatever it takes to win." Then he told me I should always do the unexpected, and do it as fast and hard as I could because speed and force were also critical elements in a fight for your life when the enemy was literally within "spittin' range."

Finally, Sergeant Terry showed me the most lethal spots on the human body and how to get to them. None of them are deeper than four inches from the surface of the average body, and some are best reached with a slash instead of a stab. I also learned that position, balance, and leverage were essential to this kind of fight. I learned the lessons, practiced the moves, and prayed I would never have to use them. The prayers were in vain.

Fort Polk had a well-deserved reputation for realistic training. It was a place where many of the Vietnam veterans who were not our drill sergeants lived in the deep woods and swamps in their own "Viet Cong Villages." In the last two weeks of AIT, we conducted a Field Training Exercise (FTX) against these men. We tried search-and-destroy missions against them. We tried to ambush them and got ambushed by them. We also practiced escape and evasion tactics against them because some of us got captured. My squad staged a night raid on their camp to liberate some of our friends. A lot of "butt strokes" got passed out on both sides without pugil sticks. I got some bruised ribs and a broken hand, but I thought I gave as good as I got. And more importantly, as a group, we felt we had prepared ourselves fairly well for Vietnam.

DEEP SOUTHERN RACISM

Some of the Draft Class of September 1968 left Fort Polk at the end of January 1969 to join the Vietnam Class of 1969. My friends Bobby Johnson and Steve Beohne were among them. Sergeant Terry went back too. Bobby was from Cleveland, and I had taught his wife grammar when I worked in the Resident Tutor Program at East Technical High School the summer before I was drafted. We did basic training together, but we were in different companies at Fort Polk because I went into the Leadership Academy. I met Steve at the academy. He was a slow-talking Southerner who claimed he had been a drummer in a Los Angeles rock band before he got drafted. Maybe. He could play the drums, but I knew more about Motown groups than West Coast ones. Steve also had strong sense of right and wrong and a mean streak when he saw wrong.

The Leadership Academy took two weeks, so Bobby's company was ready to graduate before Steve and I were. At the end of his AIT, Bobby came to my barracks to see me. He was not getting a leave to say good-bye to his wife because he had been home for Christmas. Bobby said he had a weekend pass so he was going to Leesville, the nearest town, to have some drinks. Steve and I decided to go with him even though we had no pass. Bobby worried that we would get in trouble. I was sure of it. I predicted the Army would put me in the infantry and send me to Vietnam.

We also got in trouble in Leesville. At the club we went to, the waitress would only serve Steve because he was White. He asked why she didn't bring our beer, and she said, "I don't serve Niggers." Steve said, "Bitch, I didn't ask for Niggers, I asked for three beers." The bouncer got first-hand experience of Steve's mean streak when he followed us out to the parking lot. Steve went back to the post to ice his hand down and stow away the new .38-caliber pistol he took from the bouncer. Bobby and I got beaten up and arrested a while later by the sheriff and several deputies.

We were near the bus stop and a deputy asked us, "Where y'all boys goin'?" Bobby was still pissed about the racist thing at the bar, and he was in no mood to let getting called a "boy" pass unchallenged. He told the deputy, "If you see a boy, why don't you just whip his ass?" The deputy and a few of his friends saw two boys. We got arrested too, but we soon found it was a local scam to get bail money from soldiers. We gave them most of the money we had, got let out of jail, and went back to the fort. Bobby went to Vietnam the next morning and served with an armored cavalry unit. I heard he died there, but he didn't.[12]

THE NON COMMISSIONED OFFICER'S ACADEMY

Fort Polk was also the place where I began to make plans to spend less than a year in Vietnam, and get out of the Army in less than two years. I was the outstanding trainee in my basic training battalion, so Staff Sergeant Tony Short, my drill instructor from Fort Knox, recommended me for a two-week course at the Leadership Academy at Fort Polk. While I was there, I learned about two things that could get me out of Vietnam and the Army early. The first thing was the Army's early release program for men who planned to resume their education after discharge. This program allowed a reduction of service time of up to three months for men who got accepted by an educational institution.

To get out of Vietnam and the Army simultaneously and early, I needed to stay in the United States for a year. The only way to stay in the States for a year was to volunteer for more training, so I asked Sergeant Terry to recommend me for the NCO Academy at Fort Benning, Georgia. He wrote the letter, and I passed the entrance exam. So, instead of going to Vietnam in February 1969, I went to Fort Benning, Georgia's, Non Commissioned Officer's Academy.

The NCO Academy was another strange facet of Lyndon Johnson's "Vietnam-Only Army." It was a twenty-four-week program developed to address the vacancies in the enlisted ranks caused by the Vietnam War in general and the Tet Offensive in particular. There was a 70 percent graduation rate and the top 5 percent of each class was awarded the rank of staff sergeant. Normally, it took four to five years to become an experienced soldier with the rank of sergeant or staff sergeant. The NCO Academy compressed that process significantly. Vietnam was a small-unit war, and the sergeants who ran small units were being used up faster than the normal promotion process could replace them. The academy was centered at the Fort Benning School of Infantry near Columbus, Georgia. It produced 13,000 sergeants a year, and most of them were draftees. As a group, they were like me, relatively old men at 21–23 who tried to manage squads and platoons of men, 86 percent of whom were 19 or 20. In fact, 38 percent of them were 18 or younger.[13]

At Fort Benning, most of the instruction cadre were sergeants. Most of them had served with elite units like the paratroopers, Rangers, and Special Forces. They were also career NCOs who had a lot of experience operating small units. Most of them could run a company as well as any captain, but I think, to a man, they despised captains and lieutenants as people who had brainstorms and no practical idea of how to make them happen. They also operated on the basic principle that you never ask anyone to do something you can't do better yourself. This principle applied to everything we did there: running, obstacle courses, weapons training, radio communications, maps and navigation, reconnaissance and intelligence gathering, or any of the other classes we took. No senior NCO ever told a junior one to run us through the obstacle course or the combat range. In their eyes, politicians and officers led from the rear. These NCOs were men who led from the front, so they went with us from start to finish.

The first month as a Non Commissioned Officer Candidate (NCOC) consisted of a mix of strenuous physical training and classes in the same high-tech classrooms used by the officer candidates. The Rangers in the cadre usually led the physical training and it was tough. We started with a five-mile run and increased a mile every day, until we hit twelve miles. When the distance held steady, the size of the pack increased. The academy had an overall 30 percent failure rate, and most of them left in the first weeks because they couldn't adjust to the physical demands. It was the first time in the Army that I was physically hard-pressed to keep up.

The physical side of the NCO Academy was to teach us not only how to extend our personal limits, but also teamwork and loyalty. We did everything in fire teams (half an infantry squad) and no task, whether it was a climb up a cliff or field-stripping a weapon in the dark, was considered complete until everyone had done it perfectly. The very nature of our work caused injuries, and some of them were serious. There were concussions and sprains and things got broken too. The teamwork ethic forced us to deal with those. We learned enough first aid to step in for a medic in most emergencies, and except in cases of life endangerment, ambulances and Medevac helicopters were not used. We carried our wounded until the exercise was over. This was where we learned the rule that no matter what, you never leave a man behind.

Fire teams were arranged alphabetically. Mine had men whose names began with G: Ed Gardiner, Jim Gillam, Fred Golladay, and Robert Graves. We started calling ourselves the G Men. Gardiner was a tall guy who really liked a new sci-fi show called *Star Trek* and Clint Eastwood movies. He actually looked like Eastwood. We were all draftees, but Golladay and Graves were the sons of Lifers, professional military men. Golladay was a short, stocky White guy who liked the music of Jimi Hendrix, the Temptations, and drugs, especially LSD. His dad was a World War II vet who had served with Merrill's Marauders in the Pacific theater. The Marauders, according to Golladay, were one of the toughest units in the Pacific theater. They fought five major engagements against the Japanese in Burma, and every one of them received the Bronze Star for Valor. Graves was a tall, slender African-American, and so handsome the drill sergeants always called him "Pretty Boy." His father was a colonel and so happy his son had gotten drafted he tracked him down on his honeymoon to give him the good news.

Golladay went off one day and got high on LSD. He was dismissed from the NCO Academy and sent directly to Vietnam. A guy named Mike Mullen replaced him on our team. Everybody called him "Mulligan." Mullen was a small, imperturbable Irishman from Iowa. In fact, no matter what was happening, he never swore. We found it so comical that he was so well mannered that we started calling him "Goody Two-Shoes." We knew it was goofy but, as Mike pointed out, if we stuck with that name for him, we could still be the G Men.

The curriculum at Benning was centered on the cold, practical instruction of how to do the work of an infantryman: destroy your enemy and stay alive. The syllabus also followed a logical progression from the simple to the complex and the personal to the unit-sized considerations that an NCO had to make. There were too many to describe here, but the class on ambushes is an example. The class began when the instructor asked rhetorically, "What is an ambush?" He answered himself, "Ambushes are murder, and murder is fun." Then he explained that they were only fun if you survived them. Next, he explained how to make several different kinds of ambush: linear, L-shaped, X-shaped, and mechanical, using command detonated mines like the Claymore mine. Essentially they were all based on the idea of putting as many high-velocity projectiles into a killing zone as fast and efficiently as you could.

The next thing we did was to move from theory to praxis using ourselves and other candidates as subjects. We ambushed our classmates, then we got ambushed to learn how to survive them. To survive, you had to get out of the killing zone and mix yourself among the attackers so that they couldn't fire indiscriminately for fear of hitting their own men. The nature of the fight then became a matter of combat up close and personal. It became a brutal test to see if you wanted to live another thirty seconds and what you were willing to do about it. It was during these classes that I realized I had to learn more about what to do with a combat knife.

Staff Sergeant Clay, a small, scarred survivor of two tours in Vietnam, took our personal combat classes to levels we had not contemplated before, and aside from a lot of pain, I took some lifesaving lessons with me from those classes. The first one was that a long personal fight was thirty seconds and that you were going to get hurt no matter what. As Clay explained it, "The thing to do is accept the pain, minimize the damage to you, and kill the Motherfucker as quick as you can." If you couldn't do that in thirty seconds, he said, "you need to find a way to 'un-ass the area,' " In other words, run away.

Staff Sergeant Clay also believed size and numbers were immaterial to the outcome in personal combat. According to him, the man with inhibitions and a conscience was the one who died. "Best thing to do Gillam," he said "is to spit those things right out on the ground." Clay and the other instructors taught us by painful example not to do the expected and not to telegraph our intentions. I suppose what I learned about using a combat knife against a rifle with a bayonet is pretty representative of what we were supposed to learn, but that story is best told in another context.

We ended the NCO course with a two-week FTX. We operated in platoon-sized or smaller units and carried out reconnaissance, ambushes, and search-and-destroy missions against the men in Ranger and Special Forces training. Amazingly, we won as many times as we lost. We graduated in May 1969, and after just ten months in the Army I became a sergeant. Then, after graduation ceremonies and a week of leave, we reported to various infantry AIT locations to train a squad or a platoon for Vietnam.

TRAINING TROOPS AT FORT MCCLELLAN, ALABAMA

I was sent to Fort McClellan, Alabama, and two of the G Men, Ed Gardiner and Mike Mullen, were there, too. Like all Army posts and assignments, there were up sides and down sides about McClellan. The biggest up side was that I knew that taking a platoon through AIT would keep me in Alabama until the end of August. It meant that by the time I finished training my men, I would have been in the Army for a year and I was not going to spend a year in Vietnam. Initially, I thought the other up sides about McClellan were its proximity to the small town of Anniston and the big city of Birmingham, and the weekend passes that I thought sergeants frequently received. Not! I soon found out that "instant NCOs" like us were on post pretty much for the duration. Lifers were in charge of making out the list for passes.

Lifers also made rooming assignments. As a buck sergeant, I was assigned to one of the two rooms at the end of the barracks. I shared mine with Mike Mullen. Ed Gardiner was across the hall with another Benning grad named David Frosty. Dave had been in our barracks at the NCO Academy, but we had not worked with him. At that time, the singer Jerry Butler had an album out called *The Ice Man Cometh* so, predictably, Frosty became "Iceman." He and I shared a liking for motorcycles, and we often talked about getting a Harley when we got out of the Army and making a run to California.

The first day at McClellan, we went to breakfast about 4:30 in the morning. We also met the man who was to become our nemesis: Sgt. John Nail. He was the senior drill sergeant in charge of our platoon. Sergeant Nail was at the top of the list for the down side about McClellan. Our relationship with him was symptomatic of some of the problems with the Vietnam Only Army. He let us know in the first sixty seconds that he was not pleased to work with us. He called us his "instant NCOs," and "shake and bake sergeants." He was in mid-harangue when he told us he had been a corporal for eight years. I interrupted him to say that must be a record for being passed over for incompetence. Aside from securing my place at the top of his permanent shit list, this exchange was typical of the professional and philosophical gulf between some career NCOs and draftees.

Nail and men like him felt nothing could justify making a sergeant except surviving combat. So their ideas about training men were founded on a combination of a cursory treatment of the training in AIT with a large dose of petty harassment over things like beds that were not made to their satisfaction or floors that were not shiny enough. When the summer ended, I expected to go to Vietnam with some of the men we were training. So, I went to Nail privately about his priorities and treatment of the men. He made it abundantly clear that as the senior drill sergeant for our platoon, he would set the priorities for training regardless of what I or the other "shake and bakes" thought.

Nail and I finally had it out when he turned over all of my squad's beds and dumped the contents of their footlockers in a pile for the third time. I told him I wouldn't tolerate it anymore. He told me in front of my men that I should "drop and give him twenty," just like I was a basic trainee. I told him to kiss my ass and walked straight into the office of Captain Grogan, the company commander. I told the captain I was not a trainee and that I would be treated with the respect that my rank required. I ended my little tirade by telling the captain that I was there to train infantrymen, not butlers. I didn't know it, but Captain Grogan was a former master sergeant who had taken a field promotion some years before. He had Nail in his office for a short time, and after that we got on with the business of AIT.

Frosty, Gardiner, Mullen, and I trained the men as we had been taught, never asking anything from them that we couldn't do, and do better. It just seemed to make better sense than the harassment mode. Nail was a pretty big, intimidating guy, but just looking around the barracks, we knew that wasn't going to work for us. Ed Gardiner and Dave Frosty were the biggest of us, and they only weighed about 160 pounds. Mike Mullen and I were about the size of the average Vietnamese. We had one guy who had been a linebacker at Louisiana State University. There were also a couple others who I think had been linemen at the University of Georgia. I knew getting in their face about something was not going to happen. The best I could manage was an undignified shout into their chest. So, we decided that since all four of us had been college students, and there were a number of former college students in the platoon, we should take a more cerebral approach to training.

We called a platoon meeting after Nail had left for a weekend in the Birmingham bars to explain our approach to training. We told them that for us, AIT was a class about killing and not being killed. We also said there would be a pass-fail final exam held in Vietnam. You pass, you come home and get on with your life. You fail, you come home in a body bag. You get any one of your sergeants killed, and we will haunt you and your family forever.

The cerebral approach seemed to work pretty well. We put the brightest of our trainees in positions of leadership similar to what I had held during my own basic training and AIT. Yet, in selecting these men, we noticed a piece of the class bias in the draft. To a man, the most capable soldiers we trained were not going to Vietnam with us. They were all well-connected guys who were in the National Guard or Army Reserve. They were going home when the training cycle ended.

The summer of 1969 ended and America put a man on the moon while we held the customary Field Training Exercise (FTX) at the end of AIT. I heard about the landing a week after it happened while I was in the battalion aid station. I had an infected forearm from a fight between my squad and a squad of Vietnam veterans in the "Viet Cong Village" we had to search during the FTX. Things had gotten pretty physical and several of us ended up in a tussle in a pigpen. There was a graduating ceremony, and I got a trophy for being the outstanding NCO of the training cycle. Then, everyone went home for three weeks' leave knowing that our part of the Draft Class of September 1968 would soon become the Vietnam Class of September 1969.

THE FIRST WAVE OF THE VIETNAM CLASS OF 1969–70

The men in the Draft Class of September 1968 became the Vietnam Class of 1969–70 in two waves. The first and largest one got to Vietnam about six months ahead of me. They went in February 1969. They had what was considered the normal amount of training and shipped out right after AIT. Bobby Johnson and Steve Beohne were in that wave. Bobby Johnson wrote a few

times to tell me that he and Steve Beohne were serving with the
1st Squadron, 10th Armored Cavalry on patrol on the highways
in the Central Highlands. The last letter I got from Bobby told
me that both Steve and Sergeant Terry were dead. According to
Bobby, Sergeant Terry had returned to Vietnam and rejoined the
LRRPs. He and his entire team got killed in an ambush while I
was at Fort McClellan. I read the letter and wondered if the attrition rate for the entire Vietnam class of that year was as high as it
had been for my friends.

RESETTING THE BATTLEGROUND: A STRATEGIC SHIFT
IN THE CENTRAL HIGHLANDS

Bobby, Steve, and many of the men in the Vietnam Class of February 1969 arrived just in time for a new strategy initiative by
the enemy in the Central Highlands. The ranks of the Viet Cong
had been decimated by the earlier phases of the Tet Offensive,
so the gaps were filled with main-force units from the NVA. At
the order of Group 559, Hanoi's Central Military Command, "a
river of revolutionary forces" and the supplies they needed to
continue the fight were ordered southward on the Ho Chi Minh
Trail. The main stream of the "river of revolutionary forces" was
21,600 hard-core NVA infantrymen and an artillery regiment.
They were as tough and well-equipped as any unit in the U.S.
Army. A 500-man engineering battalion came with them to keep
the supply trail open and build their base camps that were scattered throughout the Plei Trap Valley. They also brought 500 elite
sapper commandos from the NVA 305th Airborne Brigade at
Xuan Mai.[14]

Bobby, Steve, and the Vietnam Class of February 1969 who
went to the 4th Infantry Division were part of the effort to stop
this flow. They were part of three brigades commanded by Col.
Gordon J. Duquemin. Their mission was officially named Operation *Putnam Panther. Putnam Panther* lasted from February 1 to

June 16, 1969, and like the Tet Offensive, it was a series of battles between maneuver-sized units of one or more battalions at a time. There were major battles at or near every American base in the Central Highlands. The fights at Kon Horing and Polei Kleng, two firebases set up to stem the flow of NVA into the Highlands through the Plei Trap Valley, were examples of how fierce the fighting became. An NVA battalion staged a diversionary attack at Kon Horing and then sapper commandos got inside the base and destroyed the heavy equipment used to wreck sections of the Ho Chi Minh Trail. At Polei Kleng, NVA tanks and artillery attacked the base, infantry overran the perimeter and both sides used artillery at point-blank range, flame throwers, and hand to hand combat to take and retake sections of the camp.[15]

The 1st Battalion, 22nd Infantry Regiment was the unit I joined in Vietnam, and it was part of Duquemin's force in the Central Highlands. By the time I got there, they were what the Army calls "an experienced, blooded" unit. While they worked on *Putnam Panther*, they had fifty-four men killed and 342 wounded.[16] In July 1969, the 1st Battalion, 22nd Infantry was assigned to a new operation called Operation *Putnam Tiger*. It was a continuation of *Putnam Panther*, but it shifted the focus of the unit from Kontum Province to Pleiku and Binh Dinh Provinces. It was supposed to last until the end of July, but it was extended until almost the end of September. I joined the battalion in September 1969 when it was in last the stages of Operation *Putnam Tiger*.

3. ✴

Joining the Vietnam Class
of 1969–70

ARRIVING IN VIETNAM AND FIRST EXPERIENCES: GOING TO VIETNAM

I started the process of joining the Vietnam Class of 1969–70 in the middle of August 1969, when I finished my assignment at Fort McClellan, Alabama, as an infantry instructor. There was a formal graduation ceremony immediately followed by a sorting-out process. The lucky, well-connected, wealthy, White men in my platoon went home and resumed their civilian lives except for one weekend a month when they showed up for duty with the National Guard. We called that weekend warrior work. The rest of us got a two-week leave. Then we boarded airplanes that transported us from membership in the Draft Class of 1968 to the Vietnam Class of 1969.

CRITICAL NEWS ISSUES—VIETNAMIZATION AND HO CHI MINH'S DEATH

The orders to go to Vietnam had hovered over my shoulder like a ghost for a year. I often thought about them in the same childish way I had thought about facing my father when I got into trouble at school or broke a window playing baseball. I would just keep telling myself, "Maybe something good will happen and I won't have to deal with it." In fact, during the midsummer and early fall of 1969, there were two critical news items that actually encouraged my naiveté about a last-minute reprieve. Then, at other times, I thought I would go to Vietnam but that I would not be there for very long. The sources for these flights from reality were the press coverage of the policy of Vietnamization and the announcement of Ho Chi Minh's death.

Vietnamization was the centerpiece of Richard Nixon's Vietnam policy. The central idea was to transfer as much of the responsibility for combat from American forces to the ARVN as quickly as possible.[1] Presidents Nixon and Nguyen Van Thieu met on the island of Midway in late May 1969 to discuss implementation of the policy. It was an important meeting because it signaled the departure from President Johnson's policies of escalation and attrition. After their Midway meeting, President Nixon held a press conference to announce that the first stage of Vietnamization would involve the "redeployment" of 25,000 Americans. Of course, I read the word "redeployment" as "withdrawal," and I also speculated on the possibility of those 25,000 becoming the first of a flood of troops coming home. That naïve hope was bolstered by a press conference on July 21 when President Nixon, with the new MACV commander Gen. Creighton Abrams in attendance, told the world that the troops in question would be home by the end of August 1969. The fact that Abrams specifically named an infantry unit (the 3rd Battalion, 66th Brigade of the 9th Infantry Division) as part of the redeployment process raised my hopes of avoiding Vietnam even higher.[2] That degree of specificity and the fact that he mentioned infantry troops made me feel this was something more than empty propaganda to assuage the anti-war sentiment in the nation.

Major J. F. Harris, the assistant judge advocate general at the Army War College, wrote a report on the mechanics of

Vietnamization called, "Lessons Learned, Bulletin Number 76, Vietnamization, 1969." Major Harris's work explained how the process worked for the 9th Infantry Division in the upper Mekong Delta, and how it was applied to the 9th Regimental Landing Team of the 3rd Marine Division in I Corps, the northern part of South Vietnam. The redeployment plan was called Operation *Keystone Eagle*. According to Harris, "Each [of those units] contained all categories of redeploying personnel, some of whom had to be *released* before their unit's redeployment."[3]

The key word in this segment of the report was "*released*." It referred to all the men who were released from the 9th Infantry Division or the 3rd Marine Division, and *reassigned* to other units in Vietnam because they had not served a minimum ten-month tour of duty. Those men who had served less than ten months were transferred to other units and men in those other units who had served ten months were *released* from their units and *reassigned* to the 9th Infantry Division or the Marine Regimental Landing Team.[4] In effect, the 9th Infantry Division and the 3rd Marine Division's Landing Team were populated with "short timers" who were coming home because they had served their tour of duty. The men who had not done so were sent to other combat units to complete their ten-month tour of duty.

The reality of Operation *Keystone Eagle* was revealed in a *Newsweek* magazine article called "Beginning of the End." The article noted that the 9th Division's 3rd Battalion had a total of 814 men who were boarding ships to leave Vietnam. But, when the men were interviewed, it was found that only 158 of them had actually fought with the 3rd Battalion. The rest were "short timers" gathered from other infantry units all over Vietnam.[5]

While the *release* and *repopulate* method of Operation *Keystone Eagle* was being applied in the Mekong Delta and I Corps, there was another more forthright plan for the withdrawal of troops from the Central Highlands. It was called a "Memorandum of

Agreement on Responsibilities of ARVN and United States Forces in Kontum Province and Along Route 14 North of Pleiku City." A copy of the memorandum was appended to the report written by Major Harris.

The signatories of the agreement were Maj. Gen. Lu Mong Lan, the Vietnamese commander of II Corps, and Lt. Gen. Charles A. Corcoran, Lan's American counterpart. Their agreement was signed in April 1969. A four-page document that specified the military responsibilities of both ARVN and American forces in II Corps during the first phase of Vietnamization was part of the document, but it was withheld from the public for the security of the troops involved. The pertinent part of the agreement was page A 2. It specified the types of units to be redeployed or withdrawn from Vietnam. According to the agreement, seven artillery battalions, two Army aviation units from Kontum City Airfield, nine engineering battalions, and three signal battalions were to be withdrawn. "*No infantry or mechanized infantry were to be sent home.*"[6] (Italics added). The agreement between Lan and Corcoran was part of a complex plan to allow Gen. Creighton Abrams, the MACV commander, to continue to fight the war while the president periodically made public announcements of how many fewer American troops were in Vietnam.

On September 4, 1969, my leave was winding down and Vietnam loomed large on my personal radar screen. Then, Radio Hanoi announced that Ho Chi Minh, the president of North Vietnam, had died the day before.[7] I knew Ho had been the driving force of Vietnam's resistance to colonization and foreign intervention since the Versailles Peace Conference in 1919. I began to fantasize about the collapse of their efforts now that "Uncle Ho" was dead. I even remember telling my fiancée I would probably be home for Thanksgiving. Had I been privy to the reaction of the National Liberation Front's leadership, or military efforts in Vietnam in general, or the Central Highlands, where I was headed, I would not have been so unrealistic.

A document captured in the Central Highlands shortly after Ho's death revealed the NLF leadership's reaction to the situation. In that document, Comrade Nam, the party secretary of Viet Cong Region 5, referred to the announcement of the death of Ho at the 5th Guerilla Warfare Conference held in the Central Highlands in late September 1969. Nam told his comrades, "Our Uncle Ho is dead. We are dumbfounded and confused . . . " [8] Then he made the attempt to rally them to move on with their struggle. He said to them that in the party, "We are determined to dedicate our lives to the liberation of the South, protect the North, reunify the fatherland, build socialism, and move toward communism."[9] The Vietnamese were not about to give up the struggle and it seemed everyone in their command structure and ours knew it except me. So, in September of 1969 I put my ignorant, naïve self on a plane, and joined the Vietnam class of 1969–70.

The trip to Vietnam was by no means a standardized affair. It changed over the years. When my brother went as part of the 3rd Marine Division, they spent a month on ships and charged ashore onto China Beach in the first major amphibious landing since the Korean War. I flew to Vietnam, so I got there faster, but unlike the earlier troop deployments, the Vietnam Class of 1969–70 did not arrive in the coherent units they had trained with. We came singly from our homes all over America to military installations on the West Coast. From those places, we were dispersed again, as individuals to units in Vietnam.

I flew from Cleveland, Ohio, to Denver, Colorado, to Seattle, Washington. Then, I waited a week at Fort Lewis, Washington, for the flight to Vietnam. While I was there, I was pleasantly surprised to meet up with Dave (Iceman) Frosty and two of the G Men, Ed Gardner and Mike Mullen. Dave started for Vietnam from Philadelphia. Ed started from Pittsburgh. Mike flew in from La Porte City, Iowa. No one seemed to know what had become of Bobby Graves. We knew his wife was French, and he often talked of just flying to France and leaving the Army behind. Then again, maybe Graves deserted because of the rain. He had done his basic training at Fort Lewis, and when we were at Benning he often told us how depressing it was to be wet all the time. I don't know if he went to France or not, but I never heard from him again. We stayed in the mildewed barracks of Fort Lewis for a week. It rained the whole week.

September 11 has been important in America since 2001, but it has been important to me for much longer. It marks, for example, two important birthdays. My first daughter Jessica was born on September 11, and so was Mike Mullen. September 11 was also an important day for the rest of the G Men, the Iceman, and about two hundred other members of the Vietnam Class of 1969–70. It was the day we boarded a plane for the twenty-four-hour trans-Pacific flight bound for Cam Ranh Bay, Vietnam.

We stopped once for fuel in Yokota, Japan. While we stretched and walked around, we met groups of men going home. There was the expected and morbid teasing about our chances of survival. One of the jokes I remember was a sergeant with dead-looking eyes asking me what size body bag I wore. Our brand-new, bright green jungle fatigues (they didn't call them BDUs back then) drew these comments like a magnet. What I didn't expect was the fear I saw in the faces of many of the men wearing the old faded fatigues who were going home. Some were wounded, and there were good reasons for their fear; after all, what does a one-armed high school dropout, whose only proven success is firing an M-60 machinegun, do in America?

There were also men whose wounds were emotional, and thus, less obvious. They were the ones whose spirits had faded right along with their clothes. They all had the "thousand yard stare" of the combat veteran. They were indifferent to, or unaware of, their surroundings. They appeared focused on something far away. Months later, when I was on the way home, I knew from personal, bitter experience, what they were doing. Some of them were turning their minds and spirits inward as they relived some aspect of the recent but violent past. Some were living with survivor's guilt or one of the other emotional consequences of moving from combat to civilized life in twenty-four hours. The "thousand yard stare" was a facet of fear I had never seen before the summer of 1969. Yet, by the fall of 1970 I knew it well. My fiancée irritated me often and deeply in quiet moments when she asked me what I was looking at and thinking about.

ARRIVAL AT CAM RANH BAY

It has been forty years since I went to Vietnam the first time. The memory of that first day and the year behind it has become a remarkably consistent mental slide show. The slides always come up in the same order, and they each capture an essential part of my first day in Vietnam.

Frame one is the landing during which the pilot did his best imitation of a falling stone. He barely managed a last-second flare-out before crash landing. His explanation for what we all felt was an intentional crash dive was that it was the standard operating procedure for preventing the promotion of an enemy soldier who had just been issued a brand-new B-40 rocket.

Frame two is the assault of the heat and humidity when the plane's doors opened. It felt like an attack by a living, malevolent being determined to kill us all before we could fire a shot. Cam Ranh Bay is on the South China Sea, in a climatic zone where August and September are months when the temperature and humidity readings race to reach 100 every day. To me, it felt like they always made it before ten in the morning.

Frame three is the battered blue bus we rode to the terminal. Once aboard, someone made a comment about heat prostration being as dangerous as combat. No one laughed. As the temperature in the bus rose, we discovered we couldn't open the windows. They were covered with heavy-gauge wire screens. The driver told us the screens were meant to keep grenades from

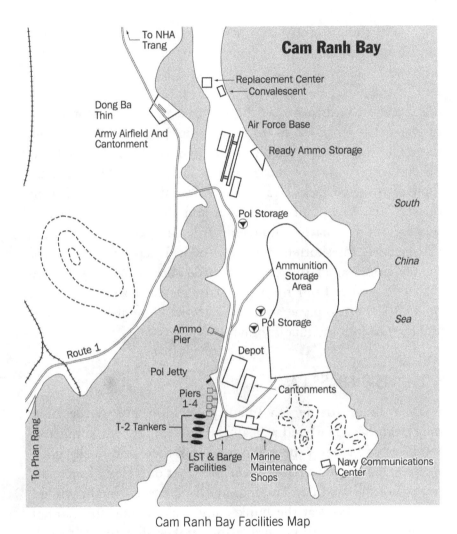

Cam Ranh Bay Facilities Map

Source: Kelley, *Where We Were, Map 32*, Dept. of the Army, *Vietnam Studies, Base Development in South Vietnam*, 1965–1970, p. 56.

being tossed into the bus. I wondered aloud how long before we would be issued weapons. An infantry master sergeant starting his third tour in Vietnam assured me we would all get weapons sometime in the next week to ten days. I knew right then, it was going to be a long year.

Frame four is always my first combat experience. It came during my first night in Vietnam, about ten days *before* I got a weapon. I was in the troop replacement depot on the northern end of the outer peninsula at Cam Ranh. The depot was several hundred yards north of the air base, and just east of a strip of water that separated us from the main Army base. That night, several large sampans pulled into the midst of some fishing boats on the eastern side of the peninsula and started firing mortar shells into the barracks area of the replacement depot. So I went through my first combat unarmed and hiding under a bed. It was too soon to have a thousand yard stare, but I did a perfect, if somewhat foreshortened, version of it. I had my eyes locked on the floor under the bed and made sure it never got more than two inches from my face. Early the next morning, I got on a C-130 cargo plane and flew into the Central Highlands of Vietnam to join my infantry division.

4TH DIVISION BASE CAMP

I was assigned to the 4th Infantry Division and, at the time, they were headquartered at Camp Enari, just twelve kilometers southeast of Pleiku. I spent about a week there and finally got a weapon. I also got mortared again and went on a base camp security patrol the next day. The mortar attack came at night while I was on guard duty at the bunker line surrounding the camp. I had plenty of time to get inside the bunker after the first shells landed. They were far short of the bunker line, and the enemy adjusted fire by dropping them three at a time, with each group of three landing progressively closer.

In the relative quiet between volleys, I heard rustling in the leaves and trash inside the bunker. I lit my cigarette lighter and discovered I was sharing the bunker with a hooded cobra. We both kept to opposite sides of the bunker until the shells stopped. As soon as the mortars stopped, I got to the door first, and I dropped a grenade through the window. The sergeant of the guard was not pleased about the damaged bunker, so when dawn came, I spent several hours repairing it.

The day after the mortar attack, all the new "Grunts" went to the rifle range to zero their weapons. Infantrymen were called "Grunts" because that is what they did every time they hefted their large packs. "Zeroing" is the basic method of making sure the weapon fires properly and that the battle sights are set for the individual who uses the weapon. After we were as certain as we could be that our M-16s were in working order, we were separated into platoons for base camp security patrols. Initially, I was not overly nervous. I figured that although the enemy might drop a few mortar rounds in stand-off attacks, they surely wouldn't dare approach something as large and well defended as a division base camp.

Ignorance is bliss. An experienced sergeant was in charge and, just before we left for the patrol, he told us Camp Enari had been named for a lieutenant who got killed there during Tet. That is when I got nervous. I got even more nervous when the sergeant made each one of us walk point for a while. During my turn, I heard voices a few yards away through the brush, and I almost started shooting. The sergeant in charge pushed my weapon down because he knew it was only some Montagnard women and girls passing by and they were unarmed. They were making one of their frequent trips to the camp to barter or beg for food.

The day after I almost killed those unarmed women and children, I met "Top White," my company first sergeant, and PFC Greg "Bo" Bodell who had been in the division hospital to get stitches in his scalp. Top told us to be packed and on the landing pad at dawn the next day to join B Company whose men were working the area near Landing Zone (LZ) Ruth. I was at the pad on time and really scared because I knew I was finally going to a line company on patrol in Vietnam. We were loading C-Rations and ammunition on some choppers when I heard the company was in a firefight on LZ Ruth. I immediately started wondering how bad it hurt if you got shot. The next thing I heard was the order to saddle up (get your pack and weapon) and get on a bird. As I moved to the chopper, Top White jerked me by the arm and started yelling at me that he didn't allow young buck sergeants to wear mustaches. He said I should go and shave mine off but I wasn't to miss my lift to the LZ. At the time, I thought Top had lost his mind. I also thought it was a great opportunity to avoid getting shot, so I made sure I took long enough with the shaving to miss my lift. Only later did it occur to me Top White didn't want to go into a landing zone firefight with an inexperienced "instant NCO."

LZ RUTH

From August 1 to October 31, my battalion, the First Battalion, 22nd Regiment, and my company, B Company, worked from three different firebases: LZs Bass, Ruth, and Hard Times.[10] The day I was supposed to join them their move from Bass to Ruth was contested by the enemy. I landed at LZ Ruth in the late afternoon the next day with Bodell, another experienced grunt named Terry and two other new guys. The fighting was over, and my company had already left for a search-and-clear operation in the surrounding mountains, so we were all temporarily assigned to the mortar platoon of D Company. They had put out some rolls of concertina barbed wire before dark on the day before I arrived, and another attack stalled against the wire that night. At dawn, there were three dead men tangled in the wire. Shortly after I landed, a lieutenant gave me a pair of wire cutters and some heavy leather gloves and told me to cut the three dead "Gooks"[11] out of the wire and bury them somewhere in the minefield outside the perimeter.

All three men had been dead almost twenty-four hours in the heat of Vietnam, and they looked and smelled just like what they were: road kill. One was partially disemboweled and he smelled the worst. All three had numerous bullet holes. Also, they were almost naked. They wore what looked like leather jockey straps, and they were covered in a black, greasy substance that I assumed was camouflage for a nighttime infiltration. My first thought was that these guys didn't even have uniforms to wear. Someone told me they were sappers and they usually dressed like that for a night attack, but since I had no idea what a sapper really was, I just thought "what a stupid name." By the time I had made a hole big enough for the three of them outside the wire and another one for myself inside the wire, it was almost dark. I wrote two one-page letters: one to my fiancée and one to my parents. By then, it was dark, so I ate cold canned food called C-Rations because I knew better than to show any kind of light at night. I couldn't tell what I ate by sight or taste. I fell asleep wondering what it would be like to go to war wearing nothing but a leather jockey strap.

I woke up thrashing on the bottom of my hole with a hand on my shoulder and another one across my mouth. It was the pit boss from the mortar squad who had come to wake me up for the 3:00 a.m.-to-dawn shift of perimeter guard. Shortly after dawn, I tried to eat a can of C-Ration ham and eggs. The label on the can said it had been packaged in 1946, the year before I was born. I puked it up and went to help build bunkers.

There was a lot of digging to be done on a new firebase, and I kept at bunker building and guard duty for another three days in the sun. Firebases were basically hills with all the trees knocked down on the top with an outer ring of fighting bunkers on the military crest of the hill. Once those were done, squad-sized living bunkers for the enlisted men were dug. Conexs, which are essentially half a tractor trailer for officers' housing and were named after their original manufacturer, Continental Express, were delivered by flying cranes. I dug holes and filled sandbags in the bright sun for three days, and I got the first sunburn of my life on my back and shoulders.

B COMPANY IN THE FIELD

I was in a lot of pain from the sunburn, and I was wondering why White people ever put themselves in danger of such agony by going to the beach when Top White showed up. He told me to get saddled up because Greg Bodell, Terry, a new guy named José Rocha, and I were supposed to fly out to the company with supplies as soon as they set up a perimeter for the night. It was dusk above the landing zone when the chopper began its descent, but below the triple canopy of the jungle, it was pitch dark. I dragged some cases of ammunition and C-Rations to the middle of the perimeter and started shaking the hands of people whose faces I could hardly see at arm's length. Bo and Terry were from the second platoon, so they went to join their guys. José Rocha, a Mexican-American, and I were new guys, so the company commander, Capt. John Derricco, told us to dig a hole together and help with radio watch that night.

Before dawn, Captain Derricco told Rocha he was to be kept as part of the Company Command Post (CP). He was assigned to carry one of the many radios used to contact base camp, artillery batteries, and the tactical aircraft we called in emergencies. I felt sorry for Rocha. As part of the CP, he would not have to walk point, or go on ambushes, but Radio Telephone Operator (RTO) was not a job I would have liked. The ANPRC ("Prick") radios we used weighed about twenty-five pounds. The spare batteries the RTOs carried weighed five pounds each, and they usually carried several spares. We both agreed the weight of his radio equipment together with his basic load of ammunition, food, and water would probably herniate a healthy pack mule. And more importantly, the antenna for the radio waved around as a convenient marker for snipers. Rocha and I were discussing all those liabilities for his assignment when the captain called Bodell on the radio and told him to come to the CP. When Bo got there, the captain told him I was in charge of Bo's second squad, second platoon, and that he should introduce me to the men.

There was no officer in charge of the second platoon. There were so many officers in Vietnam they only had to spend six months in the field. Our lieutenant had done his time in the bush and rotated to the base camp. NCOs above the rank of staff sergeant were also scarce in the field. They were either dead or in base camp because they had the connections to avoid combat. So there were only two other sergeants in the platoon, and both were NCO Academy graduates. "Bear" was a staff sergeant who served as the platoon sergeant and platoon leader until we got a new lieutenant. I never heard anyone call him anything else. The other one was Sergeant Wevadeaux. He was in charge of both machinegun teams for the platoon. I never heard his first name either. We just called him "Weave."

FIRST COMMAND

An infantry squad is supposed to have ten men. My squad had seven: Greg Bodell, Steve Lehman, Luis Ybarra, Bud Rose, Bob Frost, Ed Bennet, and Terry. Terry was an Hispanic looking guy who was "short." This meant he had little time left in Vietnam. Actually, he was so short he left the next week. He was also very different from the rest of the squad. He would not tell me his first name, and I don't think anyone in the squad knew it either. We all had nicknames but, somebody, somewhere always knew your real name just in case you got killed and your family had to be notified. Terry never said what his whole name was or even mentioned a family. Some said he never got mail either. I also noticed he traveled extremely light. He had an M-79 grenade launcher, and he wore a vest that held about two-dozen rounds for it. He didn't carry the huge rucksack the rest of us had either. He had a pack frame with cardboard backing. On that he tied a poncho and camouflaged poncho liner and a sandbag. In the sandbag were three canteens, his C–Rations, and extra rounds for his weapon.

Terry had seen the sunburn blisters on my back and shoulders at the firebase, and he told me point blank I needed to dump some of the heavy crap they had issued me at base camp. I did have a lot of extraneous gear, but I wasn't sure what to dump, so I told him to do what he thought best while I went to get a map from Lieutenant Tijerino, the company executive officer. Terry took out my rain suit, shower shoes, air mattress, two towels, two extra sets of jungle fatigues, T-shirts, and boxer shorts. He cut them all up with a knife and threw them in a foxhole as we were getting ready to start the day's patrol.

I noticed some of the men smirking, but I had no idea why. I was going to ask what was so funny when a filthy, disheveled man who smelled bad and had red–rimmed eyes charged up to me and gave me a bear hug. It was Fred Golladay, the G Man from the NCO Academy who had been canned for getting high on LSD. He was in the third platoon and had spent the night on an ambush on one of the trails leading to our position. I looked at Fred and his machinegunner, and wondered how long it would take me to look and smell like they did. The rigors of the past months had rendered Fred almost unrecognizable. The gunner was a Black guy who looked like a body builder, and he just eyed me up in an amused way. Then he said something to Fred about draft boards scraping the bottom of the barrel for short skinny guys. To me, he just said, "Sarge, we gonna hump yo' little ass in the ground today." Despite the load lightening Terry had done for me, they almost did, too.

I still had a helmet, a web belt and battle harness called "Lifer Straps" with ammunition pouches, a .45-caliber pistol and four clips of ammunition for it, an M–16 and twenty magazines of ammunition, five canteens, a case of C–Rations, a Claymore mine, six grenades, a kilo of C-4 plastic explosives, a machete, a poncho and liner, a shaving kit, and a waterproof ammunition box for stationery, photos and, cigarettes. After a couple tries, I got this mess on my back and walked to the head of my squad. I felt like screaming when it hit the sunburn on my back and shoulders. The whole pack and ammo weighed seventy to eighty pounds, and the shoulder straps felt like they were going to tear my arms off.

The platoon moved off through the jungle and up a slope covered with elephant grass. When I walked out of the trees, I couldn't believe the heat. In minutes, the barrel of my weapon was almost too hot to touch. I was already tired and panting and we hadn't been moving a half hour. I was also hyperventilating from fear. That was because, in training, we always skirted open grassy areas, and I was really worried about being out in the open. In my rush to get up the hill and into cover, I fell a lot. When I started grabbing at the elephant grass to keep from sliding back downhill, I cut my hands and arms to ribbons. No doubt about it, I provided lots of humor for my squad. In about an hour, we had topped the ridge and gone down the other side to a stream. I was sure I would die from heat and exertion before anybody shot me. When we got near the stream we stopped for a minute, and I left my squad up the slope from the stream. I abandoned all thoughts of staying under cover in the trees and sat down in the water. I was still sitting there, drinking water out of my helmet when the last man in the platoon came by. I was hoping we could stop for the day, but no such luck.

It was only about 8:00 a.m. when we crossed that stream. By 2:00 p.m., I was in agony. The straps from my pack had debrided my shoulders and I had bloody patches on both shoulders of my shirt. Salt from my sweat had seeped into them and the sunburn on my back, and that hurt too, but I was still standing. I took some comfort from the fact that Fred's machinegunner wasn't. He had been sipping only small amounts of water and eating the salt tablets the Army prescribed at that time to keep from sweating. We know now that was a bad idea. He couldn't cool himself properly and he passed out. We climbed one more hill, cut a landing zone, and called a Dustoff (medical evacuation helicopter) for him.

The Dustoff landing had marked our position for any enemy in the area, so Captain Derricco sent all three platoons in different directions for the night. When Bear got us to where we were supposed to be, we dug our daily fox holes, put out Claymores, cleared fields of fire, and ate some dinner cooked over glowing dabs of burning C-4 explosives. After dark, the air cooled quickly, and I noticed a white powder on everybody's shirts. It was the residue from salt we had sweated out in the heat. The temperature dropped from the high 90s to the 60s and it started to rain. Everyone but Terry and I got on a rain jacket and inflated their air mattresses so they wouldn't have to lie in the mud at night. I finally figured out what had been so funny that morning. Terry never acknowledged weather conditions, or much else. It was just his way. I, on the other hand, did. I shivered through that night and about a week more of them until the resupply bird brought me another rain jacket and took Terry back to base camp so he could go home.

MISSIONS AND LEADERSHIP FOR 4TH DIVISION AND 2ND BRIGADE

When I joined B Company, it was part of the 22nd Regiment, of the 2nd Brigade of the 4th Infantry Division. The brigade and its constituent units had spent the summer patrolling through Binh Dinh, Pleiku, and Kontum Provinces as the division and brigade commanders shifted them to help with three simultaneous operations. The 4th Division's mission was called Operation *Dan-Quyen-Hines*, and one of the operations the 2nd Brigade was assigned in furtherance of the division's mission was called Operation *Putnam Tiger*. *Putnam Tiger* came to an end on September 22, 1969, and judging from the After Action Report submitted for it, it had been a costly enterprise for the enemy and our brigade too. The 2nd Brigade killed 562 NVA that summer. They took only ten prisoners, and one person surrendered to them.[12]

The relatively small number of weapons captured by the brigade is perhaps a testament to the caliber of the enemy and their discipline under fire. Whenever possible, the enemy always tried to carry the weapons of fallen comrades from the field of battle. The After Action Report for *Putnam Tiger* says they left behind thirty-seven AK-47s, and five SKS Carbines. They also left behind several weapons they had taken from French and Americans: thirty-six French MAS rifles, two M-16s, an M-79 grenade launcher, five M-1 carbines, and a Browning Automatic Rifle. Their largest material loss was in the category of small arms ammunition. The enemy lost 13,265 rounds of small arms ammunition and nearly 900 rounds for light machineguns along with a few rifle grenades and rockets. But all in all, these losses were not nearly the fighting load or armaments that would have been issued to the 562 NVA who were killed.

The After Action Report for *Putnam Tiger* also listed the American casualties, and it is there especially that the difficulty and danger of the mission can be seen. Eighty-one Americans were killed in action and 245 more were wounded on that one operation during the weeks immediately before I joined my unit in Vietnam.[13]

The 2nd Brigade also spent time on another operation whose duration slightly overlapped Operation *Putnam Tiger*. It lasted from August 1 to October 31 of 1969. It was called Operation *Putnam Cougar*, and my battalion and my company spent most of the summer and fall on these operations.

The division-level goal during the summer and fall of 1969 was to support the South Vietnamese pacification program, provide reaction forces to attacks on key military installations, and screen the Cambodian border to interdict enemy infiltration of supplies and men. There were, of course, a lot of NVA who entered the Central Highlands through the tri-border area bound for base areas in the region. In fact, the presence of thirty-five different units, with a total of 20,510 troops, was confirmed. The largest and most aggressive units were the K–16 Tank Battalion with 30–35 tanks and 240 crewmen. Then, there were the 18th NVA Regiment's 1,200 men, the 28th NVA Regiment's 1,400 men, and the 66th NVA Regiment's 1,250 men. There were 2,475 Viet Cong there, too.[14]

Colonel Harold Pinney commanded the 4th Division's 2nd Brigade, and it contained my battalion and company. The first task for the 2nd Brigade during the summer and fall of 1969 was to deny the enemy the use of his main infiltration routes that went past the Special Forces Camp at Polei Kleng to the cities of Kontum and Pleiku. Next, 2nd Brigade was supposed to secure Highway 14 from Pleiku City to Kontum City and Highway 19 from Pleiku to the Mang Yang Pass. As the brigade pursued these tasks, they were up against a force of 4,335 men; about half of them were thought to belong to the 18th NVA Regiment.[15]

The infantry battalion is the basic maneuver unit of the brigade, and Colonel Pinney moved my battalion, the 1st Battalion, 22nd Infantry, to three different areas of operation between August 1 and the end of October. For two weeks the battalion was twenty-four kilometers northwest of Kontum City at LZ Bass. Then from September 14 to 20 they patrolled the area around LZ Ruth, which was eight kilometers northwest of Pleiku. Finally, from September 21 to October 28, the battalion was based at LZ Hard Times, twenty kilometers northeast of An Khe.[16]

Lt. Col. Michael P. Juvenal became our new battalion commander on September 3 so most of these moves meant that he and his staff flew to three different firebases to direct the four companies in the battalion. B Company, the one I was assigned to, also got a new commander just before I joined them. Capt. Arthur Hicks was replaced by Capt. John Derricco on September 10.[17] Derricco had been in Vietnam before as a platoon leader in the Mekong Delta with the 9th Infantry Division. In the 4th Division he was not very popular, and I think it was because he didn't adapt his patrol tactics from the swamps in the delta to the mountains of the Central Highlands.

Two of his most irritating ideas were about ambushes. First, he allowed no raingear on an ambush. He said the enemy could hear rain falling on a poncho or rain jacket. No one believed that. When it rained in the jungle, you had to shout to be heard three feet away. Also, he thought the best way to start an ambush was to toss a grenade into the killing zone. When you throw a grenade, the safety lever falls off and there is an audible pop when the striker activates the four-second fuse. That would give the victims five seconds to react. I guess the last strike against Captain Derricco was part of the caste and class system in the Vietnam Only Army. He was a lifer and all but ten men in his 140-man command were conscripts. Also, most of the men thought he was a petty professional who was just around to get his promotion ticket punched.

In November 1969, someone dropped a tear gas grenade in the captain's bunker. It had a note on it that a deadly fragmentation grenade would be next. Officers were required to serve six months in the field and Captain Derricco stayed until March 1970. Then he left us abruptly, with no prior notice. No one I knew was sorry to see him go. I think he really believed he would be a fragging victim if he didn't leave soon.

It was not until the summer of 2003, when I was conducting research for this book, that I got a clear bird's-eye picture of how my company fit into the overall mission of the division and the brigade. What I found led me to believe it had been a rough summer for

B Company and for the battalion. For example, B Company had started the operation with six officers and 158 enlisted men. Of the four companies in the battalion, B Company lost the most men. In May, two were killed and one was wounded. In June, six died and five were wounded. In July, another three were killed and two more were wounded. Three of Colonel Pinney's Headquarters Group were also wounded.[18]

FIRST PATROL

While I was participating in Operation *Putnam Cougar*, I had some first-time experiences common to the infantry. Looking back on them, I think my performance ranged from cowardice to near competence. In fact, I don't believe my work could ever have been described with adjectives like excellent or brave for the whole time I was in Vietnam. I led my first squad-sized patrol that fall, and even then, I didn't have to look back in retrospect to evaluate my behavior. I, and more importantly the men I was with, knew I was being a coward. It was a reputation I eventually repaired by simply doing the job of squad leader as I had been taught at Fort Benning, but it took a while for me to do it.

I led my first patrol on September 27, 1969, when my company was working from LZ Beaver, near the An Lo River in Binh Dinh Province. We were expecting helicopters to take us on a combat assault. Captain Derricco told Bear to send out a "pancake" and Bear told me it was my turn. A "pancake" was a security patrol that took a circular route from the firebase to make sure there was no enemy around. Bear gave me a machinegun team of four men headed by Jesse Johnson, a red-haired Californian with a handlebar moustache. They were reputed to be the best gun team in the company. I took Ed Bennet and Johnny Wayne Brown, Terry's replacement, from my squad too. Bennet carried the radio and Brown had a grenade launcher.

Looking back on that patrol and what I did, I don't believe I could have set a worse example for my men. As a sergeant, the men expected me to walk point. I was afraid to, so I told Brown to load his weapon with a shotgun round and walk point. He said he would not walk point with a single-shot weapon, so I gave him my M-16, and I took his M-79. Jesse and his team watched this exchange in silence, and we left the perimeter shortly after that. I was in the middle of the gun squad with Bennet carrying the radio right behind me. Since we only carried "fighting gear" of a basic load of ammunition and no packs, the patrol moved pretty fast. I called frequent halts to consult my map. I think the men thought I was tiring from the fast pace, but actually I wanted to know exactly where we were at all times in case I had to call for mortars or a gunship. On the first break, Jesse came to me and said he didn't want to tell me my business, but he didn't think it was a good idea to have anyone between him and his ammo bearers if a fight started. I reluctantly moved up behind Brown to walk as his "slack."

The "slack" on a patrol is supposed to make sure the point man survives any contact until the machinegun sets up to provide covering fire. A good slack man also works as a team with the point man. The point checks the ground for tracks of the enemy, booby traps, tripwires, and such. The slack watches the surrounding bushes and trees for signs of an ambush. I was not ready for that, so after a couple more breaks, I turned the patrol back to the base. Jesse told me again that he didn't want to tell me my business, but he was sure we had not gone as far as we were ordered to. I told him I had the map and I thought we had, so we went back without further incident or conversation. When we got back to the perimeter, Bear told us to pick up our packs and get ready for the combat assault. Jesse picked mine up and heaved it as far as he could. It landed in a shell hole full of water. I was too ashamed of my behavior on the patrol to say anything about it. I was also worried about making my first combat assault.

FIRST COMBAT ASSAULT

A combat assault, or CA, was a tactic in which a unit of men was landed by helicopter in a clearing to engage and destroy the enemy. It was a tactic made popular in 1966 when the 1st Cavalry Division (Airmobile) came to Vietnam. As a tactical maneuver, CAs were both simple and complex. They were simple because they got you to the enemy quickly. They became complex if the enemy contested the landing and you had to get out of a helicopter in a clearing while they were shooting at you. I was thinking about that as Captain Derricco and Lieutenant Tijerino gave out the lift assignments for each helicopter. A lift was the number of helicopters expected to fit in the landing zone (LZ). Sometimes a landing zone could only take one helicopter at a time. As it was done with walking point, and most other things dangerous, the first platoon and the first squad of a platoon to go into an LZ were rotated. It was my platoon's turn to go first. Six men from our first squad, followed by another three men and Bear, would be on the second bird, and my squad with me and five other men would be on the next bird. If the enemy decided to fight, each bird's occupants were expected to do what they could to survive until we got enough people on the ground to kill them or drive them off.

In our pre lift-off briefing, we were told the LZ was twenty-one miles northeast of An Khe, and that twice in the week before, helicopters had been fired on in the area. The first time, on September 20, a 4th Division helicopter gunship was on patrol fourteen miles northeast of An Khe. It was struck by rifle fire and the deadly 12.7-millimeter heavy machinegun the NVA used. Yet, sixteen NVA were killed before the gunship returned to base. Three days later and two miles away from that site, another 4th Division gunship reported it had drawn fire from an "unknown number of enemy" in bunkers. The gunship opened fire and killed thirty-seven of them [19] The point of the briefing, I guess, was to let us know to expect a fight.

When I sat in the open doorway of the helicopter between Greg Bodell and Bob Frost, a guy from Oklahoma who was known to be a tough fighter, I had three things on my mind. The first one was that the 12.7 machinegun was the equivalent of our .50-caliber heavy machinegun and that it could bring down fighter planes, let alone fragile helicopters and even more fragile people. Second, the term "unknown number of enemy" really worried me. The way I saw it, if thirty-seven had been killed, there must have been a lot more of them who didn't die, and they were probably going to be pretty pissed off when more helicopters showed up. Finally, I thought a lot about the fact that the two previous contacts in the area had been made by gunships. Gunships didn't land unless they were on fire or shot down. We, on the other hand were Grunts, and were going to land.

We circled the LZ once and saw that it was on the side of the hill rather than on top. It was also big enough for three birds at a time. We dropped quickly into a hover above the grass and rocks in the clearing, and the door gunner fired his M-60 machinegun into the tree line just in case anyone was there. He scared me so badly I almost fell out of the door. We got close to the ground and I jumped off the skids and discovered the ground was farther away than I thought. We were hovering three or four feet above the grass, but it was tall grass. I think I fell close to ten feet and landed in a bunch of boulders. Even though our door gunners were the only ones firing, I crawled on my belly over a lot of rocks to a good firing position facing the trees to wait for the rest of the platoon to land.

When the rest of the platoon came, Bear called the captain and said we had secured the LZ and the rest of the company should come. Robert "Stretch" Bostwick, one of the tallest, skinniest men I ever saw in the Army, sat on a rock next to where I was lying and said, "Relax Dude, there ain't no Gooks around here." Then he flipped over backwards when a burst from an AK-47 knocked chips from the rock he was sitting on.

The firefight was over pretty quickly, and none of us got hurt. We killed nine NVA, and found one AK-47.[20] I fired my weapon that day, but I have no idea if I hit anyone. If I did, it must have been an accident, because I never saw any enemy until they were dead. I just fired because everyone else did. I was just glad to survive my first CA. In the ten and a half months I was in Vietnam, I made forty-six more of them. Some were easier than the first, and some were not.

FIRST KILLING

B Company spent most of October 1969 on the miserable task called Operation *Putnam Cougar*. The monsoon rains had begun and we were climbing mountain trails in triple canopy jungle in Binh Dinh Province, thirty kilometers northeast of An Khe. Intelligence reports said that the 18th NVA Regiment's Base Area 226 was in the area. We were looking for their headquarters staff and about 1,700 men they commanded as well as the supply caches they used. The rain, fog, and jungle limited sight to about fifteen meters, and so the hunt was slow and dangerous. There were almost daily firefights involving squads or snipers who were sent to slow us down but, still, substantial caches of supplies were found. In fact, early in the morning of October 17, my company found a cave complex that had been used as a staging area. We found a printing press in one of the caves.[21]

Maj. Malcom Dixon, the battalion adjutant, wrote an After Action Report on *Putnam Cougar*. In the customary tally of enemy losses of men and materiel, Dixon noted that the 18th NVA Regiment had 114 men killed and two captured by our forces. The Republic of Korea troops working with us killed another 113 and captured 21 prisoners. In addition to the printing press, Major Dixon also included a long list of arms, ammunition, food, and other supplies that were found during the operation. A partial listing of what we took included two AK-47's, fifty-three

SKS Carbines, three World War II–vintage American M–1 rifles, six nine–millimeter machineguns, 61,000 rounds of small arms ammunition, 1,300 grenades, several hundred shells for mortars, and over 6,000 pounds of rice.[22] Major Dixon's report concluded with a section called a "Chronological Summary of Events." It was basically a list of what happened to the battalion on a day by day basis. The entry for October 19, 1969, noted that at 16:55 the second platoon of B Company found and killed one NVA.[23] That NVA was the first man I killed in Vietnam.

October 19, 1969, was a typical day for a Grunt in the Central Highlands. The monsoon rain was in its fifth consecutive day. Major Dixon described what we did as "Search and Clearing Operations," but from our perspective, it was basic search-and-destroy stuff: two opposing groups of men searching for and destroying each other. We walked the same trails the enemy used and had gunfights at close range when we met them or saw them going to their supply caches. Each squad in the platoon took turns on point and, with some help from Greg Bodell, I had finally learned how to do it correctly. In fact, I was starting to prefer it because I knew a careless point man would walk us into an ambush and get us all killed. We rotated the point squad every day, and I spent most of October 19 worried about how good the point was because my squad was last in line that day.

As sergeant of the last squad, my duty was to make sure nobody shot us in the back, so I was the last one in line. We stopped for a break, and I took a rear security position. I walked back down the trail until I couldn't see or hear any of the men. I sat on a slope with a bend in the trail in front of me. My squad was behind me and to the right. The empty trail was to my front and left. I had my weapon across my lap and divided my attention between glancing over my right shoulder for someone to come get me when the break was over and looking for the enemy walking up the trail from my left. I turned to the right, and no one was coming to get me. I turned to the left, and an armed man had appeared without a sound. He was in khakis, and he had a rifle on a long sling on his right shoulder. The butt was behind his right shoulder, and the barrel was pointed down to keep rain out of the barrel.

Time froze, and we stared at each other for an eternity. Neither one of us moved until we heard Jim Higgins, the platoon's radioman, coming to tell me the break was over. The NVA soldier started to raise his weapon but he only had one hand on it. I was sitting with both hands on mine so I had an advantage. I got my weapon up first, and we started shooting at each other from a range of less than twenty feet. He had an SKS carbine. It's a semi-automatic weapon that fires one shot from a seven-round magazine each time you pull the trigger. I probably would have died if he had had an AK-47 set on automatic. He fired twice, and both shots were low. They hit the ground under my knees, between my butt and heels. I learned later that an AK-47 set on automatic would have kept firing and cut through both my legs and body because they tend to rise to the right from the recoil of firing. My M-16 was set on semi-automatic because I had found I was a more accurate shot on that setting. I pulled the trigger three times, as fast as I could. The first shot hit him above the belt. The second hit higher, near the collarbone. The third one hit a tree behind and to the left of his head. He dropped straight down to a sitting position, staring at me with his weapon still pointed at me. But I knew the damage an M-16 did at close range, and I knew he was dead with his eyes open.

Higgins calmly called Bear and Captain Derricco to report one enemy killed in action (KIA). He picked up the man's rifle and asked me if I wanted it. I opened my mouth to speak and threw up all over myself. Higgins took that as a "no" and kept the rifle. I think he took it home with him when he left Vietnam a month later. That night, Jesse Johnson, the gun team leader who had been disgusted by my cowardice a month earlier, stopped by the foxhole I was digging. He knelt next to my hole, leaned over, and gave me an AK-47 round on a black shoestring for a necklace. I found out later that such ornaments were a kind of tribalistic award given to a man on the occasion of his first confirmed kill. I didn't sleep much that night. I kept waking up seeing men with blank faces staring at me and reaching for me.

FIRST AMBUSH

The biggest and most difficult part of my brigade and battalion mission was to deny the enemy the use of the infiltration routes into the Central Highlands from Laos and Cambodia. Since the trails were first opened in 1959, the Air Force had employed everything from B-52 air strikes from bases in Guam to high tech solutions like infrared photography and seismic sensors to halt the flow of men and materiel. Yet over time, those efforts were largely unsuccessful. In fact, the traffic increased over the years as Hanoi shifted from small-unit warfare to the use of larger units. For example, in the late 1950s and early '60s, small-unit warfare only required an average of sixty tons of goods, or the equivalent of twenty truckloads of supplies a day. But in 1965, when America escalated its involvement in Vietnam, the weekly tonnage on the Ho Chi Minh Trail jumped to 400 tons per week. By 1969, they were sending 10,000 tons, or the equivalent of 2,000 to 3,000 truckloads of supplies per week.[24]

Troop numbers on the Ho Chi Minh Trail also increased. In 1959, 1,800 men came south. In the mid '60s, about 5,000 per year were on the trails. Then, when Hanoi made the decision to move to large-scale attacks like the Tet Offensive, "a river of revolutionary forces" of about a million men per year came south.[25] The American response was to return to the old fashioned, low tech method of using patrols and ambushes to slow down the infiltration. A critical part of preparing for the ambushes was a three-year project of mapping out the trails that were being used. It was dangerous, bloody work carried out by small units because the triple canopy jungle in the area prevented aerial photography in most cases. The mapping was finished by the last week of September 1969, and then in October, the old-fashioned low tech killing began in earnest.

John Prados wrote a monograph about the Ho Chi Minh Trail called *The Blood Road: The Ho Chi Minh Trail and the Vietnam War*.[26] The introduction to Prados' book noted that when the ambushing was done and the war was over, there were seventy-two cemeteries along the trail. Ralph Blumenthal, a *New York Times* journalist, also wrote an article about the trail called "Maps of Infiltration Trails Guide GIs Stalking Foe." Blumenthal actually went on several ambush patrols in October 1969 and his article gave an account of what an ambush patrol was like. He also presented a startling accounting of the numbers of NVA killed on the way into the Central Highlands of Vietnam. He wrote that from September 24 when the mapping was finished and December 15 when he finished his patrols, 1,177 NVA, including 400 guides, died on the trails. That was twice the number killed in the preceding three months.[27]

I made my contribution to the killings on October 27, 1969. It was my first ambush. It was in the Vinh Than Valley (Happy Valley), near LZ Hard Times, twenty kilometers northeast of An Khe.[28] We were just a stone's throw from the site of my first combat assault, and I was still not very confident about some aspects of my role as a squad leader. My first patrol as part of a firebase security sweep had not been a shining moment in my military history, but in the next few weeks, with the help of Greg Bodell, and a lot of dumb luck, my squad was starting to think I was a competent point man. That was despite the fact that I had been in three point-blank firefights in which I was not hurt, and I didn't hurt anyone else either. The squad was just grateful that I spotted the ambushes before I walked them into the killing zones.

Then I suppose after I finally managed to kill a man, the captain must have thought I was ready to lead my first ambush. I, on the other hand, was not so sure. Ambushes were more complicated and dangerous than a quick check of the area around a firebase or a frightened reflex action. One of my NCOC instructors had told us ambushes were murder, and murder is fun, especially if you survive. I survived my first ambush, but it was not fun.

As the squad leader, I chose the place where it happened. I scanned my map and found a ridgeline that ended in a sharp drop and faced the inside curve of a horseshoe bend in a high-speed trail. I checked with Sergeant Richey, our artillery forward observer to make sure he and Captain Derricco knew where we were going, in case we needed immediate help. Next, I gathered the seven men of my squad and the four men of Jesse Johnson's gun team for a briefing. I told them where we were going, what we were supposed to do, and I told them that on the way there, I would point out rally points in case we were ambushed before we set up our ambush and had to run for our lives.

Then, I put on a flak jacket. They were pretty heavy. I think they weighed about fifteen or twenty pounds. We usually only wore them if we were in a convoy, but I thought I might need mine. Finally, since I had stopped telling people to do things I was afraid to do, I took the point again that night, and I put Bodell as my slack. I preferred him there because he was not only experienced, he was left-handed. A left-handed person naturally points his weapon to the right with no awkwardness and, as a right-handed person, I could easily cover the left side.

We got to the trail bend in about an hour, and it looked even better in reality than on the map. The area between the end of the ridgeline and the trail was a flat space about ten feet wide with good cover behind boulders and large fallen trees. Behind the flat area, the ridgeline rose up in a cliff several meters high. I thought it was perfect protection for our backs because the firebase was at the top of the ridge, and anyone trying to move in behind us

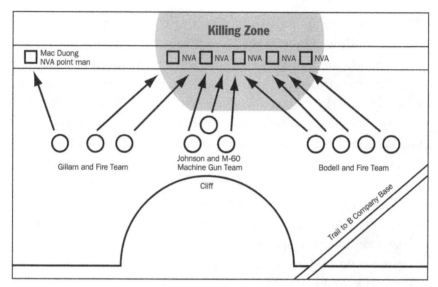

Diagram, Layout of Gillam's First Ambush

would have to come by the men at the bunker line there. The ends of the bend in the trail were to our right and left, and this meant we could all fire into the killing zone without danger of hitting each other. I placed the gun team in the center and one fire team (half my squad) on either side of them. Bodell was in charge of the one on the right and I took the left side. After everyone was set, I dashed across the trail to see if I could see my men. I couldn't, so I came back and we settled in to wait.

Ambushes require patience and discipline and, with the prospect of lying in the rain most of the night, I was running out of both. It had started to rain on the way to the ambush, and we were supposed to stay in place for twenty-four hours unless we had contact. Captain Derricco didn't let us take rain jackets on ambushes. He said the rain sounded different when it hit jackets instead of leaves and the ground, and the enemy would hear the difference. I think he didn't want us to be comfortable and go to sleep. I was already shivering, and I also knew the leech on my hand had some friends inside my shirt and pants. I was telling myself for the tenth time that the rain was a good thing because I was shivering so much I knew I wouldn't fall asleep from boredom when Luis Ybarra threw a pebble and hit me on the side of my face. I looked to the right, and he was staring at a single NVA who was ten meters away in the middle of the trail. He was a point man and moving about twenty meters ahead of five other men on the trail. I knew then that there would be some murder happening in a matter of seconds, and I hoped I would not be on the receiving end.

The proper way to start an ambush was for the man on the end to let the enemy point man walk completely through the killing zone. Then, when all the men behind him were inside the killing zone, you were supposed to spring the trap by shooting the point man in the back or hunting him down after you killed the people behind him. If everyone was not in the killing zone when the shooting started, and they were well trained, you could find yourself in big trouble. While you were busy shooting to your front, the people outside the killing zone would attack your flank, and you would end up trapped in a crossfire. The men I could see had no packs. They had rifles, grenades, and helmets. That meant they were either based nearby or scouting the trail ahead of a larger unit of supply carriers. In either case, I figured their six against our eleven was the best odds I could get, so I decided to initiate the ambush. The point man walked along the trail until he was about thirty meters to my left. He stopped and turned around to look at or signal the men behind him, and I shot him.

Instantly, all seventeen people on that trail started shooting at each other. Sixteen rifles and a machinegun firing at a range of ten to fifteen feet make a lot of noise and confusion. I wasn't aware of everything that went on, but I knew right away that these scouts were well trained and aggressive. Instead of looking for cover in the killing zone, or jumping off the other side of the trail, they brought the fight to us by charging right at us. They knew that if they got among us, we had to worry about hitting our own men and there was going to be some vicious fighting at arm's length to see who wanted to be alive in thirty seconds.

They were well trained, brave and, unlucky. They were also dead after a twenty-second firefight that seemed to last an hour. Foolishly, Luis Ybarra and I both came to our knees to fire at the same man. Then I fell on my left side. I thought Luis had knocked me out of the way to keep me from getting shot by someone I couldn't see. I jumped back up and stood behind a tree. I was trying to figure out why I was having trouble breathing as I watched Jesse fire a burst of six into the last man still moving in the killing zone. Then it was over.

I saw five really dead NVA on the trail and in the rocks in front of me. While I counted my men, I saw that I had missed the point man. I saw him running on the other side of the trail. He was headed back in the direction he had come from, probably to get help. So I started shooting again. My magazine ran out. I reloaded and stupidly ran alone into the bushes in pursuit. I found an SKS carbine on the ground with some blood on it. I figured I had seen the last of the point man, and then common sense or fear bit me on the ass and I got back across the trail to my squad. I knew that it was important for us to clear the area quickly in case the scouts had friends. So, I snatched up the SKS, told Bodell and Jesse to have the men grab what weapons they saw, and we headed back up the ridge to Hard Times in a hurry.

LZ Hard Times was built high up on a long narrow ridge overlooking the Vinh Than Valley, so once we cleared the tree line and got inside the wire, we could see dawn breaking. I found Captain Derricco to make my report. He was with Capt. Steven Robinson, the battalion surgeon in front of his bunker. The doctor interrupted my excited blabbering and asked me if I wanted him to look at my side. I looked at it myself, and saw that blood was leaking from beneath my flak jacket.

The doctor sat me on top of a bunker, took off my flak jacket and found a hole in the right side of my shirt. He took off my shirt and found a 7.62-millimeter bullet just barely sticking out of my right side below my ribs. I think when I got on my knees in the ambush, the bullet had hit the flap covering the laces that held the front and back of my flak jacket together. Doctor Robinson said that was probably why I fell on my side and had trouble breathing for a few minutes. He thought it was probably a ricochet that had lost much of its velocity. He knew AK-47 rounds, fired at close range, usually punched right through a flak jacket. He pulled the bullet out with a pair of forceps, poured some disinfectant into the hole and then packed it with cotton. He added a strip of tape to hold the cotton in place and that was that. Cleaning and packing the wound hurt more than getting it. I knew the flak jacket had saved me from sustaining a lot of damage, and every time I thought about how bad it could have been, I got nauseous with anxiety.

The United States Army also remembered my first ambush, and all the other "firsts" that I experienced when I joined B Company during the fall of 1969. They were folded into the unemotional, impersonal, bureaucratic system of reports generated by brigade and battalion commanders for their superiors at the division and MACV level of the war. For example, the Operations Report for the Fourth Division's 2nd Brigade describes the events during the days when its 1st Battalion, 22nd Regiment, worked from LZ Ruth, northeast of Pleiku in mid-September, and moved to LZ Hard Times on the twenty-first of September, 1969.[29] That report did not explain what it was like to pull day-old corpses into a minefield and bury them. It didn't say what it was like to sit in the doorway of a helicopter as it hovered in an area where the better armed gunships had been fired on with heavy caliber machineguns just days before.

There was also an Operations Report for the 1st Battalion, 22nd Regiment, written for the brigade commander. That report covers the three-week period when the battalion was assigned to the area around LZ Hard Times. This report makes the laconic observations that among other things, six Americans were wounded in action, six enemy were killed in action, one was captured, and five bodies were found on a trail near LZ Hard Times. This report also noted that three AK-47s, four SKS Carbines, one 60-millimeter mortar, one 9-millimeter machinegun, five tons of rice, and 500 pounds of documents were captured in that period.[30] Somewhere in that report are the terror-filled hours or minutes, or even parts of minutes when I hunted men and was hunted by them. The report also provides a bureaucratic overlay for the first time I killed a man. The report also neatly hides the fact that on the night of October 27, 1969, I was so charged with adrenaline I didn't realize I had been shot until an hour or so after it happened.

LOSING FRIENDS

There was also an unofficial record of losses that began in the fall of 1969. It was my personal record of the deaths of friends I trained with and came to the war with. It started four days after I got to Vietnam. The G Men were disbanded at Cam Ranh Bay. We got our unit assignments and boarded separate C-130 cargo planes to fly to our respective division base camps. Ed Gardiner and Dave "Iceman" Frosty were the first of the men I trained with to leave. They went to different companies in the 3rd Battalion of the 503rd Airborne Brigade. I remember thinking that I would hate to make a parachute jump in Vietnam. I had no idea that neither the 101st or 173rd Airborne units ever made a combat jump during the war. Still, Mike Mullen and I thought they would be O.K. because we had heard the Airborne guys were still tough and took care of their men. I lost Frosty's and Gardiner's addresses during my move, but Mike had theirs and mine. He wrote me before Thanksgiving to tell me they were both dead. In 1981, I bought a big Yamaha instead of a Harley. I drove it from Columbus, Ohio, to rural Virginia to do research for my dissertation. Years later, I bought a Harley. I never rode either bike, or watched *Star Trek* or Clint Eastwood movies, without thinking of Ed Gardiner.

Mike Mullen went to the American Division. It was built from the personnel leavings of several other American infantry units. He served in the first platoon of C Company, in the 1st Battalion, 198th Brigade of the 23rd Infantry Division. I have more detailed information about Mike's assignment because the Americal Division, Mike's battalion commander, and Mike himself, all acquired a lot of notoriety. The division was the same one Lieutenant William Calley belonged to when he committed the My Lai Massacre on March 16, 1968. On September 5 of that year, Calley was charged with murder, and on November 13, coverage of the incident by Seymour Hersh, a reporter for *New Yorker* magazine, was picked up by wire services across America. Then, on December 5, *Life* magazine published the graphic color photos of the massacre.[31] They showed the bodies of over four hundred dead old men, women, and children piled on top of each other or strewn about the fields where they had been murdered as they begged for their lives or tried to run to safety.

Mike and his battalion commander got famous because they figured prominently in two books and a made-for-T.V. movie. The first book was called *Friendly Fire*, written by C. D. B. Bryan, a journalist. The movie was made in 1976 and had the same title. Carol Burnett played Mike's mother Peg. The second book was *Unfriendly Fire: A Mother's Memoir*. Mike's mother Peg wrote it in 1995.[32] Mike's battalion commander was Lt. Col. Norman Schwarzkopf, the man who commanded American troops in the invasion of Grenada and Operation Desert Storm. Bryan interviewed Schwarzkopf, Mike's company commander, Capt. Tom Cameron, and several of Mike's friends. Mike didn't get interviewed for the book. An errant 105-millimeter shell fired by an American artillery battery killed him on February 18, 1970. His death was the reason for both books and the movie.[33] Here's how it happened.

At 2:50 a.m. in the morning of February 18, 1970, an American artillery round struck a tree above the sleeping position and foxhole where Mike and his squad were. Two men died and four were wounded. Mike was sleeping on the ground surrounded by sandbags with two other men: privates Leroy Hamilton and Edward Hall. When the shell exploded, two of the three died and one was left untouched. Mike, lying on the right side, was probably the first to die. If he didn't die first, at least he died quickly. His heart was pierced from behind by a crescent shaped piece of shrapnel. Private Edward Hall, sleeping in the middle, was untouched. Leroy Hamilton was on the other side of Hall. A large piece of shrapnel chopped him open from his left armpit to his hip and he bled to death.

The worst of the wounded was Private Gary "Prince" Samuels. He was sitting on the edge of a foxhole when the explosion came, and his left leg was amputated at mid-thigh. Specialist Fourth Class Ivey, the platoon's radio operator, had a fist-sized hole in his back that exposed his spine and intestines, but he survived. Sergeant Wetsel, Mike's platoon sergeant, was wounded in the hand and also survived. Private "Cactus" Gonzales, and Lieutenant Joslin, Mike's platoon leader, suffered concussions.[34]

4.

Operation *Putnam Wildcat*

November 1, 1969, to January 18, 1970

In September 1969 when I heard of Ho Chi Minh's death, I naively predicted that I would not go to Vietnam or, if I did go, I would be home for the holidays. Clearly, I had no understanding of the martyr effect on political movements or the barest appreciation of the strength of Vietnamese nationalism. So, I ended up in Vietnam and joined B Company, 1st Battalion of the 22nd Infantry Regiment while it was shifted back and forth between Operations *Putnam Tiger* and *Putnam Panther*.

When Operations *Putnam Tiger* and *Panther* ended, I had been in Vietnam for a month. It was an adjustment period during which I experienced most of the things common to infantry duty in Vietnam for the first time. I got mortared several times, and I learned to despise the random death of the explosions and the helplessness while waiting for the enemy to run out of shells. I heard that I had lost friends with whom I trained in the States. I cleared away dead bodies after a firefight, and then I went on my first combat patrols. I survived the first of many combat assaults, and I also killed a man face to face for the first time. A few days after that, I planned and carried out an ambush that killed five more men. I was also shot for the first time.

When Operation *Putnam Panther* ended, we were flown to the 4th Infantry Division's base camp at Pleiku for a two-day stand down. A stand down was a rest period where we got cold-water showers, clean clothes, more ammunition and equipment, and medical care as needed. Aside from that, we spread our air mattresses on the concrete floor in a metal roofed barracks that had screens for walls, ate as much non-canned food as we could, and drank as much beer as we could. At the end of the stand down, we boarded two-and-a-half-ton trucks called "Deuce and a Halfs," bound for LZ Beaver in the An Lao Valley in the Central Highlands province of Binh Dinh.

The An Lao Valley is thirty-five kilometers long and shaped like an L that is slightly tilted to the left. The city of Bong Son is the point where the bottom of the L turns from its north-south direction and heads northeastward toward the sea. LZ Beaver was on a hill above the An Lao River nine kilometers northwest of Bong Son.[1] That was where we started another two missions that took up thirteen weeks. The first mission was called *Putnam Wild-cat*, and it lasted from November 1, 1969, to January 18, 1970. The second mission was called *Putnam Power* and it lasted from January 18 to February 7, 1970.

OPERATION *PUTNAM WILDCAT*

The basic mission for *Putnam Wildcat* was to use two infantry battalions, the 1st Battalion, 12th Regiment, and my unit, the 1st Battalion, 22nd Regiment, to drive the Viet Cong and NVA from the An Lao Valley. They had been driven from the valley three and a half years before during Operation *Masher/White Wing*. In that operation, the combined forces of the 1st Air Cavalry, American Marines, the Korean Army, and elements of an ARVN Division were used.

The Air Cavalry unit was the principal force on the earlier mission and it was the same unit that had, early on, made a name for itself in the annals of Vietnam's military history. They were the men of Col. Hal Moore's 5th and 7th Cavalry Brigades (Airmobile). They fought Brig. Gen. Chu Huy Man's 320th, 33rd, and 66th NVA Regiments in a three-day battle for LZs X-Ray and Albany in the fall of 1965. The Air Cavalry's initial success against Man's troops in the Ia Drang Valley, and later in the An Lao convinced the Pentagon that America could defeat the enemy in Vietnam. They also made the use of helicopters as tactical assets for air mobility a primary characteristic of the war in Vietnam.[2]

Despite Colonel Moore's success in 1965, the Viet Cong and the NVA returned, in force, to the An Lao Valley and we had our work cut out for us. On the very first day of the operation, a Viet Cong surrendered to D Company of the 1st Battalion, 12th Regiment, and he told us exactly half of what we were up against. This man was a member of the 95th Battalion of the 2nd Viet Cong Regiment. He came to D Company with a "Chieu Hoi," or open arms propaganda leaflet that we dropped by aircraft over suspected enemy areas. The leaflets encouraged defections and promised humane treatment. This defector said his unit had come to Binh Dinh Province from Quang Ngai Province on October 28. He also said the 97th Viet Cong Battalion from the same regiment was in the valley too, and the 93rd Viet Cong Battalion was scheduled to arrive at an unknown time. Our intelligence officers were led to believe these Viet Cong units were attached to the headquarters unit of the 3rd NVA Infantry Division and a medical battalion. They estimated these units comprised a force of about 2,680 personnel. Finally, the prisoner told the intelligence people these units were in a place they called Base Area 226 from which they planned to conduct offensive operations against the American units in the western part of the Central Highlands.[3] I suppose the interrogators accepted the Chieu Hoi's word as the truth. We were told that were going into the An Lao Valley to destroy Base Area 226 and the 2,600 to 2,700 enemy located there.

After three months, when the operation was over, it was pretty clear we had gotten only half the story from the Chieu Hoi. Captured documents and more prisoner interrogations helped us identify and confirm the presence of three other major units in the An Lao. The first was the 2nd NVA Regiment with 980 men. The second was a 1,300-man contingent from the 18th NVA Regiment, and finally there were another 400 men who were serving with the 300th NVA Artillery Battalion. So, during the course of the operation we ended up fighting another 2,680 men who were not supposed to be there. Those extra men shielded us from locating and penetrating Base Area 226. In fact, while we were on Operation *Putnam Wildcat*, we never broke into that area and destroyed it because we never figured out where it was.[4]

All four companies of my battalion rode to LZ Beaver in a convoy. It was a wet, cold, and generally miserable trip. The "General Intelligence Report," filed after the mission was over, said the monsoon season was just beginning and I recall the rain falling in sheets for three to four days at a time. The winds gusted to ten to fifteen knots per hour, and the nighttime lows were in the 60s.[5] Sitting in the back of the convoy's trucks, it felt a lot colder. The canvas covers over the truck beds were removed so we could see to shoot if we were ambushed. So, we sat in the wind and rain, on a layer of sandbags in the truck beds that were supposed to protect us from land mines. We were soaked to the skin inside 100 yards. We huddled on those hard packed sandbags while we bumped along the fifty or sixty kilometers from Pleiku to Bong Son and then into the lower An Lao Valley.

LZ Beaver was a company-sized firebase on a hill with the An Lao River on one side and a dirt road that went past the base of the hill on the other side. When the trucks stopped, C and D Companies slogged up to the top and started enlarging the perimeter to accommodate three more companies. A and B Companies were ordered to secure the trucks over night because American convoys avoided night runs whenever possible. The trucks were left on the road at the base of the hill and we spread ourselves across the rice paddies in a horseshoe-shaped perimeter with the road across the open end.

Our first inclination was to walk along the dikes separating one farmer's property from his neighbor's, but that was not a very safe course of action. The dikes were restricted spaces where the average Grunt would rather walk instead of wading in the knee-deep water full of the buffalo dung and human waste they used for fertilizer. So, they were perfect places to plant mines or booby traps. Captain Derricco, who had served before in the Mekong Delta where much of the terrain was rice paddies, made sure we stayed in the shit-filled water. I thought we would go all the way to the wood line and set up there, but he stopped us in the paddies, and we spent the night in the water next to the dikes after carefully probing them with bayonets for mines and booby traps. In retrospect, I think he was leaving the advantageous terrain of the wood line unoccupied in order to bait the enemy into approaching our positions.

By about 2:30 a.m. it had stopped raining, and in the relative quiet that ensued, we heard movement in the woods at the edge of the paddies. The fact that whoever was there could be heard thirty meters away meant there were more than one or two people out there. We put some fire from M-16s and grenade launchers in the area and also launched some flares. After that we waited the rest of the night for something to happen, but that was all the action there was. After dawn, my squad was sent to check out the area, but all we found was a crossbow and a quiver made of a hollow bamboo tube with three arrows in it.[6] I remember looking at the arrows and shuddering at the thought of getting shot by one. They had barbed iron heads that smelled of human feces. The barbs ensured that if you got stuck with one, you had two choices: pull it out and rip a bigger hole in yourself, or push it out the other side and increase the area exposed to the shit and probably get hepatitis and gangrene at the same time.

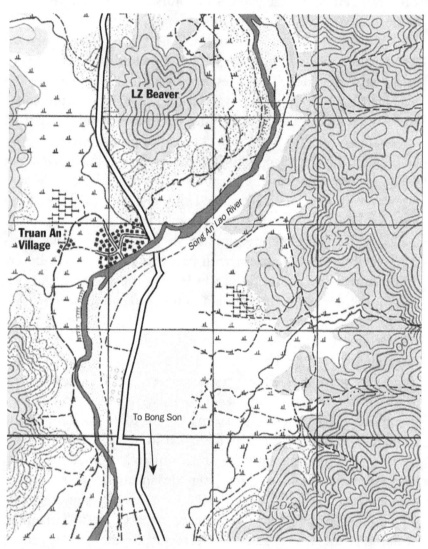

The location of LZ Beaver in the An Lao Valley

Source: This map was prepared using information from the US Geological Survey Map of the Lower (Song) An Lao River Valley, and the websites *freewebs.comjim4jet/vietmap14.htm.* and *mapquest.com/maps/map.adp?qt=mapquest&city+Qui+Nhon&country=VN.*

About two hours after we found the crossbow and arrows, we were ordered to the top of Beaver. There was not a happy camper, or a human smelling one either, in our company. The first thing we did when we got there was to strip off our clothes and get rid of the bloated four- to six-inch-long leeches that had attached themselves to us in the night. Just pulling them off or scraping them off with a knife blade left the heads in place and caused infections. So, we burned them off with cigarettes or squirted them with insect repellent. I always thought it was odd that killing leeches was the only useful thing insect repellant did. The flies and mosquitoes actually liked the stuff. Then we put our smelly shit-encrusted clothes back on and started shoveling mud to make bunkers for ourselves.

In two days the hilltop called LZ Beaver started to get crowded. In addition to the four infantry companies stationed there, mortar crews, a battery of artillery, and the Battalion Tactical Operations Center (TOC) arrived. The TOC was where the battalion commander and his staff lived and worked. They were officers, so they lived in conexes, steel boxes that looked like half a tractor-trailer with living accommodations inside. We called the TOC "officer's country," and like the emperors of Asian countries, the Colonel/Emperor required his corvée, labor tax. Each company/clan had to send a detail of men to help build sandbag walls around the conexes. We also erected a chainlink fence around the TOC to explode B-40 rockets before they hit the conexes.

The rest of the battalion busied itself with the rotation of duties for securing the area around the base. For the most part, this involved one company taking responsibility for security sweeps along the river and across the paddies into the jungle. Another company manned the bunker line for perimeter guard, and the other one would make sure the road was clear of mines so the supply trucks could get to us. D Company, our mortar support unit, never left the base. They were on permanent call to fire their shells wherever we asked.

ROADS, MINES, AND CIVILIANS

On November 2, my squad was ordered to guard two combat engineers while they swept a section of the road from Bong Son to LZ Beaver for mines. It was an experience that taught me much about the futility of the war and made me very leery of civilians. We left the perimeter carrying only our light gear, 500 rounds of ammunition per rifle, a few grenades, and a couple canteens of water. Bob Frost and Greg Bodell walked a double point covering both sides of the road. The two engineers followed them with their mine detectors swinging back and forth across the road. I took the middle of the road behind the mine-sweepers, and the rest of the squad strung out over about twenty-five meters behind me. It was the first time I had seen a real mine sweep, and I thought they were going really fast for an area where they might find a mine. I told them to slow down because they were separating themselves from the main body of the patrol, and crowding too close to the point.

They waited for us to catch up, and then they almost gave me a heart attack on the spot. One of them stopped, conferred with his friend, and then they both began to stomp around on the section of the road that had drawn their attention. The lead fire team of my squad and I dove off the road into the ditch. The others, who were farther back, dropped flat in the road. The engineers thought it was pretty funny. They said the road was so full of shrapnel from years of war that their detectors were always beeping. They said they could tell from the sound in the earphones whether they had found a mine or not. I doubted their story until they actually did find a mine.

As the engineers proceeded to clear and detonate the mine they found, a small crowd of women and children approached us from the part of the road we had not yet inspected. Most of the women worked in pairs carrying insulated food cans that were used to bring hot food to soldiers in the field. They stole them all the time from American and ARVN camps. That day they had ice-cold beer and sodas from the same source. They offered to sell them to us for a dollar each. (A can of soda in 1969 usually cost a quarter in a vending machine, and fifteen cents in the Post Exchange or PX on a base). Having heard many stories about poisonings and booby traps of ingenious kinds, I stuck to the water in my canteen until I saw some of the men who had been around a while buy a cold drink. I let them buy Cokes and Pepsis, and I really pissed some of them off when I made it clear that no one was going to drink beer on this patrol.

While I was drinking a soda, I asked the engineer sergeant if the appearance of the civilians from the uncleared section of the road meant the rest of the road was safe. He said it was more than likely we would find plenty more mines. He suspected, but could not prove, that one or more of these itinerant merchants was also planting mines in the road as they worked their way toward and beyond LZ Beaver. Actually, it was the only logical explanation for the fact that they had walked miles along a mine-infested road without any problem. I called back to Beaver and told the captain's radio operator that I had stopped a crowd of civilians and asked what they wanted me to do with them.[7] I was told to search them and let them go wherever they wanted.

The villagers said they were headed south for Truan An Village, so we let them continue. When we searched the baskets on the end of an old woman's carrying pole we found about a hundred loose AK-47 rounds beneath some half-rotten fish. We took the rounds and let her go because we all knew she would never survive interrogation by the ARVN we were obligated to turn her over to. There was a teenaged boy with her on a bike and he wore a black vest and a derby hat. His clothes and his mouth made him stand out to us, and he really made himself a nuisance about searching the old woman. He kept mouthing off until I threatened to send him to the ARVNs for a talk. Over the next couple weeks, my squad escorted the engineers a few more times, and one morning we found a wide, shallow crater in the road. Beyond the outer edge of the crater, we found a mangled bicycle, a derby hat, and several semi-human-looking pieces of road kill. One of them was the sole of a human foot, lying face up in the road as if the rest of the person had been planted upside down in the dirt.

SECURITY SWEEPS / M-16 MALFUNCTION

Two of the other duties each company took a turn at to secure LZ Beaver were security sweeps and ambushes. The sweeps were basic search-and-destroy stuff: find the enemy, kill as many as we could, and steal as much of their supplies as we could. The ambushes were supposed to catch the occasional sniper or the artillery observers who spotted for and adjusted the fire of mortars and rockets that fell on the base. Given the proximity to so many men and the firepower on top of Beaver, sweeps and ambushes were normally not considered to be extremely hazardous duty. In fact, my first squad-sized patrol had been a security sweep off LZ Hard Times.

The first week of Operation *Putnam Wildcat*, C Company did the security sweeps, and they found out unexpected events could really complicate things. My squad was preparing for another mine sweep on the road when we heard a single rifle shot followed by several more in the jungle west of the firebase. I grabbed the radio and tuned to the battalion "push," or frequency, to find out what happened. What follows is a reconstruction of what happened based on my recollection of what I heard and what I found in the National Archives when I read the Battalion Duty Officer's Log in the summer of 2003.[8]

A squad from C Company had been out all night on an ambush and in the morning, five NVA walked into their killing zone. The sergeant responsible for initiating the ambush raised his M-16, pulled the trigger, and nothing happened. He was exposed to the enemy but close enough to lay hands on their point man so he knocked him down with a butt stroke to the head. While the enemy point man lay on the ground, the sergeant pulled the charging handle to clear the chamber of his weapon. The extractor pin broke the ridge on the side of the jammed round leaving it in the end of the barrel and another round moved up from the magazine to create a double feed. He had two bullets inside the chamber, and neither one would fire. One of the other men on the ambush opened fire on the other four NVA as they scattered westward into the jungle.

The squad of Americans took off in pursuit of the enemy but to little avail. They called to report they had "captured" a pith helmet and a B-40 rocket launcher with a round in it, and they were following a blood trail. After almost an hour's searching, they called again to report they had found one pair of Ho Chi Minh sandals on a large trail with tracks from approximately thirty-five to forty people.[9] There was no mention of what happened to the enemy point man. Presumably, he regained consciousness and made his escape while the Americans were chasing his comrades. In the end, five NVA escaped near-certain death because an M-16 failed to function, and the squad leader had to explain to his company commander how all that effort only netted a hat, some sandals, and a rocket launcher. No one would bother to explain to the sergeant why his weapon failed.

When I stood atop LZ Beaver and looked down on the An Lao River in the valley, I expected there would be many labor-intensive "water parties" hauling water in five-gallon cans up the hill from the river for our daily needs. That was not the case. To do so would mean a predictable parade of men on the way to the river, and predictable travel always invited ambushes. So, we got the water for the base from a tributary stream of the An Lao that cut through the paddies a half mile from the base. A portable purification station was set up there and manned by a team of three enlisted men from the corps of engineers. They pumped the water into a 500-gallon open-topped canvas tank, treated it with chemicals, and then pumped the clean water into a 500-gallon water tank/trailer. Then, a 54-A flying crane or a Chinook troop carrier helicopter hauled it to the top of the hill. This "water point," as we called it, was guarded by an infantry squad at all times. It was considered part of the task of perimeter security. So when B Company rotated off the road security or security sweeps and ambushes, one of its squads was dispatched to protect the water point and its three engineers.

In early November my squad was assigned to a two-week rotation guarding the water point. We considered this pretty soft duty. There would be no patrolling and no ambushing, just sitting in the shade, a mere half mile from the firebase shooting the breeze with the engineers who were always in a mellow mood because of the huge bamboo dope pipe they had. The stem was about three feet long and about the size of a man's wrist in diameter. The bowl was quite a bit larger. It would hold a "nickel bag" at a time. In Vietnam, a $5.00 or "nickel bag" was a sandwich baggie stuffed full of marijuana. I was also particularly pleased to get this assignment because we had gotten a couple new men in the squad, Sgt. Richard Beunzel and Pvt. James Hinzo, so we had the customary ten-man squad. This meant that guard duty at night would be shorter and we could get some rest.

WARNING: HIGHPOINT ATTACK

On November 3 the 300th NVA Artillery Battalion moved into the An Lao Valley. On November 11, they attacked LZ English, another of the firebases in the valley, with their six-foot-long 122-millimeter rockets and heavy mortars. The men of the 173rd Airborne Brigade were on LZ English, and they had two men killed and fifteen wounded that day. There was also damage to two helicopters that were there at the time.[10] Our intelligence officers felt that attack and other information they gathered indicated things were going to heat up quickly in the An Lao Valley. So, my squad's respite was shorter than expected.

At 2:45 a.m. on November 16, the brigade intelligence section radioed the TOC at Beaver that they had information confirming the enemy would conduct what they called "highpoint" attacks in provinces of the Central Highlands. LZ Beaver was on the list of potential targets. The message also advised that "4th Division addresses" (units) should go to two-thirds alert. Up on Beaver, B Company went to 50 percent alert on the bunker line and they expected to go to full alert at any time.[11]

Jim Hinzo, one of the new men in the squad, was standing radio watch/guard duty and heard the intell message, and he woke me up immediately. I got on the radio to Captain Derricco and asked permission to bring my men and the engineers inside the wire right away. He said the men on the bunker line were pretty nervous and that we might get shot. He said we should stay put until daylight.

I was not pleased, and neither were the men in my squad. We were starting to feel like bait in the captain's quest for a higher body count. I put the squad on full alert. Once they were hunkered down in a circle of sandbagged fighting positions, I got on the radio to the mortar platoon assigned to help us if we needed it. They were the same guys I had spent my first night in the field with and gotten sunburned helping them build bunkers. We carefully rechecked the pre-set defensive coordinates for the water point. These were the coordinates of likely enemy approaches to our position that we could have the mortars fire on. Or, in case the enemy came from an unexpected direction, we could use these coordinates as reference points to adjust fire on the enemy. After that, we sat, waited, watched, and worried.

It was a day and a half before we got back inside the firebase, and I made the decision to abandon the water point on my own initiative. At dawn on the sixteenth, Captain Derricco sent our third platoon out to search for signs of the enemy. When they didn't find anyone, he gave us more proof for our bait theory. He assigned third platoon to be a rescue force for my squad if we were attacked, and told us to stay in place for another night.[12]

The next day, November 17, the captain sent out three dawn patrols. We tracked them by monitoring their "sit reps" (situation reports). We knew they were working in a pretty small area near the river but the enemy was too elusive for them. The hide and seek game went on all day, and at 6:15 that evening, we listened in anger as we heard the battalion's plan summary for the next twenty-four hours. The plan summary was basically the daily orders given to each company in the battalion. This particular one ordered B Company to continue with perimeter defense, send out two patrols in the daytime, and set two ambushes at night. There was no mention of bringing my squad in from their exposed position at the water point.[13]

Less than an hour after the plan summary was broadcast, about a company of the elusive enemy finally showed up. Unbelievably, they were directly across the river from the water point, wading across with torches! Ten men against about 140 was no contest! I got on the radio and told Joe Rocha, one of the CO's radio men, that my squad was coming in, and asked him to notify the perimeter guards so we didn't get shot by our own guys. As soon as I got off the line, the two Dusters on the firebase opened up on the enemy in the river. Dusters are tracked vehicles with twin 40-millimeter cannons. They make a sound like a mortar tube firing at a machinegun's rate of fire, and the rounds explode on contact. We could see them exploding amid the torches on both sides of the river and sending up geysers of water mixed with parts of people.

We used the Duster fire as a diversion and started back to the base. The half-mile trek to the perimeter was one of the longest, darkest, scariest, half miles I ever traveled. I think I aged at least a week, and I also almost opened fire on three shadows and two trees along the way. About five minutes into the trip, we heard the artillery battery come up on our push to warn the entire battalion net about troop movement on their radar and that they would be commencing fire immediately.[14] That was when we threw caution and stealth to the wind and sprinted the rest of the way to the perimeter.

My squad got itself inside the perimeter without incident, but I was sure the intelligence report and the fact that the enemy was moving in large numbers with lights meant we were in for at least one frontal assault on LZ Beaver. We waited for two days and the assault never happened. So, on November 19, our battalion stood down from alert and went back to the normal rotation of assigned duties on and around the base. My company's first platoon drew ambush duty, and my platoon, the second, went back to road clearing. The only excitement we had was trying to hold back a crowd of women and kids who were trying to scavenge equipment from a downed helicopter. The "slick," as it was called, had set down due to mechanical difficulties, and the crew had walked up the road to Beaver rather than wait by themselves in an exposed position in the paddies.[15]

While we herded the crowd of scavengers away from the slick, our first platoon called in to say they were returning from ambush duty with a prisoner. There was a little excitement about that, but the description sounded strange. The platoon leader said their prisoner was nine feet long. They had captured a nine-foot boa constrictor, and were happily making plans to cook it as soon as they got back inside the perimeter.[16]

At first, the return to our normal firebase routine was fairly boring. Then it got ridiculous with my squad trying to herd women and kids around and another one wrestling a huge snake up a hill for dinner. Then, in the middle of the afternoon, C Company's first platoon called in with the first serious business of the day. Their point man had found a cluster of four booby traps on a trail. The traps were four one-foot-square holes about six inches deep. A copper trip wire had been anchored in the bottom of each pit, and they were covered with a straw mat and sand. The trip wires were attached to four cans that were five inches in diameter and packed with C-4 plastic explosives and a variety of projectiles including glass, stones, and nails.[17] The cans were anchored to solid trees beside the trail and camouflaged so they could function as shotguns with barrels with five-inch diameters. Like the insulated food containers out on the road, the C-4 and the large cans could only have come from an American or ARVN base. Since the teenager with the derby had blown himself up setting a mine in the road, we were pretty certain that some of the other "road side salesmen" and scavengers were working against us, but we had yet to catch them in the act. Because more of these kinds of booby traps began to show up on the trails around Beaver, we expected things to get serious in the near future.

In fact, things got serious the very next day. C Company's first platoon made a basic tactical error at the end of a security patrol and two of their men were wounded. They were in a hurry to get to the base because darkness was approaching, and they used the same route they left the base by to return. They got ambushed. At about 6:35 p.m., they were fired on from the north and south. The first two rounds were B-40 rockets from the south. When the rockets went off, everyone in the patrol took cover, but that immobility set them up for bracketing fire from three more rockets from the north. Then rifle fire from AK-47s and SKS carbines came in on them from both directions.

The patrol held their attackers at bay with rifle and machine-gun fire for twenty minutes, but one of their men went down with a sucking chest wound. Sucking chest wounds were very serious because the lungs could fill with blood and a person could actually drown on dry land unless he got immediate medical attention. The TOC on Beaver called for a Dustoff at 7:05 p.m., about a half hour into the firefight. Exactly one minute later, the enemy stepped up the pressure with a heavy increase in rifle fire and three more B-40 rockets. Shrapnel from one of the rockets wounded another man in the patrol.

At 7:30 p.m., a Medevac helicopter escorted by a Cobra gunship arrived on station above the fight. It was then the Americans' turn to step up the pressure. The Cobra started to deliver suppressive fire from its "Minnie Gun," a six-barreled, electrically operated machinegun, at the rate of 6,000 rounds per minute. That blast of fire kept the enemy down while the two wounded men were winched up to the Medevac helicopter on a jungle penetrator. A jungle penetrator was a contraption that looked like a giant grappling hook with flat blades instead of hooks that were actually small bench seats for the wounded. It was dropped from a hovering Medevac helicopter, by winch, through the jungle canopy with the seats raised against the shaft so it could "penetrate" all three layers of the jungle canopy. Once it reached the ground, the bench seats were extended, and the wounded were placed on them and strapped to the shaft. Then, the whole contraption and the wounded were retrieved when the cable was rewound.

Dustoffs, like combat assaults, are simple in concept but difficult to execute. The most basic difficulty is caused when a Medevac helicopter hovers, presenting a stationary target for the enemy. Fortunately, this was an instance when the Cobra gunship and the men on the ground were able to deliver enough suppressive fire to get both men on board without further injury to them or damage to the helicopter. In fact, the evacuation was completed by 7:40 p.m. without further casualties because the Cobra got lucky on one of its covering runs. It fired some of the 2.75-inch rockets from the pod mounted on the right side of the fuselage at a suspected enemy position. The rockets exploded on impact and caused a large secondary explosion. That was a sure sign they had struck the ammunition bearer for at least one of the B-40 gunners.[18]

MEDICAL CARE FOR AMERICANS

C Company's men got ambushed and had two seriously wounded men inside an hour. Then, within an hour of being wounded, both men were in the care of the battalion surgeon on LZ Beaver. It was pretty obvious to all the Grunts how fortunate we were to have such resources and, in fact, many times after my squad killed those five men in an ambush, I wondered what had become of the one I wounded. I also wondered about the numerous other wounded whose predicaments were always noted in our sit reps as "blood trails being followed." Truthfully, for seventeen years after I left Vietnam, I thought often about the personal side of who my enemy had been and what happened to them when they got sick, wounded, or killed, but I kept the considerations to the limited group of my brother and other combat veterans I know. I did this because my initial attempts to discuss such concerns with the men in my unit, and even the battalion surgeon, were pretty much discouraged.

I was in the battalion surgeon's care on LZ Beaver when I broached the subject of the type of care and treatment the enemy was able to give their men. As a physician, Captain Robinson didn't seem surprised by the question, but he said he had no idea and was not inclined to find out. He was the only physician for nearly 850 infantrymen and he had no time to worry about how the enemy was getting along.[19] Then he began to treat me for the various medical problems I had developed in my first six weeks in the jungle.

The first problem was the bullet wound from my first ambush. It was almost closed but still bleeding a little. So, it remained a daily attraction for leeches. Also, I had cellulitis on my shoulders and hands. The shoulders had never recovered from the sunburn from my first week. Carrying a pack every day aggravated the blisters, and then they got infected because I didn't bathe or change clothes the first month I was in the field.

The most serious problem seemed to be my hands. They were covered with infected brush cuts from elephant grass and punctures from thorns. They would not heal because I was always wet and dirty. My left thumb was twice its normal size, and my last two fingers on my right hand were the size of normal thumbs. All the other digits and places on the palms were draining pus continually. When it got to the point that I couldn't change magazines in my weapon, Captain Derricco told me to see the surgeon. The surgeon's chief medic had recently been promoted from our company. He took personal care of the surgeon's instructions for me. He numbed both hands with injections and lanced all my fingers and a couple places in each palm with a scalpel to drain them. He also took the initiative to send me to the base camp at Pleiku where I could get soaks in an antibacterial soap called phisohex three times a day.[20] Six days later, I was back on LZ Beaver building more bunkers and escorting the combat engineers while they cleared the road of mines so supply convoys could reach the LZ.

When I got back from the base camp, I approached the topic of medical care for the enemy obliquely with our new platoon leader, Lt. William ("LT Mack") MacKowan. He had just finished a briefing for a patrol we were supposed to make, and as we loaded magazines and stuffed grenades in our pockets, I asked him if he ever wondered who the enemy were and what they might be like as people. We knew of course, in general terms, that they were the NVA and the Viet Cong, and they also had unit designations, but no one knew personal details. All we really knew was that there was "an enemy unit," or some "gooks" we were supposed to hunt down. LT Mack had joined the Army instead of getting drafted and was also Special Forces trained. Maybe that had a lot to do with the way he discouraged inquiries that would give a face to the enemy. He told me it was not necessary to know about them, or to care about what happened to them. He said, "Gill, we are here to get a high body count. Just kill 'em, count 'em, and forget 'em."

I had a similar conversation with Bud Rose and Stretch Bostwick, two privates in my platoon. We were digging foxholes for the night and I brought up the topic. They were both draftees and, like me, just trying to get through the war. Rose said, "Man, I don't know, and I don't care. I just want to get through this year without having to personally kill someone. I know it might be unrealistic, but that's what I want." I guessed at the time that this was his way of retreating from the reality of our situation. I asked Stretch if he ever wondered who the people were in the photos in the wallets of the dead, or who the letters in their packs were addressed to. He stared at me for a minute, and then he said, "Dude, why do you care? Are you gonna write and say you're sorry about capping somebody's old man? Old Luke the Gook ain't worrying about you, so you don't gotta worry about him. What you best do is worry about Gillam not endin' up in a body bag."

In retrospect, I know those responses, whether they were from officers or enlisted men, were shaped for emotional protection. We were doing an emotionally tough job and like LT Mack said, it was enough that we accumulated a body count for most of our patrols. So we stressed the impersonal approach as much as we could. We made the NVA and Viet Cong into "the other," those people who sociologists and psychologists say are created in the minds of soldiers so they can do the violent things civilians find unacceptable without feeling shame or blame. We dehumanized them. We called them "Gooks" and "Dinks" instead of men or soldiers. Then, as a war of attrition demanded, we killed them and counted them. When we killed in sufficient numbers, rewards of rank and privilege in the insular world that is the infantry were given to us. It mattered not at all if we had done things that would land us in prison if we had been civilians. It was a situation in which most of us kept the emotional personal questions bottled up and buried in our psyches for later consideration, and sometimes, therapeutic treatment.

Of course, avoiding the issue of the enemy's humanity had immediate consequences, too. One of them was when I found myself hunched over in the rain covered in my own vomit, after killing a man for the first time. I kept trying to latch onto the idea that my nausea was not the result of revulsion and stark terror; it was just the physiological result of an adrenaline overload. For several days, I looked desperately for a way to bury the thoughts about whether or not the man had a family or friends. Sometimes, I even wondered if he was really dead. I only presumed he was when Jim Higgins and I stripped him of his weapon and left him wide eyed and sitting upright against a tree. I kept debating with myself whether it was better to have killed him outright, as I thought I had, or to leave him wounded and in shock sitting in the mud.

The next time I killed, I left five men lying on a trail after my first ambush. These men, I knew for a certainty, were dead. Each of them had absorbed too many high-velocity bullets at near point-blank range, to be anything else but dead. Yet, by the time I got back to the base to make my report to Captain Derricco, I had already started to reject or bury thoughts of their personalities. I even changed the facts about the wounded man. I shot him, but I laid the responsibility for what might have happened to him afterward on the collective "we" of my squad. I simply told the captain "we bushwhacked six Gooks. We got five KIAs and we wounded one. He left a blood trail, but that's all we found."

For seventeen years after I left Vietnam, like many other veterans, I repressed thoughts about the humanity of my enemies and what happened to them. Then, in the fall of 1987, Martin Yanuck, my department chair at Spelman College, asked me to create a course on the history of Vietnam from the colonial era to the present. That request not only caused me to exhume many long-buried issues, it also forced those issues into the more public forum of academia where I was required to consider them in an organized, insightful, and, indirectly, therapeutic manner. As I gathered information for that course, and later for this book, I was able to put definitive, documented answers to some of my questions about the people we called KIAs (killed in action) and WIAs (wounded in action) who left blood trails we followed.

MEDICAL TREATMENT FOR THE ENEMY

The best documentary information I found on the topic of medical treatment for my former enemies was a report written during the summer of 1969 by Brig. Gen. William E. Potts, the Assistant Chief of Staff for Intelligence for MACV. It is called "Medical Causes of Non-Effectiveness Among VC/NVA Troops (Third Update)."[21] General Potts' report was a study and discussion of the principal wounds and diseases that caused attrition (death, permanent disability, and temporary disability) among the Viet Cong and NVA forces during the war. Not surprisingly, he found that battle wounds and malaria were the most serious causes for their "non-effectiveness."

Through interrogation of prisoners and defectors, and the analysis of captured medical records for over 15,000 patients, General Potts determined that three factors caused deaths among the enemy once they were wounded. The first cause was the prolonged time between receiving a wound and arrival at an adequately equipped medical facility. The second cause of death was the generally anemic blood condition among troops of the Viet Cong and NVA.[22] Finally, General Potts noted that the placement of the wound also was critical to the soldier's survival or death. We were taught to aim for "center mass," the thorax and abdomen, whenever we could. General Potts found that the majority of enemy with those kinds of wounds died before they ever saw a hospital. There was not even much hope for those with wounds to extremities. Of 15,077 men in his study with arm and leg wounds, 13,213, or 87.6 percent, died of their wounds.[23]

Difficulties with the medical evacuation and treatment of the wounded also contributed to the high death rate among the enemy. According to General Potts, the Viet Cong and NVA aidmen on the field of battle could do little other than to try to stop the bleeding. They typically lacked equipment like sterile dressings and hypodermic needles for the injection of painkillers or antibiotics. Also, no intravenous fluids were available until they reached a battalion aid station. Those aid stations were usually eight to twelve hours away and the patients were typically transported to them in hammocks attached to bamboo poles that were carried by two men or suspended between two bicycles.

If a wounded Viet Cong or NVA soldier lived to see a battalion aid station, he was treated by either an Yi Si (Medical Technician), or a Bac Si (Physician). The medical technicians and physicians were assisted by up to eight nurses and twenty aidmen whose first duty was triage of the wounded into one of three categories: seriously wounded, moderately wounded, and minor wounds. A shocking 100 percent of those men in the seriously wounded category ended up "permanently disabled," and never returned to combat. Fifty percent of the moderately wounded also became permanently disabled, and 25 to 30 percent of the men with minor wounds also fell into this category. The dismal recovery prognosis was caused by nervous system damage, joint injuries, poorly healed fractures, and the long-term effect of infections.

In truth, there was little effective medical help available at a battalion aid station. They were basically facilities for wound cleaning, sutures, amputations, and abdominal surgery. Many of the patients in these latter two procedures died from the lack of sterile operating fields and instruments. Also, there was almost never any whole blood, and drugs like dextran, a common blood expander, were also scarce or unavailable. Painkillers were also scarce, so many died from shock during amputations or surgery. Those with minor wounds remained at the battalion aid station and the others, after stabilization, went to regimental or provincial level facilities. Again, the usual mode of transportation to those facilities was by hammock or bicycle, but there were occasional resorts to trucks. Only once in over 15,000 cases was the evacuation by air that Americans took for granted even mentioned. A small plane for a high-ranking cadre was used. The time frame for the usual mode of transport to these upper level facilities was anywhere between three days to three weeks.[24]

Like their American counterparts, the enemy soldiers were also hospitalized for non-battle related conditions and I was surprised to see that first among those causes were their own booby traps. After that, the chief causes for hospitalization were diseases. General Potts' study found that the enemy's chances of recovery from diseases were compromised because of a high incidence of anemia among their ranks. This condition was primarily the result of protein deficient diets, chronic malaria, and intestinal parasites. It was General Potts' opinion that an anemic condition in a patient compromised his overall recovery from wounds as well as diseases. For example, documents found in enemy medical facilities showed their patients' red blood cell count was 2.5–3.5 million per cubic centimeter. The average red cell count in a healthy, non-anemic patient is 4.5 to 5 million cells per cubic centimeter. It was General Potts' opinion that anemics didn't survive wounds well because they couldn't develop clots to slow the outflow of blood.

General Potts also noted that malaria was the chief non-traumatic disabler and killer of the enemy's troops. Forty-eight percent of the patients in their hospitals and 44 percent of their forces in the field were infected with it. Twenty percent of them were hospitalized for it and 2 percent of them died of it. Three of the four species of malaria that infect people were found in Vietnam, and the most dangerous one, the *Falciparum*, thrived in the Central Highlands. (The others are the *Plasmodium Vivax*, *Plasmodium Falciparum*, and *Plasmodium Malariae*.) The drug chloraquin was used when it was available, but it did not prevent the invasion of the liver or affect the disease once it spread to that organ. It did, however, protect red blood cells and suppress the discomfort of acute malarial attacks. The *Falciparum* strain of malaria is very resistant to chloraquin and Americans used chloraquin in combination with primaquin to destroy the malaria parasite in the liver. The Viet Cong and NVA had no access at all to primaquin.

Other disabling diseases that struck the enemy forces were respiratory and gastrointestinal ailments. In the former group, tuberculosis and pneumonia led the way. Sixteen percent of the patients in General Potts' study had those problems. The most common gastrointestinal ailment was dysentery. Eleven percent of the enemy's men came down with it. They were treated with sulfaquanidine, iodine, emetrine, or opiates.[25]

TALKING TO A "BLOOD TRAIL"/MEETING A MAN I SHOT

In early 1991, I added to my documentary information about the enemy's medical treatment when I returned to Vietnam as a Fulbright Fellow. During the program, I attended two weeks of seminars and lectures held in the Ministry of Education's offices in Ho Chi Minh City and Hanoi. In Hanoi, I had a cathartic moment during a lecture given by Professor Mac Duong, who was at the time a member of Hanoi University's Literature Department. During the war, he spent six years in the infantry as a guide on the Ho Chi Minh Trail. His lecture was a description of life on the Ho Chi Minh Trail during the war. He said he had been wounded in the right forearm and sent home for recovery. His doctors determined that he had sustained permanent nerve damage, and so Mac was reassigned as a training cadre at Xuan Mai, the training camp and origination point of the Ho Chi Minh Trail.

As Professor Mac answered specific questions from some of our group, three things he said brought me to the startling realization that I was the person who had shot him during the war. The first thing was the coincidence of dates. He was shot on October 27, 1969, the same date I led my first ambush. It was not a date either of us would likely forget because we were both shot on that night. Second, the map he put up for discussion showed the same terrain features in the Vinh Than Valley (Happy Valley) I had used to select the ambush site. Third, in his account, and my memory, there was only one survivor, and he had dropped a rifle when he got shot in the right forearm. I reported and remembered chasing the lone survivor and I also brought his rifle home with me in 1970. It had blood on it when I picked it up. A final confirmation of my thoughts on the matter came when I went to the National Archives to conduct research on this book. There, I found the details of the ambush recorded in a document called the "Operation Report for the 1st Battalion, 22nd Regiment."[26]

THE BRIGADE REACTION FORCE

In early November 1969, just as Operation *Putnam Wildcat* was starting, President Richard Nixon gave a speech on the Vietnamization of the war. He said that in January 1969, when he took office, the war was already four years old. In that period 31,000 Americans had been killed, and the training of ARVN troops to "Vietnamize," or take over the major responsibility for the conduct of the war was far behind schedule. He continued to say that 550,000 Americans were in Vietnam when he came to office and there were no solid plans for leaving. Finally, the president noted that there had been no substantive progress at the Paris Peace Talks, and there were deep divisions at home and abroad about our policy and position in Vietnam. President Nixon said it was these facts that led him to the plan for Vietnamization that he announced that day.

The heart of the plan required the removal of 60,000 troops from Vietnam by December 15, 1969, and 20 percent of those men were supposed to be combat troops. This was possible, he said, because infiltration along the Ho Chi Minh Trail was less than 20 percent of what it had been in 1968. He also noted that American casualties in September and October of 1969 were the lowest in three years. At the end of this encouraging piece of propaganda, Nixon said he would not publicize timetables of future withdrawals for security reasons.[27]

I read about the speech in letters from home, but I was not impressed. Nixon had made similar noises before. For example, in July 1969, he had held a press conference with Gen. Creighton Abrams, the top commander in Vietnam, in attendance. That was when he had promised to "re-deploy" 25,000 troops by the end of August 1969.[28] The fact that I shipped out for Vietnam in September 1969, and began hearing disturbing rumors about the reassignment of supposedly departing troops to other units, led me to the realization that despite Nixon's encouraging pronouncements, I was not going home for the holidays. In fact, I had a thoroughly depressing Thanksgiving to start the season off. We went on an ambush, and it not only rained, but because of a freak cold snap, we spent the night shivering in a sleet storm, dressed in wet tropical-weight jungle fatigues.

The day after Thanksgiving, my battalion was chosen to be the reaction force for the 4th Infantry Division's 3rd Brigade. As such, our battalion, or one of its companies, would make combat assaults to any area where the other units in the brigade encountered more enemies than they expected or could handle. That same day, we received orders for a combat assault from the vicinity of LZ Beaver to a field a few kilometers west, near LZ Stinger.[29] We expected the worst. The helicopters would not land for fear of mines, so we jumped the last five or six feet into the suspected minefield while the door gunners on every ship tore up the tree line with their machineguns. The landing was uncontested, and we disarmed a couple mines without incident. Those were the only breaks we got. For ten straight days, from December 1 to 10, our battalion turned up enemy supplies, and every time we did, there were firefights and killings on both sides.

B Company had three platoons in the field, and each patrolled separate areas in search of the enemy and his supplies. On the morning of December 5, our first platoon found a hut and a cave with 500 pounds of wheat in them. The next day, the same unit killed one NVA and wounded another when they showed up on a trail near the cave. The wounded one dropped his weapon, so they also captured two AK-47s. On the morning of December 10, my platoon and the third platoon were working close to each other, and we got into a running firefight with three NVA. We chased them for half a day and killed one of them. Then, around the middle of the afternoon, D company, on one of the rare times when they left a firebase, got two men wounded. It was an ambush that went awry when D Company's point man spotted the enemy before he led his men into the killing zone. They pursued their attackers and just before 5:00 p.m. they captured an NVA officer who carried a .45-caliber sidearm.[30] The fact that it was a weapon carried by Americans did not bode well for his treatment before he was turned over to the ARVN for questioning.

In general, the men of D Company, like the rest of us, were aware of the strategy and tactics of the enemy. One of their strategic aims was to cause enough American casualties and uncertainty about our safety inside our bases to turn the trickle of men being withdrawn into a flood. The August 7, 1969, attack on the American Convalescent Hospital at Cam Ranh Bay was an example of that strategy. They also wanted to demoralize the American forces still serving in Vietnam, similar to when the Viet Cong executed two American prisoners in September 1965. Capt. Humbert R. Versace and Sgt. Kenneth M. Roarback were shot on September 26, 1965. The public announcement that accompanied the executions said their deaths were "a fully justified act, severe and well deserved . . . a proper protest against the fascist sentence and execution by the lackey government of three patriots who had been convicted by the government of South Vietnam of terrorist acts."[31]

Knowing the enemy had no qualms about executing American prisoners, and the general circumstances under which we met the enemy during the rest of Operation *Putnam Wildcat,* turned the operation into a series of brutal encounters. Some were close-range firefights followed by hand-to-hand combat between point men on each side. Some were ambushes that trapped and killed a few of the enemy. Prisoners became a rarity; we took only thirty-two during the three months of the operation.[32] My squad captured one of them, and we kept him tied to a tree while we waited for a helicopter to come and take him away for interrogation. Ed Bennet, one of the men who carried the radio for my squad, wanted to cut off his ears. I found myself in the awkward position of having to defend an NVA soldier from my own men.

A CHRISTMAS DAY KILLING

I went to Vietnam naively thinking I might get home by the holiday season. I passed Thanksgiving sitting in the rain and sleet on an ambush. So when Christmas approached, I had no illusions about where I was going or what would happen. We were in the middle of an operation, and I resigned myself to treat the holidays like any other day despite the fact that we did receive some unexpected concessions from Col. Michael P. Juvenal, the new battalion commander. For Christmas Eve, each company in the battalion was allowed to gather its platoons into a single perimeter for a relatively safer position. We also got mail and hot meals flown out to us. I got a package my mother sent with a canned ham, a loaf of rye bread, and some other goodies. My sister sent some chocolate chip cookies that had gotten beaten to crumbs, but we ate them anyhow. My dad sent a miniature Christmas tree with lights and a small battery so the lights would come on. It was all very nice. I cooked the ham on a couple empty C-Ration cans with C-4 explosive for fuel, and I made ham on rye sandwiches for the whole squad. Larry Black, a guy from Texas, said he was in love with my sister and her chocolate chip crumbs and asked for her address. We all had a good laugh about that.

On Christmas day, it was back to work. The company split into platoons again, and we spent the day searching for more NVA to destroy. It was pouring cold rain, and we found no enemies at all. At the time, I thought it was probably because the only people stupid enough to come out in that weather were Americans. Just to be sure, the platoon split into squads to search a little more and planned a rendezvous on a hill overlooking a valley for later in the day. By late afternoon, we had covered our assigned area, and each squad headed for the designated hilltop. My squad was the third one to arrive and we started digging foxholes along the military crest for the night perimeter. We were just about done with the job when, much to our disgust, the battalion commander's Loach (Light Observation Helicopter) circled our position twice and landed. He had come to bolster morale, I suppose, or inspect the troops, but we cared little about that. No one was glad see Colonel Juvenal because we knew that his landing at our position had given our location to the enemy. We would have to move as soon as he left or risk getting mortared that night. That meant at least another hour's walk, part of it in the dark, and digging more foxholes.

The colonel's arrival also stirred up the ever-present class and caste antagonisms of officer versus enlisted men and professional soldier, or Lifer versus draftee. While his helicopter circled over the valley as a continued advertisement for our general location, the colonel walked around to almost every fighting position in the perimeter. I was really pissed. As far as I was concerned, he was just marking each of them for later attention by the NVA after he left. Captain Derrico seemed to be all smiles about the colonel's visit, but hell, he was a Lifer too.

The colonel stood by my foxhole for a minute or so, and what transpired in that short time summed up all the differences in rank and caste between us. Using my helmet, I had bailed the water in my foxhole down to ankle depth when he got there. He was so clean I could smell him ten feet away. I had not changed clothes or bathed since mid-November. He had on a Class A raincoat with a chrome-plated .45-caliber automatic on a web belt around his waist. We called them Pimp Guns. They were probably just flashy enough for the streets, but no Grunt in his right mind would carry anything that shiny. The raincoat covered him to a point just below his knees, but from my position in the hole, I was at eye level with the bottom of his starched, pressed jungle fatigues. The colonel's clean pants were neatly bloused into a pair of spit-shined, all leather paratrooper jump boots. Full leather combat boots were a statement of status. If they stayed wet all the time, they would rot off your feet in a couple weeks, but no one had any doubt that the colonel would be wet for no more than a couple hours. I was wearing boots with canvas uppers and I hadn't been dry since the monsoon season began in September. My whole body was wrinkled up like a child's hands that had been left in the bathtub too long.

I was just not in a civil mood when the colonel harrumphed like all Lifers did and asked, "Who's in charge here?" The first answer that came to mind was "probably some guy named Nguyen," but I bit down on that and told him I was the squad leader. Next, he said, "So how are you son? Are we winning the war?" Other than the note that came with the small tree, I had not heard from my dad in a while and the colonel's presumptuousness just evaporated what little civility I had left. I dumped a helmet full of muddy water near his boots and told him, "My dad is back in the World, in Ohio. As far as the fuckin' war goes, I got six months and a wake up here. Then you can give my piece of your circus to some other draftee."

The colonel frowned, asked my name and rank, and then he moved on like he was a politician on a campaign. I don't think he even considered that every stop could have marked the position for a rocket or mortar shell. Captain Derricco, as was required on these little inspection tours, was standing next to the colonel. He mumbled something to LT Mack, and then Mack hung back to speak to me when the other two Lifers left. He told me I needed to adjust my attitude toward officers before it got me in trouble. I said, "You know, LT, you're right. Before you know it, I could find myself drafted and in the infantry somewhere in Vietnam."

There was an enemy mortar crew lurking near us that day, but we didn't have to move to avoid them after the colonel left. They were all dead before his Loach landed to pick him up. My squad and the others on the hilltop watched them die. This is how it happened: Joe Rocha was on the radio talking to Sgt. Joe "Cat" Ackzinski, who had been ordered to use his squad as a stay-behind ambush for anyone walking our back trail. Rocha was telling Cat to stay put because we were going to change night locations as soon as the brass left.

While Rocha talked to Cat on the radio, he was looking at a tree line that bordered a field of elephant grass where Cat was supposed to be, and incredibly, he saw an enemy mortar squad walking right through the middle of the field. They were on a perpendicular course that would intersect the route of Cat's squad in about a hundred meters.

In Vietnam, darkness always comes first to the valleys, and that is probably why they were walking out in the open. Unfortunately for them, from the hilltop, there was still enough light for us to see them all. Two of them were carrying a mortar tube and base plate. There were eight more, and with the exception of their point man, they all carried a pack frame with three of the larger 82-millimeter mortar rounds on it. Clearly, they planned on making a miserable night for one of the platoons in our company. Neither the NVA nor Cat's men in the trees could see each other because of the rain, failing light, and the eight- to ten-foot-high elephant grass. So, LT Mack snatched the radio hand-set from Rocha and started frantically telling Cat's men to spread out on line facing the field. Then, the colonel said to no one in particular, that we ought to bring some fire to bear on those men from our position.

Most of us were staring dumbfounded at the NVA's stupidity when Jesse Johnson, the M-60 machinegunner I had gone on my first patrol with, opened fire. It was textbook machinegun work, and all ten of the NVA were dead in less than two minutes. Jesse was a muscular man who could hold the beaten zone for his weapon to a circle of eighteen inches at five hundred yards. The range to his targets was about three hundred yards, so when he fired his usual burst of six to nine rounds on center of mass of each man, every one of them was chopped to pieces by a hail-storm of 7.62-millimeter bullets to the chest and stomach. Jesse took his time and deliberately alternated his selection of targets back and forth from the front to the rear of the column. As soon as he took down their point man, he swung onto the last man and dropped him in his tracks. That caused the illusion that they were under attack from the front and rear, and prevented them from retreating in the direction they had come from. It was a piece of dramatic good fortune that he also set off one of the mortar rounds or a grenade at the rear of the column. The explosion made the rest of the squad hunker down in a depression in the valley seeking cover from what they probably assumed was one of our mortar teams.

The next thing that happened was Cat's squad opened fire from the wood line. The depression the NVA found saved them from direct harm by fire from Cat's squad, but it held them in a vulnerable position on the valley floor. As long as they stayed there, the line of sight from the military crest of the hill left them totally exposed to Jesse's gun. They were sitting ducks and he killed every one of them by himself. The colonel promoted him on the spot from specialist fourth class to sergeant. Then he got in his Loach and went back to the TOC.

The backslapping and dappin over Jesse's promotion lasted about a half hour. Then, as darkness came to the hilltop, Captain Derricco got a bright idea. He figured that some more NVA might come looking for their mortar squad, so he sent my squad down into the valley to set up an ambush in a bamboo grove near the bodies. My opinion was that the Lifers were getting too damn greedy about the body count thing, and I said so when LT Mack came to tell me I had the bushwhack that night. Mack said he and the captain thought it was the perfect job for a smart-ass sergeant to work on an attitude adjustment.

GETTING OVERRUN

One of the infantryman's unspoken fears is that he will be caught in an isolated tactically poor position and have his unit overrun. Since we had just seen what a tactically deficient position the valley floor was, I forgot about Lifers and their body count fixation and started getting my squad set up to make sure we survived the night. We got on our bellies and crawled into the center of a bamboo thicket about twenty meters from the dead mortar team. Then we dug body-length trenches just wide enough for two men to lie in and camouflaged them. We also set out trip flares backed up by Claymore mines on the likely avenues of approach. Then, I got on the "Red Leg Push" (artillery frequency) and made sure they knew where we were and where the pre-set coordinates were for firing shells to protect our position. After that, the only thing left to do was to settle into our trenches and wait for some more NVA to get stupid. The rain filled up the trenches in less than an hour. The good news was the cold water kept us awake all night. The bad news was even with two men to a hole for body warmth, we were still miserably cold, and our clothes were full of leeches.

It was almost dawn when my squad was overrun. We heard them coming from two sides of our position even though the wind and rain had not slackened at all. Small units in the jungle always took care to move quietly, so the fact that we could hear branches breaking and footsteps had me really worried about being outnumbered. I was about to call the artillery for a fire mission when Bud Rose shook my arm and pointed to a pair of glowing yellow eyes a few feet from us. They belonged to a baby orangutan. It suddenly made sense that none of our trip flares had gone off because the baby and his relatives had come to us through the branches of some nearby trees. They had dropped inside our line of flares to feed on bamboo shoots all around us. They were breaking off stalks and eating as they came, and that accounted for the noise we heard.

I had just started to relax and consider the humor of the fact that we were sitting in the middle of their breakfast when Bud Rose brought all hell down on us. He picked up a fist-sized stone and threw it right at the baby orangutan. When the stone hit, the baby squalled, and its parents surged forward to protect it. I had no idea until that morning how big orangutans were. I think the one that jumped Rose and me was about five feet tall and probably weighed a lot more than either one of us. One thing for sure, it was a hell of a lot stronger than both of us together. I also made the painful discovery that they can swing sticks like clubs. At least, I think that is how four of my ribs got cracked. I was in the midst of a general melee of running shouting people and snarling animals, so I wasn't very clear about details. For all I know, the damage could have happened when one or more of my men trampled me.

None of us were dead, but there were a lot of bruises. I was just glad no one had shot and wounded one of the apes. It was a sure bet that none of us would have scored a one-shot kill, and a wounded parent ape had to be worse than just an angry one. All the trip flares we set out were tripped in the flight from the apes. So there we were, bedraggled, ass kicked, and crawling around in a bright circle of light for every NVA in the valley to see. It was time to get out and get out quick. We retrieved our Claymore mines and other gear that was scattered around the thicket. Then we limped back up the hill to the perimeter, and I explained what happened to the CO and LT Mack.

Joe Rocha said he called in the "contact" to the battalion duty officer as soon as he got his giggles under control, but my search in the archives in the summer of 2003 turned up no such record.[33] At the time though, we took a lot of teasing about being "overrun." The up side was we got orders for only a lightweight short-range patrol for that afternoon. That allowed me time to get my ribs properly taped and wait for a handful of percodan tablets to take effect. For the rest of my tour in Vietnam, my squad was also referred to as "Gillam's Gorillas."

WINS AND LOSSES FROM *PUTNAM WILDCAT*

Operation *Putnam Wildcat* officially concluded on January 31, 1970. That same day Captain Derricco rotated his headquarters group back to my platoon, and I had the chance to talk to Joe Rocha. He was still serving as the captain's radio operator, and that allowed him to monitor information on the battalion push. Joe was a conscientious soldier, and I think he actually cared if we won the war or not. He said from what he heard on the radio, it seemed like we had done a pretty good job on the operation. In the summer of 2003, I located two documents in the National Archives that gave specific details of what we accomplished. The first was the "Enemy Strength, Tactics, and Losses" section of the "Operation Report for *Putnam Wildcat.*" The second was a sub-section of that report called the "After Action Report, Results." Those two documents gave a sharper focus to what Rocha called a pretty good job.

The 1st Battalion, 22nd Infantry killed ninety-nine enemy in action, and captured thirty-two more of them. We captured forty-nine AK-47s, one of the newer AK-50 assault rifles with the folding stock, seven SKS Carbines, three rocket launchers, two French MAS rifles, a Soviet-made PPS sub-machinegun, a Soviet-made Makarov pistol, three Chinese-made 9-millimeter pistols, and seven crossbows. We also recovered several American-made weapons. One of them was a World War II vintage .30-caliber carbine. There were also three .45-caliber pistols and an M-79 grenade launcher.

Since depriving the enemy of his ammunition and supplies was also an important part of the operation, there was also a careful accounting of the munitions seized during the operation. Some of what we collected was the ammunition of the dead after a firefight or an ambush, but we also took significant amounts of ammunition from caches we discovered. The "After Action Report" said that we took 118 of their smaller 60-millimeter mortar rounds, and 29 of their larger 82-millimeter rounds from caves and camouflaged bunkers. There were also the thirty rounds we collected Christmas day and blew up before we left what I called "Orangutan Valley." One hundred and nineteen B-40 rockets came into our possession, mostly from arms caches, but also a few from dead or captured enemy. We accounted for 7,453 rounds of ammunition for rifles from the same sources. We recovered twenty-three American grenades and seventeen grenades of Chinese manufacture. Finally, we captured eleven Viet Cong uniforms and over 3,864 pounds of rice.[34]

We were in a war, so it was expected that our operational successes would be balanced by exactions of dead and wounded. The enemy collected from us without respect for rank or position. For example, the personnel information in the "Operations Report" for *Putnam Wildcat* showed that an officer in our battalion headquarters was killed and another was wounded during the operation. Such casualties were clear reminders that even if you worked in what most enlisted men thought of as the relative safety of a conex standing duty officer's radio watch for the battalion commander, you were still not beyond the reach of the enemy. The two officers in this case were part of the fifteen men wounded in the standoff attack with rockets and mortars on LZ English. We lost three other men who were killed in the search–and-destroy operations in the An Lao Valley. Then, there were the wounded. Most of them were in D Company. Fourteen of their men were wounded. My company was either lucky, good, or a combination of both. We had no one killed, and only two men were wounded seriously.[35]

5. ✸

Operation *Putnam Power*

January 18 to February 7, 1970

The 1st Battalion, 22nd Infantry was the 2nd Brigade's reaction force, so we got pulled in from the field in mid-January for a three-week assignment called Operation *Putnam Power*. We were picked up by choppers from a hastily cut landing zone and flown to LZ Stinger. We got a two-day stand down, during which we bathed, changed clothes, and drank ourselves silly. Then they told us where we were going and what they expected us to do. The brigade intelligence people said they had finally confirmed the location of Base Area 226 in the Vinh Than Valley, so they were sending us back to destroy it. The English translation of Vinh Than is Happy Valley. I had been there before, but I had no happy memories of it. The Vinh Than had been a redoubt for Vietnamese forces during their 900 years of resistance to the Chinese, so I guess the Vietnamese would be happy with the place. In fact, from their perspective, it probably made pretty good sense for them to return to the scene of a past success.[1]

On the morning of January 18, 1970, B Company began its three-week assignment on Operation *Putnam Power*. We were part of a battalion-sized combat assault from LZ Stinger that dropped four infantry companies into separate landing zones. My company got on the ground with no casualties because nearly 900 men from the 4th Infantry Division's 1st Battalion, 12th Regiment were already in the valley to give us a hand. As soon as the enemy knew they were there, they stopped shooting at our helicopters and temporarily withdrew.[2] But despite the relatively uncontested landing, everyone guessed we were in for a concentrated dose of what the war was all about.

The struggle for Base Area 226 involved elements of the air war, the ground war, and a part of the Vietnam War that few who were not there knew about: the war *in* the ground. In the three weeks I spent in the Vinh Than Valley, I got the up-close and personal version of all three. The combined experience had an effect that was both immediate and long-term on the land and all of us who were there. In fact, for my part, the experience forced me to accept the fact that if I were to survive my tour of duty, I would have to grow a callous on my soul and become a hardened, relentless killer. The problem I had with that resolution then, and sometimes even now, is how hardened and relentless I had to be.

PUTNAM POWER AND THE AIR WAR

The largest, and perhaps most devastating, part of the air war in the Vinh Than Valley were "*Arc Light*" missions flown by B-52 strategic bombers. The B-52s were huge planes built by the Boeing Aircraft Corporation as part of the Cold War against the Soviet Union and the People's Republic of China. They were never used against either of those nations, but they had been in Vietnam since June 1965. Lyndon Johnson first considered using them in early November 1964 as a retaliatory measure for a Viet Cong attack on American aircraft at Bien Hoa Air Base, but he put off using them and instead opted for smaller, tactical aircraft in a bombing program called *Rolling Thunder*. *Rolling Thunder* was supposed to gradually increase the pain quotient of Hanoi and force them to accept a negotiated peace. It didn't, so Johnson finally made the decision to initiate bombing by B-52s in Vietnam. They called them *Arc Light* missions.

On June 16, 1965, thirty B-52s launched from their base on the island of Guam to strike at a suspected concentration of Viet Cong near Ben Cat, not far from Saigon. A spy warned the Viet Cong, and so the first *Arc Light* mission killed no one. Still, Lyndon Johnson and General Westmoreland, the MACV Commander, elected to continue their use because they delivered devastating payloads onto a relatively small area. That first non-lethal strike was typical in its concentration of destructive power. Each of the first twenty-four planes carried fifty MK117 bombs, and the other six carried thirty-six AN-M59A1 armor-piercing bombs. MK117s weighed 750 pounds, and the AN-N59A1s weighed 1,000 pounds. Altogether, 1,300 bombs with a combined weight of 558 tons fell on an area one mile long and two miles wide.[3]

The first *Arc Light* mission in the Central Highlands was launched on November 14, 1965, when elements of the 1st Air Calvary discovered an NVA base camp with two regiments of troops in the Ia Drang Valley near Cambodia. Two days later, 18 B-52s dropped 344 tons of bombs on the target. By the end of the month, they had unloaded 1,795 tons of ordnance on that single troop concentration.[4]

By January 1970, *Arc Light* missions had been used in the Central Highlands for five years, and one was employed against the location of Base Area 226 in preparation for *Putnam Power*. The devastation I saw when it was over was incredible. The drop was made in an area of triple canopy jungle where the trees were eighty to one hundred feet tall. They were stacked up like matchsticks on the edges of the craters. The craters were about thirty or forty feet across, and deep enough to hold a basement for the average two-story house in America.[5]

Arc Lights were devastating, but the Air Force also had other, larger means of delivering death from above. Their largest piece of explosive ordnance was the BLU 82/B General Purpose High Explosive Concussion Bomb. It was 4.5 feet wide, 11 feet long, and weighed 15,000 pounds. Twelve-thousand six-hundred of those pounds were explosives. They were the largest bomb in the American arsenal short of nuclear armaments, and like nuclear bombs, they were dropped one at a time. In early 1970, these bombs, known as "Daisy Cutters," were also employed in Vietnam against suspected troop concentrations and to create instant landing zones. When they were dropped on the side of a mountain, they caused landslides. When they landed on flat ground, they uprooted everything within a square 100 yards on each side and killed or seriously injured all animal life within a mile of their impact.[6]

In Binh Dinh Province, where the Vinh Than Valley is located, the Air Force also employed what we now call weapons of mass destruction. They combined the use of chemical warfare with conventional explosive ordnance in a program called Operation *Ranch Hand*. During the Vietnam War, *Ranch Hand* was described as a deforestation effort to deprive the enemy of cover, conceal-ment, and crops. It relied primarily on the chemical agent known as 2,4,5-T, or what we now call Agent Orange. Agent Orange was developed in the 1950s by the DuPont Corporation and first deployed in Vietnam by the Kennedy Administration over the objection of some of his senior military advisors. The Johnson Administration continued and expanded its use despite evidence in studies done by the National Cancer Institute and the Embry-ology Department at Yale University that Agent Orange was a carcinogen linked to cancer in laboratory mice and infant defor-mities in Vietnam.[7]

In the nine years preceding the *Putnam* operations, 1,086,000 hectares (439,676.11 acres) of forest and cultivated land in Viet-nam were sprayed with Agent Orange. Three hundred thousand of those poisoned hectares (121,457.5 acres) were in the Central Highland forests. We also poisoned crops. The usual method was to employ C–123 cargo planes equipped with 1,000-gallon tanks and wing-mounted spray nozzles during growing season to poison as many crops as possible. Ineffective crop salvage operations, runoff during the monsoon season, and seepage of the chemical into the groundwater spread the contamination to people far removed from the Central Highlands. From 1961–69, 1,293 people suffered damage to their eyes and lungs, and some were also paralyzed. Then, in 1970, the pace of poisoning accelerated. Around 185,000 people were contaminated and 3,000 died.[8]

In response to the questions raised about the danger of Agent Orange, Dr. Lee A. duBridge, the White House science advisor, announced in October 1969 that the chemical would be used only in areas remote from population, but the dramatic increase in contamination reports in 1970 indicates there was no appreciable change in the way the defoliant was used.[9] Its purpose was to deny cover and crops to the enemy, so it made no sense to spray it in places where there were no people or crops.

Dr. duBridge's propaganda notwithstanding, Agent Orange was part of Operation *Putnam Power* in Binh Dinh province. One of the places sprayed was a twenty-by-five-kilometer stretch along Highway 19. In fact, this area along the roadway was targeted for combined action by planes from Operation *Ranch Hand* and conventional tactical aircraft. First, the *Ranch Hand* planes sprayed the area's homes, crops, and orchards. Then, the tactical aircraft followed up with sorties to seed the area with steel pellet bombs that exploded when touched or vibrated from movement nearby. In effect they booby-trapped the area from the air in order to prevent the rescue of people and livestock and the salvage of homes and crops.[10]

PUTNAM POWER AND THE GROUND WAR

In spite of the rain of explosive and chemical death that fell over the Central Highlands, the North Vietnamese Army continued to pour men into the mountains in and around Base Area 226. Eventually, we were able to confirm that Base Area 226 held 5,860 soldiers divided among 13 different units. We had fought against two of them before. One was the 95th NVA Regiment. They were reputed to have 1,500 men. That made them the largest unit we hunted. The second unit was the 18th NVA Regiment. They had 1,310 troops. They were second in size to the 95th, but from our experience, they were just as tough. Besides those two familiar units, there were the 407th and C2 Sapper Battalions. We never confirmed how many men were in these last two units, but the boldness of their attacks on our firebases and small–unit perimeters in the jungle taught us very quickly that these smaller units were more dangerous than the larger ones.[11]

COMBAT ASSAULT ON A HOT LANDING ZONE

When we boarded the helicopters for the combat assault on what we thought was Base Area 226, we didn't know exactly which of those units might be there, but we did know it was likely to be a dangerous job just because of what a combat assault required. When you ride a helicopter into a landing zone on a combat assault, three men sit side by side in the open door, along with the door gunner who sits behind an M–60 machinegun mounted on a swivel. There is nothing to hide behind if the enemy is on the ground and aiming at you. Some men always jockeyed for a position away from the door gunner, at the other end of the door near the pilots. They didn't want to be near him for fear that ground fire intended for the gunner would hit them. I eventually gave up worrying about where to sit because pilots and door gunners were both pretty inviting targets. The door gunner was there to provide suppressing fire when the bird slowed and settled over the landing zone, but we knew from hard experience that often door gunners were the first to get shot on a hot LZ. If that happened, the infantrymen who were balancing on the skids of an unstable helicopter were easy targets while they looked for a safe place to jump. We always had to jump because the birds never landed for fear of mines. Good pilots would come within three to five feet, and it was up to you to make the jump onto uneven, often rocky, ground carrying a seventy-pound pack without breaking anything.

If you made it to the ground in one piece, there was one final thing to do: stay alive until the rest of the unit got on the ground. If the landing zone was small and contested by a determined enemy behind good cover, this was not always easy to do. Lying on your belly and low crawling toward the enemy left you exposed for too long. Even a poor marksman could put a bullet in your head if you gave him that kind of time. So if the landing was really hot, the men of the first few birds to land would have to respond as though they were in the killing zone of an ambush. They would have to stay on their feet and get in among the enemy so they would have to worry about hitting their own men. Once they got that far, there would be some vicious close combat. Then, the survivors of that fighting had to repel any reinforcements the enemy might send until more of their men landed.

The assignment to the first troop ships, or "slicks," into a landing zone, was rotated just like being on point, and I got lucky that day. The landing zone was big enough for two slicks at a time. I was assigned to the third lift, or group of two. That meant I was on the sixth slick while it circled over the landing zone and I was able to watch most of what happened to the first two lifts from a position of relative safety. It was a short, vicious fight. This is what I saw.

There were few open areas in the Central Highlands' jungles and, over the years, the enemy dug fighting positions around many of them in anticipation of combat assaults. So the first thing that happened in our assault was two Cobra gunships swooped over the landing zone to "prep" it for the slicks. On the first pass, they fired rockets into suspected enemy positions. On the second pass they fired their 40-millimeter cannon that expended explosive rounds at a rate of 400 per minute. Their final pass was a few bursts from their six-barreled mini guns. Each barrel of those weapons unleashed a thousand rounds of 7.62-millimeter bullets a minute. They could cover an entire football field in about three seconds.

There was a secondary explosion from one of the gunship passes, so we knew the landing zone was going to be hot. The Cobras stayed over or near the LZ to deliver as much firepower for as long as they could while the troop slicks landed. Every sixth round from their six-barreled mini gun was a red glowing tracer round so they could see where their fire was going. From where I sat, it looked like there was a steady stream of red hitting the landing zone from twelve mini gun barrels and the four M-60s of the door gunners. The fourteen machineguns chopped the jungle around the landing zone to pieces and raised a cloud of flying rocks and debris just as dangerous as the bullets. From where I sat, it was a pretty frightening demonstration of firepower, and I could not imagine what it must have been like for the enemy. Terms like "maelstrom," "hailstorm of bullets," and "rain of death" came to mind. They were all inadequate for describing what happened to the enemy that morning. I didn't care either. The landing zone was not much larger than the infield of a baseball diamond, and I really hoped that they were experiencing their own hell in that very small place.

The Cobras and the door gunners on the first two slicks kept the enemy's heads down until our first lift was on the ground and right on top of them. There was some really nasty close-in fighting, but it didn't last long. The first twelve Americans on the ground cleared out four bunkers with an M-60 machinegun, M-16s, an M-79 grenade launcher, and what appeared to be a pump shotgun. When the killing stopped, I heard a sit rep on my squad's radio that there were fourteen dead NVA and twelve rifles on the edge of the landing zone. The discrepancy between the number of dead men and weapons was because of the discipline under fire that units like the 18th NVA Regiment showed. They usually carried away as many of their dead, wounded, and weapons from a firefight as they could manage. That way we were always left to wonder what damage we had done to them.

My lift landed and moved off the landing zone immediately to make room for the next lift. As we went down a ridge into the jungle, I had no doubt the enemy had suffered serious damage. There were a lot of the ubiquitously mentioned "blood trails" that were often called in to the TOC after a firefight. There were also a lot of major body parts the loss of which could only have resulted in many more than the twelve dead NVA recorded that day. On my side of the perimeter, I counted a torso and most of what looked like three separate upper legs. I don't have any idea what was found on the other side of the landing zone.

We also took three prisoners that first day of Operation *Putnam Power*, but that was not a sign that the enemy was in a mood to give up. They were actually preparing a disciplined withdrawal of as many of their supplies, munitions, and people as they could from the valley, while doing their best to make us pay a price in blood for every cache we found and every one of their men we killed.

On the sixth day in the Vinh Than Valley, B Company's third platoon made contact with the enemy. Fred Golladay, one of the G Men from the Fort Benning NCO Academy, was involved in the fight, and when we were on stand down at the end of the mission, Fred told me what happened. He said that on January 24, around eleven in the morning, he was on point leading his platoon into a ravine where they thought they might find some supplies or enemies. They found the latter. He and his slack heard movement nearby in the brush, and they took cover just as the shooting started. It was a lucky break for them. The enemy fired twenty-five rounds of small arms fire from either an AK-47 or an RPD machinegun at them. Two men in Fred's squad were wounded and evacuated by means of a jungle penetrator because there was no place to land a helicopter.[12]

By the end of January, we were sure the enemy was using small units to screen us off from Base Area 226 while they moved their men and supplies out of the valley. So the order came down from the battalion commander for us to operate in platoon-sized units to cover as much ground as possible in the shortest amount of time. Some of the platoons were successful in finding arms or food caches before they could be moved. One of the biggest finds was made on February 7, the last day of the operation. B Company of the 1st Battalion, 12th Regiment made the find. After a prolonged harassment by several snipers, they found two caches very close together. The snipers held up their advance for awhile, and porters carried away some of the supplies in the area, but they were not entirely successful. They had to leave two caches behind. The first one was in a hut. It had 765 pounds of rice in burlap bags. The other one was in a nearby cave that had another 100 pounds of rice and two rifles. One was an AK-47, and the other was an M-2 carbine of American manufacture.[13]

That period of small patrols in late January and early February was a dangerous time for us. There were thirteen firefights in the first seven days of February. Small units moved more quietly so the frequency of surprise encounters between point elements on both sides increased dramatically. Typically, they started with opposing point men blasting away at each other from a distance of ten meters or so when they encountered each other at bends in the numerous trails in the area. We had six men wounded that week in those close-up firefights.

Cecil Dykes, a new man in my platoon from South Carolina, and I almost became numbers seven and eight. Dykes insisted on walking point right away, and he was going way too fast and making too much noise. I was his slack that day, and I warned him he was getting too far ahead for me to help if he got in trouble. He kept going, and when he crashed through a bush, there were two NVA only twenty feet away, looking at us over the sights of their AK-47s. I got a big tree between me and death and Cecil got behind a rock. He was face down screaming for help as the NVA shot the part of his pack that stuck out above the rock to pieces. I threw a grenade and followed up with a magazine load from my M-16. Eighteen shots and a grenade, and I missed them both. Not even a blood trail.

Besides the close-range firefights on jungle trails, there was also major action along Highway 19, the main roadway in the area. The most significant of those firefights involved a mechanized infantry unit, B Company of the 1st Battalion, 35th Regiment. They had been assigned to patrol Highway 19 and its nearby environs when they were ambushed. Two of their armored personnel carriers were disabled by fifteen- to twenty-pound land mines. The troops from the undamaged vehicles dismounted to provide security for repairs and evacuation of the wounded and they immediately got into a larger firefight. They had dismounted in an area where there were thirty-five bunkers with space for living quarters and an arms cache.[14]

Operation *Putnam Power* ended on February 7. I remember thinking that for a short operation we had cost the enemy considerable numbers of men and materiel. We counted twelve whole corpses and a lot of parts on the landing zone on the first day of the operation. We killed nineteen more and took four more prisoners in the next two weeks. We also found blood and weapons left on the ground after most of the brief, fierce firefights on the jungle trails. Even though we didn't find bodies to go along with the blood trails, in many of those instances, we felt that the weapons left behind counted for something. For example, we gathered up five AK-47s, three M-2 30-caliber carbines, a 9-millimeter sub-machinegun, a Mauser rifle, an M-16, and three rocket-propelled grenades and launchers.

We also took a lot of the enemy's ammunition. In all, there were 27,572 rounds of small arms ammunition taken. One American grenade and one of our Claymore mines were also recovered. There were also two big anti-vehicle-sized mines. One weighed twenty pounds, and the other fifty pounds. Four 82-millimeter mortar shells and seven 60-millimeter shells were recovered, and a total of 8,555 pounds of rice along with three transistor radios rounded out the accounting.[15]

THE WAR IN THE GROUND

In the general reporting of the enemy's losses on Operation *Putnam Power*, there was one cache of mortar rounds and one enemy death that were unreported. I know about those two lacunae in the record because I blew up the cache and I also killed that soldier. Both incidents were part of the war *in* the ground. I blew up the cache because I didn't want to have to chop a landing zone to have the mortar rounds hauled away, or carry the crates until we found a natural clearing. The soldier was a different story. This one was not a casualty of the air war or the ground war. This one died in a vicious fight in the pitch-black darkness of a tunnel deep inside a mountain. Both events occurred on the same day.

It was February 4, 1970, and I was walking point for my platoon. This was a time when I lived by my reflexes and intuition about what would happen if I stepped around a rock or moved a tree branch out of my way. Because of the ambush I had conducted in October during *Putnam Wildcat*, I was also very mindful of the fact that a careless point man could drag his whole unit to their deaths. Greg Bodell and Bob Frost, two of my platoon's best point men, had helped me learn a lot of the subtleties of the job. Frost was a tough cowboy straight off a ranch from Oklahoma. He was an expert shot and just the kind of man you would take to a war or an alley fight. We called him "Rawhide." He and

Bodell both told me in different words, but no uncertain terms, that war is unforgiving, and body bags were usually filled with people who had excuses or made mistakes. They also helped me get better at the point. Frost gave me a very useful tip for close-range shooting. It was to use my middle finger on the trigger and my index finger on that hand to point at the target. I didn't kill anyone with that technique in February, but I got close enough to two opposing point men to drive them off the trail. Bodell not only helped me learn to be a silent, aggressive point man, he walked my slack. It was a perfect match. He was left-handed so his rifle was pointed to the side of the trail opposite mine when we teamed up, so we had natural coverage of both sides of the trail.

About midmorning, I was on a trail when the three of us decided to look inside a cave I saw near the trail. It had twenty cases of mortar shells in it. It was a good find, but we knew right away that the Lifers would want them all hauled to a clearing and taken to base camp. Nobody wanted to haul that kind of load for two or three days and fight at the same time, so I decided to booby trap them and leave. I stuck a thin wire into the top of a white phosphorous grenade to block the striker from hitting the primer and setting off the four-second fuse. Then I took the handle off the grenade, dug a hole under one of the cases and put the edge of the crate on top of the striker. Finally, I eased the wire out of the hole in the grenade top and pushed the dirt carefully back around the bottom of the crate. It would have taken a close inspection with a big flashlight to spot the tampering. My platoon was 200 meters and ten or fifteen minutes away from the cave when we felt a shock wave, heard an incredible explosion, and saw a massive white and red fireball erupt from the cave. Frost walked up to me, gave me a big grin, and then we did a quick "dap," the elaborate handshake between Black men in Nam. Bob "Tiny" Pederson, the radio operator who replaced Jim Higgins, called the captain and said he wasn't sure, but he thought the explosion might have been a short round from some artillery mission. Then we continued on down the trail.

About midafternoon, the rain had slackened to a mist, and I noticed a footprint made by a Ho Chi Minh sandal, pointed toward me in the mud. Ho Chi sandals were common footwear for both Viet Cong and NVA. They were made from the treads of old tires cut to appropriate length and held in place by strips of inner tube. I stopped and noticed that the next two prints were heading off the trail into the jungle to my right. There was almost no water in them, so I knew they had been made within the last few minutes when the rain had slackened. It was also clear that the wearer of the sandals had heard us coming along the trail, and made a quick dodge down the side of the ridge. Bob Frost and I dropped our packs to track this soldier as quietly as we could.

The tracks led us to an area with moss-covered rocks on the side of the ridge. Scuff marks in the moss took us to a very shallow cave under a rock ledge. There was a hole in the back wall of the cave and recently turned semi-dry dirt on the floor of the cave. The dirt was there because someone had recently dug a tunnel into the back end of the cave. Frost said his shoulders were too wide to get into the tunnel and, unaccountably, I had an attack of stupid. I decided I would find out what happened to our quarry.

Greg Bodell and I had talked about tunnel ratting on a number of occasions. He thought I had a lot of advantages if it came to a fight in a tunnel. First, I was small enough to get in one, and I had been a varsity wrestler in high school. I won third place in the state tournament, and later, I beat the state champ in a college gym class and an intramural tournament. I was also used to wrestling blind because my coach, Paul Mowery, had insisted we wrestle several practice matches every week blindfolded. He wanted us to become intuitive wrestlers who could feel an opponent's moves in his body before he actually finished them.

When I told Bodell about the blind wrestling, he didn't believe it until I bested him three times in a row even though he was twenty pounds heavier than I was. While we rested up from our matches, he told me some other things about tunnels. One of the things he said was, "If you're going to go in, do it quick, otherwise they get far enough ahead of you to set traps or wait at a turn in the tunnel for you to come by head first and defenseless." He also told me that tunnels turn every five meters or so to prevent cave-ins without cutting timbers to shore them up. The slight turns made it easy to estimate how far you had gone. Finally, he told me, "If you ever see a flashlight coming your way, you can fire away, but more than likely, you're already a dead man." So, I armed myself with those pearls of wisdom, a .45 automatic, a combat knife, and a flashlight that I had no intention of turning on. That was because sight was the last of the senses a tunnel rat relied on to find and kill his enemy.

By the time I made the second turn in the tunnel it was pitch black. I felt like I was trapped in a narrow sewer pipe. I could move on my hands and knees, but from time to time, both shoulders scraped the walls. As I inched along, I made every forward movement in almost slow motion. And before I made them, I tried to lightly touch every inch of the ceiling, walls, and floor. I was feeling for trap doors, trip wires, and turns in the tunnel to tell me how far I had gone. At the tenth turn, I had to lie flat. A couple turns after that, I could feel that I was moving noticeably downhill when my hands told me both sides of the tunnel moved away from me at right angles. The angles on both sides, and the fact that I could also feel a hint of breeze on the sweat on the left side of my face, meant I was at an intersection with a branch tunnel instead of a slight turn. The breeze also meant the tunnel had another opening.

The possibility of another opening could mean the guy I was following was gone, or it could also allow someone to get behind me. That was when common sense bit me on the ass, and

I decided I had gone far enough. I was lying there thinking about backing out when I thought I heard a scraping sound and felt a vibration in the floor. I went absolutely still for a few minutes. While I lay there, I was almost certain that whoever else was there would hear my heart beating on the ground. Then, as slowly as I could, I gathered myself onto my knees and unsheathed my combat knife. The .45 was cocked and locked, but I was afraid to use it because I thought the sound of unsnapping the holster or taking the safety off would give me away.

The sound I thought I heard and the breeze I thought I felt were both to my left, so I put my left side against the tunnel wall and pulled my head back just inside my branch of the tunnel. I knew I was positioned just right when I lost the breeze on my cheek. I stayed there on my knees long enough to start believing I had imagined the noise when I smelled nuoc nam, the rancid sauce made from fermented fish and salt most Vietnamese ate with rice. I immediately covered my mouth with my left hand and tried to breathe slowly through my nose. If I could smell someone else's breath, I was pretty sure he would smell mine. I held my breath while I moved to the middle of the tunnel, and I gripped the leather handle of my knife with the point forward as hard as I could. I knew for sure that there was an enemy only inches away. I also knew we would struggle in the dark until one of us was dead. I had that thought in my mind when a solid blow landed on the left side of my face, and I started the wrestling match of my life.

The hand on the left side of my face told me exactly where the enemy was. He was to my left, and I knew it was a right hand because the thumb was near my eye. I looped my left arm over the top of my opponent's right arm and locked it in my armpit and jerked it toward me. At the same time, I drove forward, intending to stab for the chest or throat with my right hand, but somehow I had lost the knife. I jerked up on the arm I had trapped in an attempt to dislocate the elbow. Then I delivered an openhanded palm strike to where I thought the head would be. The heel of my hand connected and I felt teeth break. I kept battering the head, driving it down and away from me while I drove forward on my knees. We surged forward about three feet and then we slammed into the far wall of the intersection.

We were both stunned, but I recovered first. I had only taken that one blow to the head. He had taken several, and I kept battering him as hard and fast as I could with forearm smashes to his head and face. When I felt him weakening, I jerked the arm that was locked under my left arm and that flipped the man onto his left side and pinned his left arm underneath him. His legs were in the tunnel branch to my left and of no use to him for leverage.

As he struggled to roll onto his back to free his arm, I felt my chance to end the fight. My right forearm was across his mouth, and he bit me. I jerked away and slammed my right elbow down across his throat. I rolled halfway onto my right side for better leverage and pressed as hard as I could. At the same time, I pulled the arm trapped in my left armpit as hard as I could in the opposite direction. We both knew he was dying, and I could feel him trying to free his left arm before his time and air ran out. My arms were cramping, and I was hoping this would end before I lost my grip when I heard and felt his larynx collapse. A crushed larynx is a fatal injury. I don't know exactly how long it took, but this soldier did not go easily. He struggled until the very moment when death claimed him. Gradually, I sensed that his movements had become less coordinated and more like convulsions. Then, suddenly, even the convulsions stopped. It was over, and I collapsed across the body.

When I recovered, I untangled myself from the dead man. I tried to find a pulse on the neck to be sure it was over. The face was so bloody I decided to check for a heartbeat. I got nothing. All I felt was just the soft limpness of the newly dead. As I knelt over him, my left hand brushed against what I immediately knew was the haft of a knife on his belt. It was on the left side, and he had been trying to get it and his left arm into the fight when I crushed his throat. I pulled the knife out and cut his belt to get the sheath. Then I put them back together and stuck the knife in my belt. I also groped around for my knife but I couldn't find it. Then the thought came to me that this guy might not have been alone and that I should get out of there.

I knew I was moving faster on the way out than I did coming in, but it still seemed like I had crawled backwards forever before the blackness of the tunnel turned to gray. When I got close enough to the entrance to hear Bodell calling my name, I yelled that I was okay and would be there in a minute. I stretched out full length on the tunnel floor to rest and think about what I had just done. While I lay there thinking about it, a disturbing thought hit me. I realized that when I checked the soldier's chest for a heartbeat that I might have put my hand on a breast instead of a pectoral muscle. Then my friends grabbed my ankles and pulled me out of the tunnel. Bob and Greg asked me what had taken so long and if I was okay. I told them I was fine, but I think they both knew better. Bob looked at my right hand and arm and gave me a sarcastic "right." The hand had a cut on the palm near the heel that was still bleeding. The right sleeve of my shirt was bloody, too.

We put on our packs and continued the day's search without further incident. At the first break we took, I got a good look at the knife I had brought out of the tunnel. It was small and utilitarian. The blade was short and thick. The end of it was almost rounded instead of pointed, but the edge was very sharp. The handle was made from a piece of bamboo split down the middle and lashed to the haft of the blade with a bootlace, just like the ones in my boots, and covered with white tape from a medic's M-5 kit. As a weapon, it wasn't much, but it could have made a difference if the dead soldier could have gotten it into play. I used the knife to cut the lower half of my right sleeve off. I threw the sleeve away and put the knife in my pack.

In 2005, I told my therapist what had happened in the tunnel. I never told anyone in the platoon. In February 1970, I rationalized my denial by convincing myself that if I said anything, some Lifer would want me to drag the body out to confirm the killing for their damned body count. So I retreated to the practical considerations of staying alive that day. I replaced my lost combat knife with an "Arkansas Toothpick" I had taken from another dead NVA. It had a staghorn handle that wouldn't become slippery if it got bloody and a long, heavy blade that wouldn't break if it hit a rib. The name "Clem" was carved into the leather sheath. After that I just kept repeating the mantra that almost every Grunt repeated in times of stress: "It don't mean nothin'." We said it when it rained for weeks. We said it when we got shot at. We said it when someone got killed. We always said, "it don't mean nothin'" and just kept pushing. I told myself what happened in the tunnel didn't mean nothin' too. But I knew, deep down, that it did. I knew it did because from time to time, the sight or touch of a small breast would leave me in a flaccid state of depression.

Operation *Putnam Power* ended three days after the fight in the tunnel. Helicopters extracted B Company from a tiny landing zone where a slick had crashed and burned. We could tell there had been a firefight over the weapons and any useable equipment at the crash site because there were skeletons all around it. One of the skulls looked like it had three eyeholes.

Only one bird could get in at a time and my squad and Cat's squad were left out overnight. No one slept. We were probed by enemy who had probably come back to see if we had left anything of value behind. The next morning, when the choppers came back for us, we knew we had left a lot of piles of expended brass shell casings, and we hoped we also left some dead NVA in the bushes around the landing zone, but we didn't bother to check.

When our slicks landed in Pleiku, we also didn't bother with looking for a shower or clean clothes. We went straight from the landing pad to the enlisted men's club for hot food and cold drinks. Most of B Company was there, drunk before 10:00 a.m. Richie Beunzel, Cat Ackzinski, Bob Frost, Greg Bodell, and I came in together. Richie had the skull with three eyeholes in it. He put it on the bar in front of the Vietnamese bartender and ordered two beers, one for himself and one for his friend. The horrified bartender left in a big hurry. We had a good laugh about that while we served ourselves and the rest of the company too. There was a Vietnamese band there to entertain us. We noticed right away that they were all draft-aged men and that they played really poorly. Jim Hinzo, who had been a drummer in a band back in the world, decided that he could do a better job than their drummer. Cat, Jesse Johnson, a few others, and I convinced the band to lend us their instruments. We were having a really good time when the Military Police (MPs) came to break up the party.

General Tran Van Tra. General Tran commanded the National Liberation Forces (Viet Cong) through the French and American phases of the Vietnam War. He was also the commander of the Tet Offensive of 1968. This photo was taken by the author at a seminar on Vietnamese history in January 1991.

Two of the "G Men." Robert Graves and Frederick Golladay, in the barracks at the Fort Benning NCO Academy. *Photo provided courtesy of Michael Belis, Website Administrator for 1-22.org, the First Battalion, 22nd Infantry Website.*

Three of the "G Men." The end of training at Fort McClellan, Alabama, for three of the "G Men," and one other sergeant from the company. Left to right are Sergeants James Gillam, Edward Gardiner, Unknown Sergeant, and Michael Mullen. Gardiner and Mullen were killed in Vietnam.

Sgt. Gillam at LZ Ruth. LZ Ruth was on the edge of the Vinh Than Valley, and Sgt. Gillam joined the First Battalion, 22nd Regiment there. This photo was taken during a break from bunker building and burying sappers (commandos) from an attack the night before he arrived.

Frederick L. Golladay. Fred was one of the "G Men" from the Fort Benning NCO Academy. He left for Vietnam in April 1969. Sgt. Gillam arrived in September 1969 and they served together in B Company, 1st Bn, 22nd Regiment. *Photo provided courtesy of Michael Belis, Website Administrator for 1-22.org, the First Battalion, 22nd Infantry Website.*

Sgt. Gillam after first combat assault. Sgt Gillam made 47 combat assaults or helicopter landings on unsecured landing zones. This is a picture of him reading his first letter in Vietnam. It was delivered once Sgt. Gillam's company secured the hilltop.

Patrolling the road near LZ Beaver. This is Larry Black, one of the men in second squad, second platoon. He is buying snacks and drinks from the black marketers who traveled the road and sometimes mined it.   *Photo provided courtesy of Michael Belis, Website Administrator for 1-22.org, the First Battalion, 22nd Infantry Website.*

Results of the Air War. This is Sgt. Gillam standing in the bottom of a crater from an *Arc Light* strike's 1,000-pound bomb.

Combat assault in progress. This is the view from the ground as the second helicopter in a combat assault landed. Note that the gunner on the right is missing. He was shot by a sniper as this photo was taken.

Jesse Johnson. Jesse was our best machinegunner. He was promoted to sergeant on the spot by our battalion commander when he killed an entire NVA squad on Christmas Day 1969. *Photo provided courtesy of Michael Belis, Website Administrator for 1-22.org, the First Battalion, 22nd Infantry Website.*

Cobra gunship. These were assault helicopters that carried 122-millimeter rockets and a six barrel Gatling machinegun capable of firing 6,000 rounds per minute on the right side. They also carried a 40-millimeter cannon in front capable of firing 400 explosive rounds per minute.

The war in the ground. Sgt. Gillam is removing Vietnamese food and American weapons from a tunnel in the Vinh Than Valley.

This photo was taken in a small village in the highlands. It was shortly after the fight at the amphitheater and the grenade shrapnel from that fight is visible over my left eye.

Sometimes on search and destroy I carried the M-79, a 40-millimeter grenade launcher/ shotgun. I used it this day to destroy the bamboo hut and the men inside it who were shooting at us.

This photo was taken moments before we were attacked while I sat on the hammock with Bob Frost and Richie Beunzle. Bob was shot three times in the chest as we sat shoulder to shoulder.

Lieutenant/Captain TJ. Gilbert Tijerino was a first lieutenant in B Company. He returned to the field after his mandatory six months were done and became our company commander. Captain TJ was a West Point graduate, an aggressive officer who I think believed we could win the war. We disagreed often because I just wanted to be as safe as possible and get home

Photo provided courtesy of Michael Belis, Website Administrator for 1-22.org, the First Battalion, 22nd Infantry Website.

Second Platoon on the landing pad. This picture was taken on the landing pad at Pleiku while we waited to go to Cambodia. Shortly after, we got in the gunfight in Pleiku with black marketers over a truckload of ammunition. Standing second from left, Jim Hinzo, center with ammo belt Jesse Johnson, right with helmet, Jim Gillam. *Photo provided courtesy of Michael Belis, Website Administrator for 1-22.org, the First Battalion, 22nd Infantry Website.*

POW cage. This photo was taken at the National POW Museum in Andersonville, Georgia. It is a replica of the smaller POW cages we found inside Base Area 226.

Jesse Johnson's gun team. Another photo from the pad at Pleiku before we left for Jackson Hole and Cambodia. Left to right, Jim Killian, Jimmy "Smoke" Carter, unknown, Jesse Johnson. *Photo provided courtesy of Michael Belis, Website Administrator for 1-22.org, the First Battalion, 22nd Infantry Website.*

CA to Cambodia. We circled LZ Jackson Hole until the entire battalion was loaded up, then we flew to Cambodia on May 7, 1970. This is a picture of one of the lifts as it circled the jungle below us. *Photo provided courtesy of Michael Belis, Website Administrator for 1-22. org, the First Battalion, 22nd Infantry Website.*

A man I shot. Professor Mac Duong teaches literature at the University of Hanoi. I met him during a seminar there in January 1991. I also met him in October of 1969 when I shot him in the first ambush I carried out.

Jimmy Hinzo. Jim was an Apache from Arizona. He was also an irrepressible and energetic guy. Also a good man with a rifle, and he proved it in Cambodia. Photo provided courtesy of Michael Belis, Website Administrator for 1-22.org, the First Battalion, 22nd Infantry Website.

6. ✸

Operations *Hines* and *Putnam Paragon*

February 16 to May 18, 1970

From mid-January to the first week of February 1970, B Company was assigned to Operation *Putnam Power*. The objective was to find and destroy the NVA's Base Area 226. As a unit, we failed. As an individual soldier, I saw and participated in the Vietnam War on all its levels. I saw the air war carried out by B-52 aircraft of the Strategic Air Force when they performed their *Arc Light* missions. I also saw the after-effect of the chemical rain of death called Operation *Ranch Hand*. It was the kind of warfare America went to war in Iraq to prevent: the use of chemicals as weapons of mass destruction. The chemical agent 2,4,5-T, known as Agent Orange, defoliated thousands of acres of land and spread a poison over the Central Highlands and its people. We polluted the environment for decades and caused cancers and birth defects for a generation.

I also continued my part in the ground war searching out enemy supply caches and hunting their troops in vicious small-unit actions, but finally, and most frighteningly, there was my part of the war that was fought *in* the ground. I beat and strangled an enemy to death in a tunnel. After that, I thought I had seen it all, done it all, and things would get no worse for me before I left

Vietnam. I was wrong. I was a serving NCO in the reactionary force for the 4th Infantry Division's 2nd Brigade. Our job was to move in and help the brigade when new enemy bases were found, or when unexpectedly large numbers of enemy appeared. You don't drop in to rob the enemy of his supplies and expect your arrival to go uncontested. Neither do you get called to a firefight and not get shot at.

LIFE IN THE REACTION FORCE

On February 15, the First Battalion, 22nd Infantry Regiment was ordered to join Operation *Hines*. B Company, my part of the battalion, left the division base camp at Pleiku by helicopter. We landed fifty-four kilometers north of An Khe on LZ Louis. LZ Louis was originally a fire support base for the 1st Cavalry Division (Airmobile). It was closed for a while and reopened and expanded when my battalion's three infantry companies and one mortar company arrived there on February 15, 1970.[1]

B Company landed early that morning and we were ordered to do an immediate security sweep of the area. My platoon led the company single file, down a trail into the jungle toward a junction with three other trails. The junction was about five hundred meters from the fire base. The plan was to have each platoon follow a trail all the way to the floor of the valley. We only got about 100 meters from the fire base before we made contact with the enemy.

The point man for our first squad spotted an NVA soldier on the trail. He fired at him and missed so he and his slack gave chase. They dropped that idea at the first bend in the trail because they found themselves in a small camp with three freshly built thatched huts. The huts were raised on platforms and about twenty by fifteen feet. One of the huts was obviously an eating facility with a long table and benches. The interesting thing was that all three were built over underground bunkers.

First Lieutenant Tijerino, our company executive officer and soon to be company commander, called for an over-flight of the area by a scout helicopter.

We stayed on the side of the mountain for two hours while the over-flight was done. First, a light observation helicopter (Loach) from the ARVN K-75 Rangers flew over the area. It flew low, trying to draw ground fire. They didn't get shot at, but after an hour or so, they called to tell us that we were on the eastern edge of an enemy encampment. That was about 11:45 a.m. We were ordered to hold in place another hour while the K-75 people put a squad on the ground for a closer look. The Rangers dropped a squad into a small natural clearing. They conducted a reconnaissance by fire that produced screams and moans. My platoon was sent down to render whatever assistance the Rangers needed. We searched the area and turned up one Vietnamese man and a half dozen or so blood trails and drag marks where people had been pulled along the trail or off into the jungle. The man who was left behind was unarmed and dressed in gray clothing. Through an interpreter, he claimed he had been a prisoner of the NVA and Viet Cong. He said his captors had fled to the west with several more prisoners.[2] We left him with the K-75 Rangers for further interrogation.

First Lieutenant Tijerino ("Lieutenant TJ") was a Pima Indian and a West Point graduate. For some reason, many of the men felt those two things made him a good man in the jungle and a good leader. Since he was a Lifer who had spent four years in a military college, I automatically had my doubts. Besides, the Central Highlands was a long way from the American Southwest, and few people knew that the Pima were the only tribe in that region who did not forcefully resist the settlers. Lieutenant TJ also carried a Ranger Handbook in his shirt pocket, and the fact that he made frequent references to it was not reassuring to me. I didn't think a good leader should need to check his notes to decide what to do. We got an example of his handbook-guided leadership that day. As recommended in the handbook, he frequently called his NCOs together to assess the tactical situation and give us our orders face to face. He called us together and gave us facts that were obvious to even the newest of the men: we were closer to one of the main infiltration routes from Cambodia than we had been on our last mission, and there was a good chance there was a lot more enemy around. Jesse Johnson leaned over to me and muttered, "Right, I'm damned glad we got that cleared up."

Once Lieutenant TJ explained the vagaries of our tactical situation, he often made what some of us considered to be risky tactical moves. That day he held true to form. He sent the third platoon back to the top of the hill. They were to take a CA that would drop them ahead of our intended route of march in an unsecured landing zone to the west, the direction the enemy had supposedly fled. The third platoon was to act as a blocking force, while the first and second platoons worked toward it from the east. Given the fact that we had been on the ground less than an hour and found evidence of a unit larger than our company, I thought dropping the twenty men of third platoon off by themselves was a bad move, and I said so. I also wondered aloud if the camp we seemed to be on the edge of might be the Base Area 226 we had never seemed to nail down on our last mission. Lieutenant TJ let me know he was in charge, and he would decide the tactics. It wasn't the last time we would disagree about such matters.

By 5:00 p.m., the third platoon was on the ground at their landing zone. They sent a squad out to check out a high-speed trail they had seen from the air. It was about a yard wide and led from their position back toward us on a general azimuth of 90 degrees. Lieutenant TJ told them to follow the trail toward us. He obviously hoped to catch somebody between the two forces. Everyone knew you couldn't wear a track nearly three feet wide in triple canopy jungle with occasional use by a few people, so everyone got ready for a close-range firefight. Riflemen took the safeties off and set their weapons on full automatic. Grenadiers loaded 40-millimeter shotgun shells in their weapons and loosened the flap on the holsters for their pistols. A machinegunner was moved up from the middle of the platoon to walk slack for the point man. The gunners took their heavy weapons off their shoulders where they usually carried them and held them across their chests with a 100-round belt of ammunition hanging out. The final preparation was to use a three-man point team. That meant two men walked ten meters off either side of the trail, keeping pace with the point man.

The precautions paid off for the third platoon. Fred Golladay, the only living G Man from the NCO Academy besides me, was on point that day. He told me later he and his men spotted two NVA. My platoon was a kilometer away, but we heard the gunfire as Fred, his right hand flanker, and the slack man, with the M-60 machinegun, all fired on them. A half-hour later, at 5:35 p.m., third platoon called Lieutenant TJ and Captain Derricco to say they had found a pack and a box with a radio transmitter inside.[3] The fact that they found no bodies or blood was an indication of the thickness of the jungle and approaching darkness. As darkness fell around us, all three platoons linked up. We spread the three platoons in a circle astride the high-speed trail and dug two-man foxholes for the night.

It had been an eventful day, but things were not yet over. Around 9:00 p.m., a trip flare went off on the trail on the west edge of our perimeter. Three NVA were caught in the light and the third platoon killed two of them immediately. The third one escaped. Then, unbelievably, Lieutenant TJ got out a big flashlight and inspected the bodies and what they had dropped on the trail. There were two AK-47s, an SKS carbine, and two bags of rice. One was really big and weighed about 150 pounds. The other was a more manageable twenty-five pounds or so. There were also two packs. Lieutenant TJ dumped them out and found the usual junk the enemy carried: two hammocks, four shirts, six pairs of pants, some pens, paper, and eating utensils.

Some infantry units gave careless soldiers an Article Fifteen (monetary fine, reduction in rank) and/or a beating by squad members for lighting a cigarette after dark. Yet, that night, Lieutenant TJ kept walking up and down the trail with his flashlight. He wandered a few meters up and down the trail until he found the place where he assumed the two dead men came from. It was another large hut like the ones we had found that morning. It had a bunker under it suitable for about twenty people. Probably these three men were either going to or leaving their camouflaged hut just a few meters from third platoon's position with their load of supplies.[4] Finally, after much begging, we got Lieutenant TJ to turn off his light before he got us all mortared or attacked.

The next day, February 16 when he could see without a flashlight, Lieutenant TJ was back on the trail literally digging intelligence information out of the pockets of the two dead men. Around 9:30 a.m. he was on the radio to the TOC with the results. One of the men wore baggy gray clothes with Vietnamese writing on the front and the numbers 4000 on the front and back of the shirt. Those clothes and his position nearest the large bag of rice indicated he had been a prisoner being used to carry supplies. He also had a Chieu Hoi slip in one of his pants pockets. A Chieu Hoi slip was a piece of psychological warfare propaganda often dropped from small planes over suspected concentrations of enemy troops to encourage them to Chieu Hoi, or surrender. The Chieu Hoi slip in his pocket meant he probably had been an NVA or Viet Cong and had thought about surrendering. No one felt bad about killing him. Once an enemy, always an enemy, was the way we thought.

The other dead man wore a khaki NVA uniform. There was a typed list in his shirt pocket that we assumed were names. At the top of the list "Q/Y Bac Si" was written. (In Vietnamese "Bac Si" means doctor.) The bottom of the list had two signatures: "Chung Nhan Cua and Thu Truang Don."[5]

The gray clothing with the numbers had to be a prisoner uniform, and the typed document told us that a physician was somewhere near. Together, all these scraps of information told us we had most likely found the edge of a camp for at least a battalion of troops and a major medical facility because the Vietnamese, like the Americans, did not send their physicians to serve with small units; they placed them with battalions or regiments. The permanent housing for large numbers of people, plus the numbered uniforms in a color neither the NVA nor Viet Cong wore, were also clear indications there were not only large numbers of the enemy, but that they had a prisoner camp in this facility too. No one told us what the intelligence people at base camp were thinking, but most of us at the company level were pretty sure we had found Base Area 226. Searching the area the rest of the day confirmed that opinion.

The first and third platoons made the contact and discoveries on February 16, but the seventeenth was the day when my second platoon had some of the luck too. We got a late start on patrolling because it took awhile for the sunlight to reach into the deep valley we were in. When it was fully light, Captain Derricco, with Lieutenant TJ's probable advice, made another of those risky tactical decisions that the enlisted men, especially the draftees, always hated. He broke the company into platoons and sent them in different directions. Our "Fearless Leaders," Captain Derricco and Lieutenant TJ, stayed at our night location with the company medic and their radio operators. From there, they proposed to coordinate a thorough search of the area.

LT Mack was the only other officer we had in the field, and I asked him what he thought of the division of our forces. I should have known better than to ask one officer his opinion about another officer. He told me to suck it up and do my job. He also told me that it was my squad's turn to take the point. I was O.K. with that because I always worried that another point would get me killed. Besides, Bodell and Frost were my flank men, and Jesse

Johnson was walking my slack with his M-60. I felt as safe as I could be under the circumstances.

Within an hour, we found a cluster of three thatched structures. Two were six-by-six and just behind them was one that was eight feet wide and thirty feet long. The big one had a bunker inside and signs of recent use: a large puddle of congealed blood and several bloody bandages. I was telling LT Mack that maybe third platoon had gotten a piece of more than two people on the trail the night before, when the third platoon's point man came up on the radio. He reported that they had found a pith helmet and three cultivated fields of lettuce growing under a vine network with branches in it to camouflage them from aerial observation.[6] At the same time, Carl Dover, an ammo bearer for our second machinegun team, came running over to the lieutenant to say his team had discovered a string of camouflaged fighting positions next to the trail I was supposed to follow when we moved away from the huts.

For the rest of the day, all three platoons followed trails that were roughly parallel to each other but separated by high ridges covered in triple canopy jungle. We were moving generally north and west toward the border of Cambodia. The company headquarters caught up with and attached itself to my platoon because Captain Derricco wanted to inspect another of the installations we found around 2:00 p.m. that day. Bob Frost was walking off the right-hand side of the trail and slightly behind me when he saw a smaller trail connected to the one I was on. We both heard some grunting and movement to his right so our three-man point element went to investigate. Jesse Johnson followed us with his M-60 held at the shoulder like a rifle. We found three more huts, but they were being used as barns instead of housing for people. Each barn had a bamboo pen in front, and inside these pens were a total of about a dozen pigs. They weren't the huge porkers we raise in America. They were the small swaybacked pigs common to Southeast Asia. Their bellies actually dragged on the ground, and they had small pink spots where they had rubbed the hair off rooting around in their pens. We also found several large piles of uniforms in the standard NVA khaki and Viet Cong black.[7]

We continued to follow the high-speed trail to the north and west for another two nerve-wracking hours. I felt like I was walking around inside someone's house just waiting for him to come home, pissed off and armed with an AK-47. We found all kinds of evidence of large numbers of recently departed enemy. Then, just after 4:30 p.m., I thought we would be able to leave this area because the battalion commander came up on our push to tell the captain we should move south or southeast immediately and return to a point inside the battalion area of operation. Hearing that, I got out my map and checked our position. By my reckoning, we were close to Cambodia, if not actually in it. Captain Derricco called the colonel back to ask if we could stay in the area a while longer because he thought it was "a good area to hunt."[8] The Colonel O.K.ed it, so we kept hunting in a westerly direction. Less than an hour later, we found another part of Base Area 226 and evidence of a POW camp.

THE "GOOD HUNTING" IN BASE AREA 226

The POW camp had eight buildings, and there was not much in the way of camouflage. To me, that meant they felt safe because they were either in Cambodia or close to it. The largest building was twenty by thirty feet and had rows of beds made from boards tied to bamboo posts. Each board had holes at the top and bottom for prisoner restraint. We even found a couple pairs of heavy iron manacles with thick chains and a padlock on one of the beds. The other buildings were only a little smaller, and inside them we found enough things to indicate that they belonged to the camp guards. A few rounds of the short 7.62-millimeter bullets for the AK-47 and SKS carbines were on the floor in several buildings. We also found some pieces of personal equipment:

a couple belts, malaria pills, hats, toothbrushes and the like, as well as a teakettle, some baskets of yams, and a kerosene lantern. There was even another hog pen and a chicken coop with a few scrawny birds in it.

One of the men in the platoon, I don't remember who, found an M–16 rifle. It was leaning against the wall in a corner of one of the huts. This was an ominous find for two reasons. First, and most obvious, it probably meant there was either a dead American somewhere around or maybe he was a POW. The other ominous implication was that whoever had the weapon must have left in a big hurry when he heard us coming. Rifles, even M–16s that everyone knew were not as good as an AK, were seldom left behind. Altogether, it appeared this was a relatively nice and secure camp for the enemy and, perhaps, not such a nice place for the prisoners. It also appeared the enemy might still be lurking about.

The NVA and VC built and frequently moved a series of remote bases throughout South Vietnam. They were numbered as they were discovered. The moving process usually involved a delay action by some of their soldiers while the others transferred their goods and ammunition to a new site.[9]

A BIRTHDAY KILLING

After we searched the area for two days, the battalion commander was so encouraged he sent Company A, one of the units on LZ Louis, to join us. They headed generally north and east. Inside of two hours, they had the first of several contacts with the enemy. They picked up a Chieu Hoi about 10:20 that morning. My company was finally ordered away from the border so the captain sent one platoon to the northeast, one to the south, and the last one to the east. My platoon went to the east and right after Company A reported their contact, I shot an NVA who was moving along our right flank as we followed another high-speed trail.

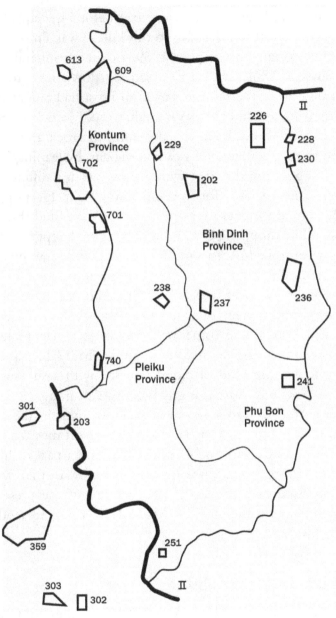

VC/NVA Base Camps. The NVA and VC built a series of remote bases through-out South Vietnam. They were numbered as they were discovered. The moving process usually involved a delay action by some of their soldiers while the others transferred their goods and ammunition to a new site.

Since I had been on point the day before, my squad was at the rear of the platoon that day, so this killing was almost a repeat of my first killing in October 1969. In my peripheral vision I saw a man in khaki with a rifle settling down next to a large rock. I fired from the hip the way Bob Frost had taught me and I surprised myself and the NVA soldier too. I knocked chips off the rock near his head. He rolled behind the rock and I got my weapon to my shoulder and steadied my aim by leaning against a tree. I was guessing the man would show up in a different place the next time he tried for me, and I was right. He popped up directly behind the rock, and inside my sights. I fired three more rounds and he dropped behind the rock again. I kept firing at the rock at a controlled pace to pin him down while my squad went on line from the trail to move in and finish him.

The fight was over in a few seconds, but we never found a body. We found a piece of wood from the stock of his weapon, and drag marks where someone I hadn't seen had pulled him away. There was also a puddle of pink, frothy blood on the ground. It was the kind of blood you see with a sucking chest wound. I was pretty sure this guy was dead, or going to die soon because there was also a fist-sized piece of lung in the puddle. The tumbling action of an M-16 bullet oftentimes made very large exit wounds, and one of mine had blown part of his lung out a hole in his back. Since he was wounded in that way and would surely drown soon, and also because of the presence of so many enemy in the area, LT Mack decided not to send us to confirm his death.[10]

SCOUT DOGS AND CROSSBOWS

For the rest of that day, both A and B Companies continued to find thatched housing units in a widely dispersed camp in the jungle. My platoon was moving from the west to the east, and we found another medical facility and got shot at by a sniper.

It was about 2:00 p.m. when we came across a large hut with medical supplies inside. There were surgical instruments and what appeared to be stacks of medical forms. Some were blank and some were filled out. We couldn't read the Vietnamese, but we did recognize recent dates written in the month/day/year pattern. The one on top had 02/17/70 on it. We also found several five-gallon clay jars with rice and corn in them.

About three hours after we left the medical facility, a sniper fired on us. From the sound of it, he was about 200 meters away. The four rounds he fired only came within about ten feet of LT Mack. In that thick jungle, we weren't sure how good his sight lines were, or whether he was just trying to delay our movement, but Mack took this personally. He called the artillery unit on the firebase and had it fire a couple of 105-millimeter beehive rounds into the area where the shots came from. After giving the sniper the giant shotgun treatment, LT Mack took our third squad with him to see what they had killed. When they got within forty meters of where they thought the sniper was, they were shot at again. I heard later that this time, the sniper got within less than a foot of LT Mack. I think discretion bit Mack on the ass. They opened fire on the sniper again but did not pursue him any farther.[11]

The next day, Company A spent the day working to a position about 1,000 meters northeast of LZ Louis. They also found more structures associated with a permanent base area and a few snipers. So, their company commander decided on a quieter approach to the situation than artillery shells. At 11:15 that morning, he called the TOC and asked for a scout dog and handler and some crossbows. Bob "Tiny" Pederson, our radioman, told me about the dogs. I thought it was a good idea. I had seen some of these animals around the base camp and heard good things about them. I had serious reservations about the crossbows, though. It was dangerous enough with a rifle on the point or anywhere else in the formation. I couldn't imagine trying to use a one-shot weapon in the area. We all expected that, sooner or later, we would find more than one enemy at a time and we knew for sure that a bow and arrow just would not cut it.

Company A got their dog and crossbow delivered around 4:00 that afternoon by a Loach. As it hovered and lowered the dog and his handler on a cable from a jungle penetrator, they took fire from five or six people in the trees nearby. Tiny told us that he heard on the radio that they got on the ground without injury, and then we started speculating on who was going to get to use the crossbow against the five or six enemy that had been shooting at them. As darkness fell, Company A was still reporting more and larger structures, and we heard their company commander order them to pull all their platoons together into a company-sized perimeter for the night. [12] It was a good move for them, because they got attacked that night.

It was after 10:00 p.m., and Tiny and I were lying on the ground near the radio, listening to the news in the area and talking about what I might do the next day because I thought it was going to be my birthday. All the days in the field were pretty much the same, and I had lost track of the date. I thought it was February 17. In the summer of 2003 when I visited the National Archives, I read the Battalion Duty Officer's Radio Logs for February 18 and discovered that Tiny was right. That document recorded the fact that someone in the last squad of B Company's second platoon had shot an NVA at close range and found a large blood trail after the incident. So I knew then, in the summer of 2003, that I had shot someone on my birthday, but in 1970, I thought that day was the seventeenth of February.

Tiny was trying to convince me it was already the eighteenth and that I had celebrated my birthday by killing someone that morning when we heard an explosion and gunfire from the direction of Company A's position. Their scout dog had alerted at about 10:30 p.m. to noise it heard outside the perimeter. When the animal stood up, the enemy set off a Claymore mine aimed at Company A's third platoon. The NVA made just enough noise to get the dog to alert and stand up, then they detonated the mine. It sent 400 double OO buckshot into the perimeter. After the explosion, we heard Company A exchanging small-arms fire for a brief time and then things got quiet. Finally, just before 11:00 p.m., we heard Company A's radioman calling the TOC on Firebase Louis to say they would need another scout dog in the morning. The TOC responded that all the companies in the battalion were going to get at least one dog and a crossbow the next day.[13]

I had no way of knowing it then, but when the sun came up on the day I thought was my birthday, it was going to be a really busy day. In fact, it was the first day of a really bad week. It began with a gunfight between a reinforced squad that I was leading against a platoon or more of NVA. It ended with a machine-gun attack on my platoon's patrol base that killed one of my best friends and wounded another one.

A VERY BAD WEEK

My bad week started with a resupply day. All the companies in the jungle had gathered their platoons around LZs to get more C-Rations, ammunition, equipment, and the crossbows no one in his right mind wanted to use. I was very pleased when the crossbow went to the first platoon and displeased when the dog and its handler also went to them. The company was going to divide into platoons again, and I always figured a dog on point would be a really important advantage. Two Vietnamese scouts, Kim and Lum, also came to the company that day. Kim had been an NVA, and Lum had been a VC, before they joined the ARVN. That was cause enough for me to distrust them. I was pretty happy when the captain decided to keep them with his headquarters group. We distributed the ammunition and supplies quickly, and at 8:30 that morning we went back to work.

Within an hour, the radio traffic on our push told us both my company and Company A were working on different sides of a really big enemy camp. The first sign of what we had between us came over the radio at 9:34 that morning when the first platoon of B Company called the captain to say they had found more buildings and evidence of women in the area within the last hour. More than one of us was wondering how you could tell there had been women in the area within an hour when Company A, working about a kilometer east of our position, called at 10:45 a.m. to report finding some backpacks among more huts and that there were panties and bras for two different-sized women in the packs. They also reported finding what appeared to be a classroom and some toys for children.[14] I missed the news about the classroom and children because I was getting a patrol briefing from LT Mack.

LT Mack had called the NCOs together because he had decided to divide the platoon in half for a while. I had been in the field longer than any of the other squad leaders, so he appointed me to be acting platoon sergeant, and his second-in-command. He ordered me to take the third squad and second machinegun team for my patrol. Because of sickness and R and R, the third squad was down from its normal strength of ten men to a five-man fire team. I had never worked directly with that squad. With the exception of their squad leader, I wasn't so sure I trusted them. One of them was Joe Kidder who had come out to us on the same resupply bird with the Vietnamese scouts.

In six months with the company, I had never seen Joe Kidder and neither had Sgt. Joe "Cat" Ackzinski, the third squad leader. I thought that was odd. When Kidder got off the resupply chopper, he did some high-fiving and dapping with the third squad, but he ignored Cat completely. That, too, was odd. I was sitting on my pack loading some magazines when I heard Stretch Bostwick ask Kidder how his detention had gone and if the Lifers were still giving him grief about smoking weed. I called Stretch over and asked him how he knew Kidder and where he had been since I came to the company. He said, "Relax Gill, Kidder's a cool dude, but the Lifers always give him a hard time just because he smokes weed in the field sometimes."

Bodell cleared it up for me. He said, "Gill, Kidder is a doper. He's been in base camp for disciplinary hearings and some jail time for insubordination and drugs. He was gone so long I thought he had been shipped back to the world." I had nothing to say to Kidder right then because he went right to Cat's squad instead of mine. Besides, the Lifers seemed to be in a hurry that day to get us back on the trail, and I just made a mental note to check with Cat about how Kidder worked in the field. Two hours later, LT Mack had made me acting platoon sergeant and given me the third squad and second machinegun team to take on a patrol. So, Kidder became one of my problems for the day.

I called both squads together to give them the "what and where" for the patrol. When we were ready to go, I started at the back of the line and walked with Cat toward the front so I could give all the men a visual once over before we started. Since I was now directly involved with the third squad, I intended to take a close look at Kidder to see how he got ready to go to work. When I saw him, I could only stare in amazement. He had taken up a middle position in his squad as they started off down the trail. He was wearing a pair of mirror lens aviator sunglasses, and a bright red bandanna on his head. He had a silver peace symbol about three inches in diameter around his neck. His M-16 was on a sling dangling from his neck. To top it all off, he had both hands in his pockets like he was on a sidewalk back in the world instead of a trail in the middle of a war.

I was still staring at Kidder in disbelief when Cat pushed me aside and slapped Kidder's face so hard that his sunglasses flew off. He told him this was no fucking parade and that he needed to get something green on his head and get his weapon in a two-handed grip and forget about dressing in base camp chic before he got somebody shot. Cat was another NCOC graduate and had also finished the Ranger School at Fort Benning. When it counted, he took a no nonsense approach to things. I also liked him because as far as I could tell, he was absolutely fearless. He was the only man in the third squad I trusted.

The group I took on that patrol was rounded out by our second-best machinegun team. Carl Dover was the gunner. He was another man I never really trusted. He was too careless about his work and was known to shirk his duty whenever he thought he could get away with it. I only agreed to let him carry the gun because Arturo Rodriguez, the previous gunner, was too slow and clumsy at reloading when a belt ran out. I would have carried the gun myself but I couldn't do that and work as platoon sergeant at the same time, so I let Dover have it. I hoped leading the team would make him more responsible. Fifteen minutes later, I found out I was wrong about that. In fact, I was nearly dead wrong about it.

THE SHOOTOUT AT THE AMPHITHEATER

Just before 11:00 a.m. on February 19, I took ten men and headed along a trail that ran on an azimuth of 270 degrees from our night position. LT Mack took the second squad, the one I usually worked with, and Jesse Johnson's machinegun team and headed off on an azimuth of 150 degrees. The first squad was left in place to guard our backpacks and secure the place as a night position for us when we returned later that day. Within minutes, both patrols were in a firefight.

I took the point that morning, and Cat walked my slack and his squad was right behind him. Dover and the gun team brought up the rear. The trail and azimuth I had been assigned took me down the side of a ridge to a narrow gully with a shallow stream about five feet wide at the bottom of it. I heard someone chopping brush with a machete on the other side of the stream. I got

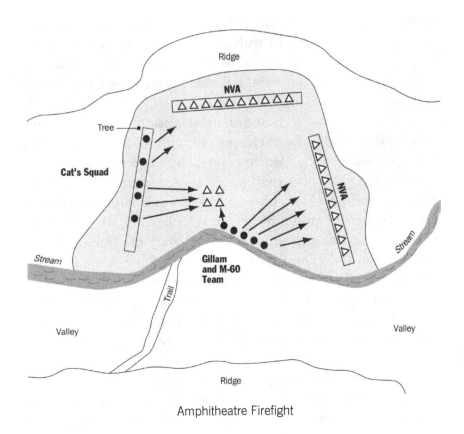

Amphitheatre Firefight

on my belly and crawled down to the bottom of the gully. I was about to slide across the shallow stretch of water when I spotted the source of the noise. It was four men with machetes clearing brush on the side of a hill shaped like an amphitheater.

The amphitheater had probably been made by an *Arc Light* thousand-pound bomb explosion. It was a huge half-circle in the side of the ridge with a lot of large uprooted trees around it. I could also distinctly hear movement and voices from the right side of the amphitheater. Those people were upstream from where I was lying, and I noticed there were enough of them to have stirred up mud in the stream while they were building their camp. The men with the machetes were so close I knew I couldn't use a radio to call for help. I definitely wasn't going to turn my back on them to withdraw to a safe distance to call for help either. I knew I was going to have to handle this one myself, and I figured with ten men, a good radioman, and the M-60's firepower, I could manage the situation.

We were on a search-and-destroy mission, so, I made some quick plans to destroy these people with as little risk to my men as possible. I decided to place Dover and his machinegun team in the gully near the bottom center of the amphitheater. I wanted to move Cat's squad across the gully and spread them uphill facing the amphitheater from its left side. If I could get the men into those positions, I could start the fight with the machinegun and kill off the largest group of enemy on the right side of the amphitheater or drive them up the hill away from the machinegun. If I could do that, Cat's men could shoot them in the back as they fled away from the M-60, or catch them in a cross fire if they went up the hill to get out of the amphitheater from the top.

I planned to take care of the brush cutters who were now to my left front with the help of one or two of the gun team. Counting me there were eleven of us, and I was confident the element of surprise and the firepower we carried would get us through this firefight. Each of us carried 500 rounds for his M-16, and everyone, except the radioman and the two sergeants, also had 500 rounds of ammunition for the machinegun. That meant we had 4,500 rounds for the M-60 and 5,500 rounds of M-16 ammunition. With that much firepower, and the fact that I knew Tiny would call a Cobra gunship for us as soon as the shooting started, I was pretty sure we would win this fight.

I hand signaled Cat to bring his squad to me. As each man came by, I whispered to him what we were up against and what I wanted him to do. Cat took about twenty minutes to place his men. I was O.K. with that. I didn't want to start this fight until I was sure I had the advantage. When Cat gave me the thumbs up that his men were ready, I waved to Dover to bring his gun up next to me. I wanted him close to make sure he didn't fire too far left and hit Cat's men and I also wanted to pick the time when the shooting started.

Dover and Johnny Wolf, his assistant gunner, lost the advantage of surprise for us and nearly got me killed. When I waved them forward, they both acted as if they had not seen the rest of us crawling around on our bellies nor heard the enemy talking and clearing brush just meters away. Both of them stood completely upright and walked the ten yards across the bottom of the gully and the stream. Their upper bodies were exposed above the brush, and I couldn't believe they weren't already dead. None of the enemy saw them, but they heard them when they got to me. Dover had grabbed the machinegun by the carrying handle on top and carried it like a suitcase dragging the ammunition belt in the dirt and water as he came. He dropped the gun on the ground and it made a loud clank at just about the same time Wolf flopped down on the ground facing the direction he had come from instead of the direction the gun was pointed.

The nearest brush cutter was ten meters away and he heard them. He dropped his machete, and started yelling while he pulled his AK-47 up on its sling. I was kneeling next to a tree trunk, and I swung my rifle up and braced my left elbow on my knee. We both started firing from ten meters away at each other. Everyone else, on both sides, opened up a split second later.

The brush cutter and I were both hit in the first volley of fire. He was hit from two directions at once. My first burst struck him center mass from the front, and Cat Ackzinski, who either heard or saw him when he shouted, blasted a full magazine into his back. We literally shot him to pieces, but when he went down his AK-47 skittered around on the ground as his dying reflexes fired off several rounds. One of those rounds nicked my left kneecap. It cut a groove in the bone, and moved it around to the inside of my knee. The grazing impact from the 7.62-millimeter slug knocked me on my left side and my left leg felt like it was on fire from the knee down. I knew I had to ignore it until this firefight was over, so I rolled onto my stomach and squirmed forward to get behind the base of a tree. I started shooting at the backs of two more brush cutters and yelled at Dover to get his M-60 working. I could hardly make myself heard because we were taking fire from people to our right and up the slope of the amphitheater too. There were people farther up the slope I had not seen and they were shooting downhill at us as they tried to protect their comrades at the bottom and right side of the amphitheater.[15]

When the shooting started from the top of the hill, four things happened almost at the same time. First, Cat's squad opened up in unison on the people I had not seen along the top and left side of the amphitheater. Then Dover got his gun working against the people on the lower right side of the amphitheater, and I saw Tiny Pederson on the radio. I knew from past experience he would tell LT Mack what our situation was and call for a Cobra gunship. I didn't know it at the time, but LT Mack was also in a firefight and would be of no help to us. But our call for a Cobra gunship was taken by a ship codenamed *Wolf Pack 32*. The ship was dispatched right away because Tiny Pederson had two skills that made him a perfect radio operator. First, he always memorized the day's verification code so the Cobras and artillery knew they were talking to an American. Second, he read a map as well as I did and always knew where we were. He flopped beside me behind the tree and yelled to me that he could talk the Cobra to our position, but we would be on our own for about a half hour until it showed up.

The fourth thing to happen after the shooting started was Dover ran away with the machinegun and his entire team went with him. He fired a couple bursts to the right of the amphitheater and when he was answered by rifle fire from that direction, he just picked up the gun and ran down the stream bed to the left. Ammo bearers are supposed to follow the gunner, so Johnny

Wolf and the rest of the team left too. Their flight took four of the rifles we needed on that side of the fight, and the 800 rounds per minute from the machinegun I was counting on to carry the day. The only people on that end of the amphitheater when the gun team left were Tiny Pederson and I. I was burning off rounds as fast and accurately as I could, but I think the enemy on both ends of the contact sensed the decrease in fire from us and they responded accordingly. They started pouring such concentrated fire in our direction that pieces of bark and hot sap hit me in the face as their bullets tore chunks off the tree I was hiding behind.

The four brush cutters were dead in the first thirty seconds of the firefight. But the people on the right side and up top began to try to move people along both our flanks to surround us. I knew that if we didn't hang on until *Wolf Pack 32* got there we were all going to be dead or prisoners. Fortunately for us, the people moving along our left flank couldn't complete their maneuver. That was because Cat's squad was spread out behind a huge tree that had been uprooted by the *Arc Light* strike. It was about three feet in diameter and sixty or seventy feet long. From there, they poured a withering fire into the enemy and drove them right off our left flank and the top side of the fight too. With the elimination of that threat Cat faced his men to the right and brought them over the log in an assault line across the heart of the amphitheater. When they came abreast of the tree where Tiny and I were, we joined their assault line and tried, together, to overwhelm the last of the enemy with the firepower of our rifles alone.

An on-line assault is physically and emotionally draining because it requires you to perform an act that defies survival instinct. You have to stand up and run five or ten meters ahead while people are shooting at you. The only way to do it is to ignore the imminence of death and focus on the rhythm of movement and fire as you advance on the enemy. I was in that rhythm when I got wounded again. I saw something brown fly through the air and land on the ground near me. My mind said grenade, and my body did a stupid thing. It moved behind a banana tree for cover. Banana trees are about as solid as celery stalks, and if the grenade had been anything other than an undependable home-made Chi-Com grenade, I would have died on the spot. Chinese Communist (Chi-Com) grenades were pretty unreliable weapons filled with old fashioned black powder. Sometimes they didn't explode because the powder got wet. Sometimes, the dampness caused a weak explosion. That was probably what happened with that grenade, but still, it knocked me flat on my back, and the banana tree fell on top of me. I was dazed, but I knew I would be dead if I stayed in the open under the banana tree. I pushed the tree off of me and crawled toward a more solid tree.

When I got to the tree, I couldn't hear or see very well. Bullets were chopping the tree to pieces, and bits of wood were falling all over me. I also had blood dripping into my left eye but, at the time, I thought it was sweat. The volume of fire had increased to the point where I didn't think we could advance any further, so I decided it was time to back us out of this place if I could. I signaled Cat to get his squad moving in the same direction Dover and the gun team had taken. He got them started and then he grabbed me by the collar of my shirt and pulled me alongside of him behind another fallen tree.

I realized then that Cat, Tiny, and I were on our own. I was pretty sure we were going to die behind that tree while we tried to cover the third squad's retreat. I don't remember being afraid, but I do remember being overcome by rage. I had accepted my death but wanted to kill as many people as I could before they got me. I got to my knees and started screaming and cursing as loud as I could and shooting as fast as I could. I didn't bother to take cover while I changed magazines, and neither did Cat. We just knelt there shooting and swearing like mad men.

Tiny was still there, too. He had been working the radio the whole time and he had talked the gunship right to us. When the

Cobra got on station, Tiny jerked me down on the ground behind the log and thrust the radio handset into my hand. I flopped onto my back with the handset, and the pilot asked me to mark my position, so I fired a white pen flare straight up through the trees. Then I had him hover over that spot and fire his minigun in an arc that began at a 90-degree azimuth and moved to the left until he was hitting just about northwest, at 280 degrees.

In about fifteen seconds, the gunner in *Wolf Pack 32* cut a swath out of the jungle that started about ten yards in front of us and extended about 100 yards deep between those two compass points. The noise was deafening, and the hot brass casings fell all over us. Some of them actually went down the front of my shirt and made a few second-degree burns. I remember thinking, at the time, that I had been shot. I had him follow up with a few of his rockets on both areas where the enemy fire had been concentrated and then it was suddenly quiet.

I looked over at Cat to see if he was okay, and I saw him raise his rifle and point it to our rear. I thought the enemy had somehow gotten behind us, and I rolled on my side, ready to fire, but there was no need. The people coming up behind us were only Dover and his gun team returning in our direction back up the gully. I was mad enough to kill Dover and his whole team on the spot, but Cat's squad was with them and I knew I couldn't claim to have killed Dover and Wolf and the rest of the gun team too by accident. Reluctantly, I turned to the things I knew I should do right away.

First, I had the men sound off one at a time to be sure they were all okay. Then I got them to set up a perimeter in case the enemy came back. I was pointing out positions for each man to take when I came across a woman hiding between the roots of a large tree.[16] She had a compound fracture of the lower left leg, and when she was sure she had been discovered, she pointed to the jungle behind her and kept sobbing out the words "baby sans, baby sans, no guns." I had no idea there were really children in the area because I was getting a patrol briefing from Lieutenant Mack when Company A reported finding children's toys in the area. I thought she was just using the idea of children in the area as a ploy to keep the gunship from firing on the rest of her unit as they fled the area.

Steve Wach, one of the gun team, held her still and clamped his hand over her mouth to keep her quiet in case there were more NVA around. When she stopped struggling and trying to yell, I used two pieces of a tree limb that had been shot off a tree to make a splint on her broken leg. While I was doing that, I noticed that blood was dripping off my face onto her leg. I also saw that my left forearm and hand were bloody too. There was also a spreading bloodstain on the front of my shirt. It was only then that I realized I had been hit by three pieces of shrapnel from the grenade. One piece had struck me in the forehead above my left eyebrow. Another was on the inside of my left forearm. The last one was in my chest between the ribs just below the left pectoral muscle.

The shrapnel holes were small, and Tiny Pederson offered to pick them out with tweezers while I used the radio to report to Captain Derricco and to try to find out what had happened to LT Mack. While I did that, Cat went scouting alone beyond our perimeter to see who was still out there and to find out what damage *Wolf Pack 32* had done. He found three bloody trails that led off into the jungle and four backpacks, all within fifty yards of our position. I got back on the radio and called a Dustoff for the woman we were holding and it arrived around 1:30 p.m. shortly before Captain Derricco showed up with the first platoon. The Dustoff dropped a jungle penetrator to haul the woman away at the same time Cat and Tiny dumped the contents of the four packs on the ground and informed the TOC of what they contained.[17]

At first, the packs looked like they held the usual junk that soldiers on both sides carried. Clothes, ID cards, pills, et cetera.

There were also a few unusual things: a spool of telephone wire suitable for a landline in a permanent camp, a large NVA flag with the red and blue panel and gold star, and twenty rounds for an M-16 rifle.[18] We knew that flags the size of the one in the pack belonged on flagpoles at big camps. The telephone wire was something that also belonged in a large camp. And then, there was the M-16 ammunition, another reminder for us that there might be an American around, either a live POW or a dead one in an unmarked grave.

While Cat and Tiny were busy on the radio, the captain told me LT Mack couldn't come to help us because he was in a firefight, too. Bob Frost was walking point for him, and he had also not gone very far when they found a cave that was being used as a command bunker for a set of ten bunkers in a row. They got fired on and had to call for help, just like I did. When the calls went out from two firefights at once, the battalion commander happened to be in the air with his personal helicopter, codenamed *Cider*. He had a door gunner on his bird, and so he went to cover LT Mack's men. *Wolf Pack 32* had been sent to cover my men.[19]

Later that afternoon, LT Mack and Frost radioed the TOC that they had found a pile of equipment similar to what my patrol had found. Their report and the one that Company A made while we were engaged in the two firefights that morning were more proof that our battalion was finally inside Base Area 226. Company A working to our east had come upon a complex of thatched buildings that were twenty-five by thirty meters each. One of them had tables inside, and there were bundles of punji stakes on some of them. They also found two classrooms or briefing rooms with three-legged easels for maps and diagrams and a dozen baskets full of corn. Company A also found two animal pens. One had five pigs and the other had thirty chickens. The final part of their report said they had found several bunkers with six to eight feet of log and dirt cover on top.[20]

By late afternoon on February 19, B Company had gathered all three of its platoons on a hill close to the amphitheater. Captain Derricco called his two lieutenants and three platoon sergeants together in the center of the perimeter to assess the tactical situation and to announce his imminent departure. The obvious highpoints of his assessment were that we were in a place where the enemy had brought his women and, according to Company A's report, his children too. He had medical personnel, classrooms, livestock, and there was evidence of permanent telephone communications along with the punji stakes that were commonly used as defensive measures around enemy camps.[21] I remember thinking to myself, "We are in deep shit. We are still inside Nguyen's house, and he is going to get really pissed about it."

The captain also told us he had finished his six months of duty in the field required for officers and had been reassigned to duty in the rear. I don't remember where he went after he left us because I didn't care. What I did care about was the fact that Lieutenant TJ was going to be our acting company commander. He was a little too gung-ho about body counts and too attached to his Army Ranger Handbook for my tastes. In fact, he exacerbated my uneasiness about his leadership just before we broke up the meeting. The battalion commander, he said, had ordered us to remain in the area to keep hunting. We couldn't really do anything about that. But Lieutenant TJ's decision to continue with squad-sized patrols for the continued hunting was different. He liked the smaller units because he felt they were quieter and had a better chance of making contact. I had just been through a firefight with less than a platoon-sized element that morning. I had four extra holes in me for my trouble. I was not a happy camper. Sticking with squad-sized patrols in an area with evidence of company and battalion units did nothing for my confidence in my new commander.

I went back to my platoon to tell them the good news-bad news and to let Frankie, our medic, work on my chipped kneecap and shrapnel wounds. We both agreed I couldn't take anything for pain because I was going to need a clear head and sharp reflexes. He said I had a dislocated kneecap. He re-centered it and stitched up the tear over it. Then, he wrapped it with an ace bandage. Frankie also tried pulling the shrapnel from above my left eye with a pair of forceps but he only got part of it. The other part seemed to be imbedded in the skull. It bled a lot, so I told him to stop with the probing and twisting. His ministrations hurt more than the damn wounds so I told him to stop the bleeding and leave the rest of my holes alone.

I ended up with a gauze pad on my forehead, held in place by a bush hat because the helmet was too tight with the pad and swelling. I put another gauze pad on my forearm and chest, and pretty soon, they were stuck in place by clotted, drying blood. I planned to have the battalion surgeon look at them when I got to a firebase or the base camp for a stand down, but he never saw them. I carried the shrapnel in my chest and arm until 1983. I was a graduate student at the Ohio State University when a weight-lifting accident tore one of my intercostal muscles, and the shrapnel came loose. A surgical resident at the university's medical school took a piece of wood and a piece of steel out of me. In 1986, I had the one in my forehead removed in an outpatient procedure while I was on spring break from Spelman College in Atlanta, Georgia.

Three days after the shootout at the amphitheater, we were still hunting around in Nguyen's house just like the colonel and Lieutenant TJ wanted. The three platoons were spaced about a kilometer apart on a ridge above a river that ran into the valley from Cambodia. My platoon was ordered to break into squads to cover more territory. The first squad stayed on the ridge top with LT Mack. The third squad and Jesse Johnson's machinegun team set up an ambush on a trail half way down the slope. I went with the second squad and the second machinegun team farther down the trail to set up another ambush close to the river.

I had relieved Dover of carrying the gun and given it to Jimmy "Smoke" Carter. Smoke was a big muscular African-American from rural South Carolina who had a voice like Louis Armstrong. He had been Jesse Johnson's assistant gunner for a long time so I figured he knew what he was doing. I moved Steve Wach in behind Smoke as an assistant gunner, and put Dover and Wolf behind Steve as ammo bearers. It was a position where I hoped they would stay out of trouble. I was wrong again.

The broad trail we used to get to the river was intersected by a smaller one that followed a tributary to the river. The two trails formed an L-shape. I left the patrol next to the main trail and I scouted for a place that we could use to cover both trails at the same time. I had not gone far at all when I found fresh footprints from two pairs of Ho Chi Minh sandals. They were fresh enough that the moisture from the damp soil by the stream had just begun to seep into them. They were pointed toward the junction of the small tributary stream and the river. That meant that at least two, if not three people were behind me on the big trail. I started tracking them. I was guessing that they were either fishing in the larger stream or had gone there to fill some canteens because the smaller stream was too shallow. I figured that if I could catch them doing either job, they would be sitting ducks. All I had to do was see them first and take care of business.

I was almost back to the junction of the two streams when I heard a single shot and a lot of voices from the area where I had left the squad. I jumped off the small trail and crashed through the jungle back to the main trail. When I got there, Carl Dover and Johnny Wolf were standing over a dead NVA. He was face up in the middle of the trail with both eyes open and a hole in the center of his chest. The rest of the squad and gun team were charging up the side of the ridge after two more NVA. I left Dover and Wolf and sprinted after the rest of my men.

I heard a lot of thrashing in the bushes and a few single rifle shots. Then I heard the hollow thunk of an M-79 grenade launcher being fired and it was quickly followed by a loud bang. The time between the thunk and bang was so short I knew Johnny Wayne Brown, the grenadier, must have been shooting at bare minimum range. I ran in that direction and found Brown, loading his weapon with one of the giant 40-millimeter buckshot rounds used for close range work. The rest of the men were there, too, and as we thrashed up hill, Brown told me he had hit the tree next to two men as they fled, and one of them was wounded. I got in front of him because I was a better tracker, and he had a one-shot weapon. I spread the rest of the squad to the left and right while we tried to herd these two men into the ambush Jesse Johnson's gun team had waiting for them higher up the ridge. Then, a few minutes later, I found a blood trail.

The color and location of the blood told me Brown had either hit both of them or hit one of them in two places. There was dark red arterial blood on the ground and low on the bushes and foamy pink blood about chest high on the bushes. I also saw footprints from Ho Chi Minh sandals that were pretty deep for a Vietnamese, even one carrying a pack while he ran. Soon, we spotted the man making the tracks. He was carrying his wounded friend over his shoulder while he went up the trail. We all gave chase, and Tiny called Jesse's men to alert them to be careful what they shot at because we were right behind them. I thought either Jesse's men or mine would get both of these men but it didn't happen. We found the one with the lung wound about a half mile up the ridge from the river. His friend had dropped him, and somehow evaded the ambush. He was wounded too, but he got away when we stopped to secure the man he dropped by the side of the trail.

Our chase had taken us almost back to our starting point, so LT Mack brought our medic and the first squad to us. The prisoner kept repeating the phrase "beaucoup chi" to the medic. Lum, one of our scouts, told us the man was saying he was in great pain. It would have been surprising if he wasn't hurting.

Brown's M-79 round had shredded the left side of his body when it exploded. He had a hole in one lung and about a dozen more wounds in his left arm, hip, and thigh. LT Mack told Lum to interrogate the prisoner before the Medevac helicopter took him away.[22] I left him to it and took Bud Rose and Joe Rocha with me back down to the river to find Dover and Wolf.

We found them sitting by the side of the trail, near the dead man. Dover told me three men had been fishing on the bank below the trail and had no idea that our squad was on the trail behind them because of the noise of the river. They walked up the bank with some fish on a string and Carl Dover, of all people, fired one round right through the first guy's heart. He said the other two men took off through the brush up the ridge just before I showed up and everyone left them standing by the trail. I asked why Dover didn't shoot the other two. Wolf just started giggling and pointed at Dover's weapon. The breach and magazine well had exploded. The bolt was sticking out the right side of the chamber housing. The magazine well and trigger guard were reduced to a few metal strips curled up like a banana peel.

Dover's weapon blew up because he had probably banged the muzzle into the side of the hill while on patrol, or just dropped it muzzle first in the dirt and plugged up the barrel. I looked at the dead man's chest, and he had a hole that was larger than the normal M-16 entrance wound. I think Dover probably killed that NVA with either a mud plug or a stone that was lodged in his barrel. A couple strokes with a cleaning rod would have fixed the problem but Dover rarely acted like a soldier at war. Weapon cleaning and maintenance were not a priority for him. He knew he should clean his weapon at least once a day. But all you had to do was look at his weapon to see it was a mess. There were actually spider webs on the inside of the metal brace for the front sight. There was green mold in the vent holes in the front hand guards of the weapon. Dover was just not into clean weapons.

We all went back up the trail, and LT Mack congratulated Dover on his shooting. Then he chewed him out soundly for having such a filthy rifle that it exploded when he tried to use it. When Mack was through with Dover, I took my turn with him. Instead of Cat's physical method, I tried menacing. I took him to the side of the trail and stood very close to him and talked quietly while I stared at his face. I said "Dover, my man, you fucked up in two firefights in a row. You just might not make it if you do it again." Then I took my .45 out of the holster, racked the slide half way back so he could see that it had a round in the chamber, and then I cocked the hammer. I got nose to nose with him and asked him if he understood what I meant. We both knew I was threatening to shoot him, but he didn't say a word. After a few seconds, I pulled his hand up and put the pistol in it. I told him he could use it until the next resupply day when another rifle would be sent out for him, and I turned my back on him and walked away.

When the fussing at Dover was over and the prisoner was Medevaced away, LT Mack put us back to work. He said I should take Smoke's machinegun team and the second squad and find another patrol base for the platoon. We found one about a kilometer northwest of the previous base. It was a nearly flat space along the top of a ridge covered by triple canopy jungle. The jungle was so thick that you couldn't see twenty meters off the trail. I thought it was a pretty good place to camp because we could dig our circle of fighting positions and they would be hard for the enemy to spot until they were really close. Then, there was the added advantage of not having to level out sleeping spaces behind the holes. I gave the coded coordinates to the place on the radio, and LT Mack told my squad to secure it for the rest of the day while the rest of the platoon finished working their assigned areas. We took the easy assignment as payment due for the KIA and prisoner and set about making ourselves comfortable.

When a unit stops in daylight, it is SOP (Standard Operating Procedure) to set out observation posts, or OPs, as they are called, on likely avenues of approach. So, before anyone started the noisy process of digging a foxhole, I sent a man off both sides of the ridge into the brush and two men along the trail that ran by our position. Those men would go far enough from our position that they could not hear us digging or talking and watch for the approach of the enemy. If they saw someone, they knew they should sneak back to the perimeter as fast as they could so we could arrange a proper reception before the enemy got to us.

After half an hour or so, most of the holes were done, or nearly done. I decided to rotate the people on OP so some of the hole diggers could get a break. Smoke volunteered for one of the OPs rather than finish digging the hole for the M-60. I told Dover to take the OP on the trail from the direction we had come in on. He started bitching about it before I could finish telling him where I wanted him to go. He said the .45 I had given him was not enough firepower, and that he wasn't going anywhere unless I gave him my rifle. I already knew how he treated weapons, and the idea that I should give him mine was just the last straw.

My temper went from calm to white hot, but I couldn't scream at him like I wanted to because we were in the jungle. Still, I let three days of built-up anger pour out. I told him that if he wasn't such a lazy son of a bitch, he would still have a working weapon. Then I called him a cowardly motherfucker for running out with the machinegun three days before. When I got around to telling him all about the fantasies I was having about ways to break things on his body, Wolf stepped between us. He traded Dover his rifle for my pistol and suggested he get out of the way while I cooled off.

Bob Frost watched the confrontation between Dover and me, and he waved me over to sit with him and Richie Beunzel in a hammock. When I got close to him, he grinned and told me to sit my old crippled ass down and check out the *Playboy* magazine he had gotten in the mail. Frost had heard I had turned twenty-three, and that made me one of the oldest men in the company. Except for the officers and First Sergeant White, most of the rest of them were nineteen or twenty. Bob started teasing me, saying I had been gimping around like an old man. I told him it was because grunt years were double dog years. Dogs aged seven years in a human year, and I felt way over twenty-three since the firefight at the amphitheater. My shrapnel holes were sore and starting to leak pus. The stitches in my left knee had torn loose. Even worse, all my holes had become a daily feeding site for leeches. I had to pour insect repellent into them several times a day when they started to itch from the wormy bloodsuckers. I was also having trouble with full movement in my left shoulder, and I had headaches from the grenade blast. In short, I was a twenty-three-year-old Grunt in a body that had some serious mileage on it.

I squeezed in between Frost and Richie to rest up and admire Hugh Hefner's latest work. The three of us had been sitting there shoulder to shoulder for about ten minutes when we looked up and saw Dover walking back into the perimeter. He went right to his rucksack, pulled out a transistor radio, attached an earphone to it, turned it on, and started back toward his observation post. Bob just groaned and said, "son of a bitch." Richie said, "I ain't believin' this!" I was back to fantasizing about breaking parts of his body when Dover stumbled and the earphone came loose. Dover's radio blasted out a few words of Michael Jackson singing, "Stop, the Love You Save Might Be Your Own." That blast was immediately followed by the sound of an RPD machinegun blasting away from the direction of Dover's abandoned OP.

In the instant before Frost, Beunzel, and I dove to the ground, I heard three solid whacks to my left and I felt something splash on my face and left arm. I ignored it for a few seconds while I burned off an entire magazine into the bushes where the fire had come from. I rolled onto my right side while I reloaded to check out Frost and he looked awful. The whacking sound I heard was the sound of him absorbing three rounds to the chest and the wetness was his blood spraying on both of us. Our eyes locked, and he said, "I'm okay," so all three of us kept shooting back at the enemy.

While we traded fire with the RPD gunner, Joe Rocha stood up and made a running dive that took him head-first into the foxhole where Smoke's M-60 was set up. In a second, he popped up and burned off a long burst of fire into the bushes too. Then, like most of the firefights we had, this one ended as suddenly as it started. In the relative quiet, I expected to hear a lot of calls for a medic, but all I heard was Rocha screaming "motherfucker, you chickenshit motherfucker."

Joe was still in the hole with the M-60 and he had a helmet in his right hand. He swung it down hard every time he said "motherfucker." Beunzel and I ran over to him and when we got there we could see Carl Dover curled into a fetal ball in the bottom of the hole to protect himself from Rocha's beating. I would have let Rocha beat him to death but I could see Joe was hurt. Beunzel and I grabbed him by the upper arms and pulled him out of the hole. He shrieked in pain, but he kept trying to kick Dover in the head as we pulled him out of the hole.

When we laid Rocha down, we could see that his shirt and pants were soaked in blood. I called for Frankie, our medic. Frankie yelled over to me to do what I could, and he would be there as soon as he stabilized Frost. I knew the first thing to do was to quiet Rocha down and find all his wounds so I could deal with the worst ones first. The first thing I saw was a compound fracture of his left forearm. I laid it next to him and told him not to move it. Then I used my knife to cut his bloody shirt open. Then I cut through his belt and opened the top of his pants. I saw three exit wounds in a diagonal line across his belly. You could tell they were exit wounds because bullets tend to make larger holes coming out of a body than going in. One was in his stomach above and to the right of his navel. The other two were lower and to the left on his abdomen just below his belt line. All of Joe's holes were the size of silver dollars and the lower two had intestines poking out. All three were also bleeding freely but the blood wasn't pulsing or squirting, so I thought he had no arterial damage.

Beunzel brought me some large gauze pads, disinfectant, and cotton balls from the medic's M-5 kit. Then we rolled Joe on his right side and stuffed wads of cotton balls in the entrance wounds in his back. As his shock and anger wore off, Joe was starting to feel a lot of pain. So I told him to tell me what happened to him as a distraction while I worked on him. He said when the RPD opened up he saw Dover drop into the hole with the M-60. He expected him to get the gun working because it was loaded and pointed in the right direction. He wouldn't have even had to expose himself; he could have just reached up and pulled the trigger, but nothing happened. Rocha said he thought Dover was dead or hurt, so he ran to the gun and got it working. The problem was, on the way there, he got shot three times in the lower back and all three rounds came out the front. One of them broke his left forearm. I knew the rest of the story; Rocha was gut shot and had a broken arm, but he still got the gun working while Dover lay on the bottom of the hole.

I left Richie Beunzel to put an inflatable splint on Rocha's arm while I went to see if I could help with Bob Frost. Tiny Pederson was kneeling next to Bob and the medic and he was already on the radio giving our position and the condition of the wounded to a Dustoff pilot.[23] Frost was sitting propped against a pack and Frankie had an IV line with a blood expander called serum albumin in his arm. That first burst of fire had struck Bob full in the chest as he sat shoulder to shoulder with me teasing me about being an old man. Like Rocha, he had fought despite his wounds. His face was swollen almost beyond recognition because he was bleeding internally and much of the blood was pumping into the pockets of flesh formed by his facial muscles. Whatever blood didn't go that way was filling up his right lung, and it wasn't long before he began to bleed from his nose and mouth. I didn't know what else to do, so I got a gauze pad and wiped his mouth. Bob looked at me and asked, "Gill, did we get them fuckers?" I told him, "No man, it was you. You got 'em all." It was the last thing we said to each other because he lost consciousness right after that.

I took the radio from Tiny and made a three-way call to inform the TOC, Lieutenant TJ, and LT Mack of our situation. I told them that we had taken automatic weapon fire from ten to fifteen meters away on an azimuth of 270 degrees. I also said that we had returned fire and the enemy retreated to the west, but I wasn't certain they had left the area so I also recommended a gunship accompany the Dustoff ship.

Both helicopters arrived on station shortly before 12:30 p.m. It took almost half an hour to get both Joe and Bob off the ground because the jungle was so thick. They took Joe up first on the penetrator because he had the best chance of survival. Strong man that he was, he almost broke my hand when he shook it while they strapped him in his seat. Bob was unconscious and couldn't sit up so he went into the litter basket. It kept hanging up in the trees. We finally had to lower him back down and unhook one end of the basket so they could pull him through the canopy.[24]

LT Mack showed up with the rest of our platoon at 1:15 and Lieutenant TJ got there just five minutes or so later. TJ ordered Mack to give the TOC an "official readout" on the firefight. I told him I had already done it and he said it wasn't official unless an officer did it. I got in TJ's face and said "what page in your fuckin' handbook said that sergeants don't know a dead man when they see one?" Bodell jerked me by the arm and told me to cool it. As I backed off, I told TJ how little I thought of his small-sized patrols inside an NVA base camp. We stared at each other for a while and then, without breaking eye contact, he told LT Mack he was taking the entire first platoon with him to track down the RPD team. I told him I wanted to go with them because I was a good tracker. I also had some serious payback in mind, but he made me stay in the perimeter. I think he was worried, and with good reason, about going off in the woods with me when there was a chance of shots being exchanged. TJ's patrol was gone for a long time, and had no success.[25]

First platoon got back around 7:00 p.m. and we made a set up with all three platoons in a very tight perimeter that night. Around 9:00 p.m. my platoon heard movement in the bushes in front of us. Johnny Wayne Brown fired a flare from his M-79, and the rest of the platoon opened fire. There was some intermittent groaning and rustling in the bushes for a couple hours. I crawled from one position to another to tell the men to throw grenades at the sounds so they didn't give away their positions. After that, it was quiet for the rest of the night except for two radio messages from the TOC. One came at around 11:00 to advise us that a so-called reliable source had indicated that there was a sapper battalion in our area and all units were to remain on high alert. The other message was that Bob Frost had died on the operating table at the battalion aid station.[26]

Frost was the first man in our platoon to die since I joined the company. We all took it badly. We expected that our company commander, Lieutenant TJ, would write a letter to his family, but I don't know if he ever did. I did find out thirty-five years later that Jim Henderson and Jim Killian, two of the relatively new guys in our platoon, wrote to Bob's sister in Oklahoma to express their condolences. Their letters and several photos of the men in our platoon were posted in a web site started by Jim Henderson.[27]

A and B Company remained in western Binh Dinh Province, between LZ Louis and the Cambodian border, until early March 1970. While we were there, the pace of our war picked up and the fighting became tougher. It was a time when it seemed either A or B Company saw action almost every day. In the tactical terms of the day, we conducted basic search-and-destroy operations. As Captain Derricco would have described it, we hunted. We hunted the enemy's supplies and camps, or we hunted the enemy who were moving the supplies and guarding the camps.

IT'S NOT BUSINESS, IT'S PERSONAL

Conducting our hunt inside the enemy's base camp is what made the contacts more frequent. It also added an element of desperation to our encounters. Also, because we stayed in the area, often times crossing and re-crossing the same trails, the killing we did often became personal. That was new for us. Before that time, our firefights had often been savage close-range encounters, but we seldom knew or cared to know much about the enemy. Even I had gotten to the point where it was enough that they died and we didn't.

Our indifference about the enemy evaporated in February and March 1970. It was replaced by the fact that sometimes we knew, or really wanted to know, who we killed. For example, Company A captured a man in a firefight. He escaped while they were waiting for a helicopter to take him to the TOC for interrogation. Some of us speculated they let him go so they could shoot him. Two days later, they killed him in another firefight. They knew it was the same man because they had shot off one of his toes in the first encounter.[28]

The killing had gotten personal for me, too. I wanted revenge for Bob Frost and Joe Rocha, and I got some measure of it. We killed many people in the days that followed Bob's death, and I stopped worrying about their friends and family, or if they would get a decent burial. When I stood staring at their corpses, I mostly wondered if any of them were the one who killed Bob, and then I left them where they lay. I was almost at the emotional place LT

Mack had told me to go months before. It was the place where I could "kill 'em, and count 'em," but even all these years later, I have not quite forgotten them.

The war was further personalized for me when I found out there really were children in the area of the firefight at the amphitheater. We were back there hunting again when our first platoon found a grave that appeared to be ten or twelve days old. We knew from experience that the enemy sometimes disguised arms caches as trailside graves and relied on our cultural and practical inhibitions to leave them undisturbed. But, after three weeks inside Base Area 226, we had few inhibitions of any kind left. First platoon dug up the grave. They found a shipping crate for rifles. They opened the crate expecting to find AK-47s. Instead, they found a child's body. Apparently, it was one of the children Company A had reported finding toys for. It was probably one of the "baby-sans" the woman we captured at the amphitheater had been screaming about when I had the Cobra gunship fire at her comrades as they fled the area.[29]

In March 1970 I heard the radio report of what had been found and I was pretty sure I had killed that child. I remember wondering what kind of idiot would bring a child to a war, but I don't recall any real regrets about it at the time. At the time, feeling guilty about it just never occurred to me. I was wearing a pretty thick layer of emotional Teflon, and so I just let the whole episode slide off me. I left the issue of the dead child on the ground with the other people I killed and walked away from all of them.

In the summer of 2003 I found the Duty Officer's Log that recorded the death of that child in a storage box in the National Archives. I opened the storage box and I had an olfactory flashback to Vietnam. The records had been packed away, smeared with the red mud of the Central Highlands for thirty-three years. I sat there, smelling the dampness of the jungle while I read the Duty Officer's Log. While I was doing that, I also had a visual flashback of the terror and misery on that woman's face as she pleaded for the lives of what might have been her own children. I sat there at my worktable and cried for a long time. When I heard one of the female archivists tell someone, "I think he's a veteran and he probably found something unpleasant." I got up and left the building.

On March 10, 1970, our entire battalion was shifted back to Operation *Putnam Paragon*. We made another combat assault into a small landing zone just below a plateau on the northern end of the Vinh Than Valley.[30] The landing was covered, as usual, by Cobra gunships, but there was only one enemy killed. He died after the Cobras left and we were on the ground. We cleared the LZ quickly and were moving toward better cover on the plateau when someone up above us shouted, "Gooks're behind us!" I turned around on the hillside and saw a man in a bright blue shirt running away from us up the hill on the other side of the narrow valley. Half of B Company fired up the woods around him. My squad was at the tail end of the company, and so I took Cecil Dykes with me to make sure this guy was dead.

We found him sitting at the base of a tree staring at us. In addition to the bright blue shirt, we had seen, he wore dark civilian-style pants. On the ground next to him was a large black suitcase. Dykes shouted for him to get up, but he didn't move. I grabbed him by the shirtfront, to jerk him to his feet. His shirt tore in my hand and he fell over because he was dead with his eyes open. I searched him for weapons and documents and discovered that he only had a wound to his calf muscle. I think he was literally scared to death by all the bullets landing around him. I opened the suitcase and it was full of Vietnamese Piasters and documents written in Vietnamese. We left the paymaster in the woods and a helicopter came back to the landing zone to pick up his suitcase.

By March of 1970, the Vinh Than, or Happy Valley, was familiar territory for me. I had been there twice before, and I had no happy memories of it. The first seven men I killed were in that valley. When we returned, I actually recognized many of the landmarks and trails. In fact, I even knew where the best cover and concealment was to be found without looking at the map. Yet even though we were working on familiar ground, there was an important difference in the way we worked the Vinh Than this time. The monsoon season was over and after the rains stopped, the upper branches of streams dried out. The lack of water drove the enemy to the trails along the shrinking rivers in the lower part of the valley. We followed them because that was the only place where there was water for them and for us. That predictability of need often put us in harm's way.

Even though we and our enemies knew the danger of riverside trails, I think Lieutenant TJ seemed to enjoy going back and forth on them. In one ten-day period, he marched the company along the same riverside trail three times. A combat assault had landed us on a hill northeast of LZ Hard Times. We walked down to a trail along the Song Kon River in the valley, and followed it for three days. When our food ran out, he ordered us to retrace our route back to the landing zone. He said it was the nearest and most convenient clearing for resupply. We got the supplies, and headed back along the same route we took to get to the landing zone. Three days later, when we were out of food again, we went back on the *same* trail to the *same* clearing for more supplies. It was a basic rule of infantry tactics to never use the same route twice in a row so, when he ordered us along the trail for the third time, I told him how I felt about it, especially since it was my turn to walk point.

Lieutenant TJ continued to troll the company up and down the trail. I was convinced he was just looking to increase his body count, but he let me take the second squad and work off the trail as flank security. We spent most of the morning leapfrogging ahead of the main column looking for trail watchers and ambushers. It wasn't long at all before Bodell stopped and pointed to a khaki shirt high up in a tree. It belonged to an NVA who was watching the riverside trail. We took our time and looked for others and we saw two more of them. All three were tied into their trees and had leafy branches in the front of their combat harness and shirts for camouflage.

These trail watchers had made two fatal mistakes. The first one was that they only camouflaged their fronts and we were behind them. The second mistake was that they had limited their mobility for a firefight by climbing up in the trees. I was thinking that maybe one of them was a gung-ho lieutenant who didn't listen to his NCOs either when one of them started waving at the other two and pointing at the river. I figured he had seen or heard our men by the river so I shot him high up in the back on the left side. He tried to turn with his weapon in his right hand so I shot him again, this time in the face. I think Bodell and Dykes shot the other two. We recovered all three weapons: two of the new AK-50 assault rifles with the folding stocks, and a bolt-action rifle with a small scope on it. I found out later that it was a Soviet-made sniper rifle called a Moisin-Nagant. None of the men fell to the ground so we just left them tied to their trees. TJ was pleased with the kills. I was more nervous about his tactics.

The next day, I thought we would get a break in my argument with Lieutenant TJ about tactics because the company was ordered to move onto LZ Terrace and secure it. We stayed there two days. We got resupplied there and three scout dogs were assigned to our company. That same night, someone on the bunker line heard voices and threw a grenade followed by some small arms fire. Lieutenant TJ took a squad and a dog and handler to search the area. I couldn't believe it but he took that damn flashlight with him too. He reported on the radio that he had found deep tracks in the trail and followed them for about two hundred meters. We watched his progress with the light the whole time, and wondered why he didn't get shot. He just came back up the hill and reported to the TOC that he had probably been chasing another trail watcher, but this one got away.[31]

FETCHING PEOPLE

At dawn on April 1, B Company took another combat assault to work the area near LZ Challenge. Challenge was twenty kilometers north of the air base in the Vinh Than Valley.[32] This move put us in the northwest of the rest of the battalion and within sight of Cambodia. Our orders were to take two weeks to work our way back south to the vicinity of LZ Terrace and clear our path of enemy. We took all three of the dog teams with us, and we weren't even off the LZ before TJ and I had another "discussion" about tactics. This time it was about how to use the dogs. The dogs were called Bart, Jinx, and Duke.[33] Bart and Duke were the largest German Shepherds I had ever seen, and Jinx was a female Black Labrador Retriever, and just as big as the others.

When these dogs got the command to "fetch," they brought you a person instead of a stick. They fetched human prey by knocking it down from behind and latching on at the base of the neck or the back of the thigh. I was pleased to hear that, and figured that Jinx and her handler who were with our platoon would be walking point. Lieutenant TJ said no. He said the Army's priorities were to conserve time, money, and equipment, not point men. In his view, the dogs were equipment, so they would go behind the point and slack man until we had a firefight and needed to chase down a blood trail. I asked him if he thought the dogs were more important than the point men. He said that dogs were more expensive to train than point men; that if the Army lost a point man, they could just draft another man and in three months, he would be in Vietnam. According to him, it took considerably longer to breed and train a scout dog. So, I ended up walking point ahead of the dog.

The patrol that day put me on a trail that followed the narrow, V-shaped end of a valley. The dry season had thinned out the undergrowth, and so, from my position on one leg of the V, I saw an NVA on the other leg of it walking in my direction. I fired three shots at him from the hip when I thought he was looking in my direction. I hit him, but he got up and ran uphill. The dog handler let Jinx off her leash. She took a moment to get his scent from the blood on the ground, and then she snarled and took off after the man. In a few minutes, we heard screaming, growling, and thrashing in the bushes. By the time we got to them, the man was dead. Jinx had pinned him face down on the ground and her jaws were clamped on the back of his neck. She was jerking him backwards down the hill towards us. There was a lot of blood on the ground, but it was hard to tell if I had killed him or if the dog did. The handler pulled Jinx away, and when I rolled the NVA over to search him, his head flopped at a crazy angle because his neck was broken. In the end, I thought, it didn't matter how he died, it only mattered that he did. Two days after Jinx and I killed the NVA, she was also indirectly related to the disappearance of our scout Lum. We were in an area that had many signs of the enemy around, and Lum was behaving in a very suspicious manner. I knew he had been NVA before he changed sides, and I also knew he was with us because we were working the area where he had been captured. Some lifer/base camp commando in battalion intelligence probably figured he would be a good source for directions to some caches or camps.

LT Mack also thought since it was the dry season that Lum would also know where we could find some drinking water. Lum, LT Mack, and I were poring over a map discussing possible ambush sites and water sources. Lum said he had no idea where water could be found because he didn't know this area. He also had no opinion at all about ambush sites or where various trails went. We ended up drinking gritty groundwater collected from holes we dug in a dry streambed. We also quietly passed the word from man to man to watch Lum's every move, especially if a fire-fight started.

The Lum watch went badly that night, and I should have killed him. I had fallen asleep near Jinx and she woke me up when she stood up and growled. She had alerted to Lum's movement inside the platoon's perimeter. In the moonlight, I watched him move quietly to one of the sandbagged sleeping positions behind a foxhole where two or three men were asleep. There was a man on guard in the foxhole, but he was several yards away and facing the jungle. I picked up my rifle and moved in that direction. Lum picked up a rifle propped against the sandbags. He fumbled with it quietly and then put it back. I couldn't tell what he was doing, but handling another man's weapon and doing it with obvious stealth seemed really suspicious to me. I got more concerned when I saw him pick up another weapon.

There was enough light for me to center my front sight on the middle of his back. I should have killed him, but instead, I took up the slack in the trigger and said, "Lum, stand still or I will kill you right now." The dog started barking when I raised my voice, and everyone in the perimeter woke up. Lum was standing there with another man's rifle in his hand. The first weapon Lum had picked up belonged to Stony Burks. Burks woke up when the dog started barking, grabbed his weapon and the magazine fell out because it was not locked into the magazine as well as it should have been. The chamber was empty too. The conclusion for me was clear. Lum was disabling weapons at one of our positions in preparation for an attack. I think if he could have gotten all three weapons disabled, he would have dispatched the guard and signaled an attack. We would have had enemy inside our perimeter in a nighttime firefight because the other men at that position would be holding empty weapons when the action started.

We stood Lum against a tree and tied his neck, arms, and legs to it. When dawn came, he kept trying to convince us that he was just checking weapons to make sure they were loaded. Nobody was buying that, and we had plans to ship him in on the next resupply bird in a few days. It didn't happen. A day after the weapons incident, our battalion commander's Loach got fired on and was forced to land on LZ Niagara. Our first and third platoons were ordered into blocking positions. My platoon was sent after the men who shot up the colonel's Loach. We never found them, and Lum disappeared.[34]

From time to time, the enemy stepped up their attempts to shoot down our helicopters and the spring of 1970 was one of those periods. In fact, it was just three weeks before our battalion commander's bird was forced down that the *Quon Doi Nhan Dan*, a Hanoi newspaper, published an article entitled "Actively Spreading a Wide Net to Down U.S. Helicopters." Xuan Phuong, the author, described various methods used to bring helicopters down, including the use of four-barreled 12.7 millimeter anti-aircraft machineguns. After noting the prior successes such as the downing of fifty helicopters from November 4 to 11, 1969, Xuan also praised a certain Comrade Long who single handedly shot down a helicopter with an AK-47.[35]

The colonel's aircraft was shot up by another Vietnamese sharpshooter, and our entire company was sent to hunt him down. We spent the entire afternoon on what turned out to be a fruitless exercise. Our third platoon almost killed the sharpshooter in an exchange of fire around 4:00 p.m. But he disappeared in about fifteen minutes.[36] The only thing our company found that afternoon was a table-model sewing machine that someone dropped by the side of a trail.[37] Lum disappeared too. I always wondered, but never asked if someone just put him on the express train to Hell like I should have done the night before.

We worked in the area between the northern end of the Vinh Than Valley and Cambodia until the last week of April when were taken by helicopter back to LZ Terrace. Once we were there, the daily routine we expected of rotating bunker duty and local security patrols around the base did not happen. Instead, much to our surprise, we were ordered through a number of training exercises reminiscent of AIT for infantry in the States. There were refresher courses on things like the use of Claymore mines, how to fire the Light Antitank Weapons (LAW), and there were even contests in marksmanship with both the M-16 and the M-60 machinegun. Given what we had been through since February, much of this seemed like a waste of time, but we knew from our work on the border and various news sources ranging from the Army's newspaper *Stars and Stripes*, and the more reliable "scuttlebutt," that we were just biding our time before we got sent to Cambodia. So, it surprised none of us when the battalion was suddenly moved back to division base camp at Pleiku.

The move to Pleiku happened so fast that a lot of ammunition for the LZ's 81 millimeter mortar tubes had to be abandoned on LZ Terrace. There simply were not enough flying cranes and Chinook cargo helicopters to get it all out. My platoon was the last one off Terrace and the battalion commander landed his personal Loach to check the closing of the firebase. He was not pleased that so much ammunition had been left behind. He remembered me from our brief, unfriendly, conversation at Christmas time. He said to me, "Son, . . . I mean sergeant, do you know how to set demolition charges?" I assured him I did, and he told me I would stay behind with him to blow up the ammunition after every one else went to base camp.

While the colonel's bird sat on the ground, I crimped a foot-long piece of standard explosive fuse onto a blasting cap and stuck it into a one-pound block of C-4 explosive. I put the package between two crates of mortar shells and then I touched the end of the fuse with a cigar provided by the colonel and ran for his helicopter. When I got in the Loach, the pilot lifted a couple feet off the ground and dove the bird off the side of the hill into the valley, picking up speed the same way real birds do when they dive. There was little time to clear the area before the explosion so it wasn't safe to do the usual slow rise, hover, and rotate maneuver that helicopters usually did off a firebase. It was a wise flying strategy because the explosion, when it came, took off most of the top of the ridge that was LZ Terrace and left a crater in the center. In an hour I was back with B Company waiting while the powers in the capitals of Vietnam, Cambodia, and America finished their diplomatic posturing and sent us off to the last big operation I participated in during the war: the Cambodian invasion of 1970.

7. ✹

Regional Politics, Diplomacy, and Military Preparations for Invasion

March 11 to May 18, 1970

DIPLOMACY AND POLITICS BEFORE THE CAMBODIAN INVASION

In the late winter and early spring of 1970, the Vietnam War intensified dramatically for the 1st Battalion, 22nd Infantry Brigade. At the same time, complications in the political and diplomatic situation in Southeast Asia set the stage for the Cambodian invasion of 1970. Of course, they also raised the war's intensity another notch.

In Phnom Penh, the capital of Cambodia, Premier Lon Nol and Prince Sirik Matok were at the end of a four-year struggle to oust Prince Norodhom Sihonouk, Cambodia's monarch, from power. A main point of contention between the two factions was Sihonouk's inability to force the North Vietnamese and their protégé, the Khmer Rouge, from Cambodia. The NVA were in Cambodia because Hanoi had extended the Ho Chi Minh Trail supply line through eastern Cambodia to avoid American air and ground attacks. Hanoi also supported the Khmer Rouge communist movement to destabilize the Cambodian government as a means to help protect the supply line and extend its power in the region.

There is a long history of Khmer/Viet ethnic antagonism that stretches back in time at least to 1471 when 60,000 Cambodians were massacred in the Vietnamese expansion that rolled over the Champa Kingdom.[1] That antagonism erupted again on March 11 and 12, 1970, when nationalistic Cambodians rioted in the capital and attacked Hanoi's embassy. There they discovered documents of a Hanoi-backed plan to seize control in Cambodia and install a Khmer Rouge government. Sihonouk, a man known for inattention to duty, went on vacation in the south of France. Lon Nol and Sihonouk's cousin, Sirik Matok, deposed him with a coup on March 17.[2] Lon Nol and Sirik Matok demanded the departure of Hanoi's delegation, the NVA, and the Viet Cong within seventy-two hours. The time expired and Lon Nol's troops attacked NVA sanctuaries throughout eastern Cambodia.

At the time, there were 400,000 Vietnamese among Cambodia's 7,000,000 people, and 75 percent of them were pro-Hanoi. Lon Nol's troops attacked them too and committed a series of ethnic massacres. On April 17, an estimated 1,000 Vietnamese bodies were seen floating in the Mekong River near the border with Vietnam. Another 100 were reported killed in the town of Takeo. Eighty-nine more died two days later in the town of Prasavat.[3] The NVA and Khmer Rouge retaliated. In short order, they took complete control of three of the nation's seventeen provinces and half of another five. So, Lon Nol appealed to Saigon and Washington D.C. for help.

The leaders in Saigon and Washington D.C. responded by moving to secure or improve their positions in the war. Saigon's immediate goal was to destroy the NVA sanctuaries in the border area, so a steady escalation of military action there was authorized. Saigon ordered ARVN artillery units to fire in support of Lon Nol's attacks on the NVA. Then, over the next ten days, Saigon's involvement in Cambodia escalated even more. From March 17 to 27 ARVN forces moved to within a mile and a half of the border, sent short-range probes into Cambodia, and finally moved armored units across the border with tactical air and artillery support from American units.[4]

In mid-April, President Thieu escalated Saigon's presence another notch with the start of Operation *Rock Crusher*, a brigade-sized attack into Cambodia's "Parrot's Beak" region by units of ARVN Armored Cavalry, Infantry, and Rangers. Then, on the twenty-ninth of April Thieu sent a division-sized force called II Field FORCEV Vietnam (II FFORCEV) to the fight. II FFORCEV's mission name was *Tuan Tang 43* (Total Victory 43). The force was authorized to work in "an operational area to a maximum depth of 30 kilometers into Cambodia."[5] II FFORCEV units swept across the border from Chau Dac, Vietnam, into the Parrot's Beak. Their objectives were the destruction of the NVA sanctuaries designated as Base Areas 367 and 706.[6]

Tuan Tang 43 was the official start of Saigon's role in the Cambodian Invasion, and their American allies were right there with them. Washington sent the equivalent of two divisions of fighting men into Cambodia. The American forces came from the 1st Cavalry Division (Air Mobile), the 101st Airborne Division, the 11th Armored Cavalry Regiment, and an amalgamated unit called the III Corps Mobile Task Force. III Corps Mobile Task Force contained tanks, mechanized infantry, and light infantry from the 4th Infantry Division's 2nd Brigade. The 1st Battalion, 22nd Regiment was part of the 2nd Brigade, so that is how I got to Cambodia. The Vietnamese units concentrated on the Parrot's Beak, at the southern end of the invasion's front, and the American units worked on the northern end called the "Fish Hook" region.[7] The Fish Hook region was the part of Cambodia just across the border from Vietnam's Central Highlands.

On the evening of April 30, 1970, President Nixon held a press conference to announce the start of Operation *Tuan Tang 43* to the nation. I was in transit to a firebase on the border of Cambodia called Jackson Hole. But, during the summer of 2003, I read the speech and several related documents. The press conference and documents were a classic example of Washington D.C. political doublespeak and denial. The Saigon government had sent the equivalent of a mechanized infantry division into Cambodia. That unit was supported by major parts of four American divisions. All the troops, U.S. and ARVN, were supported by artillery, tactical aircraft for close support, and the thousands of helicopters used in that kind of warfare. Still, President Nixon denied the fact that there was an invasion under way. He merely noted that the enemy had built up main forces and supplies in sanctuaries near the border area to launch attacks on ARVN and American forces. He said the ARVN and American attacks on the sanctuaries were "indispensable for the continuing success of troop withdrawals" and "keeping United States casualties to a minimum and ending the war sooner."[8]

Henry Kissinger, Nixon's National Security Advisor, followed up the president's comments with a 7:00 p.m. White House briefing. Kissinger admitted the military action had been in progress since the day before. Then he, like the president, provided a careful mix of fact, fiction, and denial to avoid the admission that America had invaded Cambodia. He accurately described the Fish Hook area where American forces were operating as the region above the Parrot's that stretched about twenty miles into Cambodia. He also admitted "several thousand United States troops were involved." Then, he was asked if fighting for control of NVA base areas along the border of the Central Highlands had precipitated the border crossing. Kissinger went directly into his denial mode. He said, "there hasn't really been a distinguishable combat phase in any of the base areas because there hasn't been any systematic attempt to defend these areas."[9]

I missed Kissinger's press briefing too, but again, when I read his statements in 2003, I found them as untruthful as those of the president. From February to March, the 1st Battalion, 22nd Infantry was in almost daily combat with the NVA for control of Base Area 226. Neither Nixon or Kissinger acknowledged our work. This was the two-month period when the enemy moved three divisions (the 9th, and 5th PAVN, and the 7th NVA), to the edge of the Central Highlands. It was the 5th Viet Cong Division who came into our area of operations in the Central Highlands to protect the 86th Rear Service Group. It was the troops from those combat units that B Company and the rest of our battalion fought with over the hospitals, camps, and arms caches in Base Area 226. In fact, it is most likely that it was elements from the 7th NVA division that we fought at the firefight at the amphitheater in mid-February. They were also most likely the ones who killed Bob Frost three days later.[10] Yet in spite of all that, Nixon and Kissinger stuck with the story that there had not been any distinguishable phase in combat around any of the NVA base camps.

Nixon and Kissinger also made no reference to what the enemy did in April after they salvaged what they could of their supplies and moved them across the border into Cambodia. That was the period when they stayed in the border area just out of our reach and conducted attacks by fire on the American fire support bases just inside Vietnam. Their actions at that time were part of what they called Campaign X. The goal of Campaign X was to emphasize psychological victories over military ones by ruining the pacification program of Saigon and putting pressure on the United States to withdraw from Vietnam more quickly by raising the number of American casualties.[11] I have no doubt the men injured in those attacks saw a distinguishable phase in their combat, but Nixon and Kissinger steadfastly refused to use the "I word": invasion.

THE LOGISTICAL PREPARATION FOR INVASION: BLACK MARKETEER

While the politicians lied about what we were doing, the men of the III Corps Mobile Task Forceprepared for the invasion of Cambodia that no one would speak of. Three battalions of infantry were withdrawn from operations north of Camp Radcliff, the 4th Infantry Division's base camp. They were sent to three fire-bases within sight of the Cambodian border. The 1st Battalion, 12th Infantry Regiment went to LZMeredith. The 2nd Battalion, 35th Infantry Regiment went to LZ Oasis. My battalion, the 1st Battalion, 22nd Infantry Regiment eventually ended up on LZ Jackson Hole after a short stay at division base camp to re-arm and re-equip. Our Task Force Headquarters was established thirty-seven kilometers west of the city of Pleiku at a place called New Plei Djereng. The old Plei Djereng had been one of the many Special Forces camps from which the Americans and their Cambodian CIDG troops had tried to stem the flood of men and material on the Ho Chi Minh Trail.[12]

For the men of B Company, the move to the base camp and then on to the staging area on LZ Jackson Hole was hectic, and accompanied by a lot of anxiety. We knew we were going to Cambodia, and after the fighting in and around Base Area 226, we expected to see heavy combat. When we got over Radcliff, I leaned out the door to see what was going on, and the base camp looked like an anthill after somebody stepped on it. The noisy, dusty mess we landed in was the logistical nightmare of loading up and equipping the III Corps Mobile Force for war. Fuel trucks were racing around to fuel up tanks and armored personnel carriers. Forklifts were stacking clothes and rations in huge piles for each infantry unit that landed. Flying cranes and Chinook helicopters were raising dust storms as they hauled pallets of artillery and mortar shells in cargo nets. We set down in the middle of that noisy, dusty mess.

I was used to much smaller resupply operations at jungle landing zones where only a platoon or company showed up. This operation had more troops than I had seen in one place since I landed at Cam Ranh Bay. My first thought was that it made a great target for a mortar or rocket attack. That never happened but we did have one major difficulty when we started going through the pile of supplies for our company. We had clean clothes, which we changed into without a bath. We had C-Rations that we stuffed into packs. But there was not a single bullet, or a case of grenades, or even a Claymore mine to be found! Lieutenant TJ called the company trains area and the armory to talk to First Sergeant White, the man in charge of our supplies. Oddly, there was no answer. So, TJ commandeered one of the trucks rushing around, and put Cat Ackzinski, Richie Beunzel, Smoke Carter, and me in the truck. We were told to find the first sergeant, load the truck for our platoon, and tell him there would be an ammo detail from each platoon behind us.

When we got to the company armory, First Sergeant White was still not there. A buck sergeant was locking up the side door. We had never seen him before and he had no nametag. So, I jumped off the back of the truck and said, "Hey Sarge, we're the first detail of our company to get here, but there's more behind us, and we need to draw some ammo." He just glanced over his shoulder at us and said, "Tough shit. This armory is open from 7:00 a.m.–6:00 p.m., and I already did more than an hour overtime."

It took me about half a second to go from worried about the invasion in the morning to white hot pissed off at this guy's attitude. I said, "Look asshole, we got a 6:00 a.m. lift off and we ain't got time for your REMF bullshit so just open the fuckin' door." REMF is the acronym for Rear Echelon Mother Fucker: a man who lived somewhere safe like a base camp and treated Grunts like they were practically the enemy when their comfort was compromised. This guy's response was classic REMF reparteé. He said, "My man, it sounds to me like you got a personal problem. You need to take it up with the company executive officer, or the first sergeant." Then he turned away and hustled off into the gathering darkness.

In retrospect, I should have been suspicious of this guy right away. We didn't have an executive officer at the time because

Lieutenant TJ had left that job to come to the field. Everyone in our company knew that. Also, he didn't know our first sergeant's name. I was so mad at this guy's attitude I overlooked that fact too. So, after I convinced Cat that shooting a REMF in the head was a waste of the few bullets we had, we rode the truck back to the helicopter pad to find LT Mack or Lieutenant TJ to intercede for us with the base camp commandos. Along the way, we met and turned around several other ammo details from our company.

While we sat around the landing pad waiting for the officers to deal with the clerks and jerks, we did a lot of speculating about what would happen when we got to Cambodia. After that got boring, some of the guys talked a truck driver into making a beer run into Pleiku. We had beer with us on the pad. It always came when we got resupplied with our rations, but it had been sitting in the merciless heat of Vietnam's dry season all day. Everybody knew there were Vietnamese in town that always had ice for the beer they stole from the base, and sold to us for a dollar a can. At that time, nobody really cared about buying back our own supplies. We were more into the gladiator attitude of eat, drink, and be merry, for tomorrow we might get shot. So, a bunch of us contributed to the pot and a truck full of guys from all four of the battalion's companies headed off to Pleiku's shantytown to get some beer. They took a radio with them and we promised to call them when the ammo arrived. Then, we sat around our empty ammo trucks playing cards and writing letters and trying not to think about being dead by evening of the next day.

A few minutes after the guys on the beer run left, we heard gunfire from the edge of Pleiku where our beer truck was supposed to be. In fact, we could actually see red tracers from M-16s and green ones from AK-47s crisscrossing the area. At the same time, we got a call on the battalion push that our guys needed some help. Men from every company in the battalion dropped their cards or whatever else they were doing and piled into the nearest vehicle and raced out the gate. I was on the running board of the first truck. There was a guy inside who I didn't know, and he grabbed my arm and a handful of the back of my shirt so I wouldn't fall off. I remember him joking that it would not do at all for me to get killed on a beer run when I could die in a more important battle for Cambodia in the morning.

Our rescue convoy bullied and crashed its way into Pleiku's shantytown and scattered the masses of mopeds, bicycles, and refugees in a frantic race to get to our men. When we got close to the firefight, the driver doused his lights. In the dark, we could see that most of the green tracers from AK-47s or SKSs seemed to be coming from the front and sides of what looked like a substantial building for a shantytown. The red ones from M-16s came from behind two deuce-and-a half trucks. One was parked up the street not far from the building, and the other was directly in front of it.

My truck skidded to a stop in the dusty street about fifty meters from the firefight. I jumped off when I thought it had slowed to a safe speed, but still, the momentum sent me head first into a stack of wooden crates. As soon as I pulled my helmet out of the one I had crashed into, I joined in with the others and started shooting at the front of the building. Before long, we had enough people in the fight to advance on the enemy in teams of two or three men each. It was jungle-style fire and maneuver in the shantytown. And just like our jungle fights, the enemy cut and ran before we could close in and kill them all. Most of them disappeared into the maze of alleys in Pleiku, and no one was foolish enough to chase them any farther.

When the shooting stopped, I sat on an empty oil drum and watched some of the men looking around for the guys who had made the beer run to find out what happened. I heard a lot of shouting and when the truck I had ridden on turned on its lights behind me, I could see there was a lot of shoving back and forth, so I decided to go see what was happening. When I got to the front of the building, I saw three dead Vietnamese on the ground in front of it, two more at one corner, and a crowd of GIs arguing and shoving each other around. Jesse Johnson showed up with a rifle instead of his M-60 and together, we pushed to the front of the crowd.

The center of everyone's attention was the REMF from the armory. I was a bit surprised to see him there, but I was even more surprised at the contents of one of the trucks. It was filled with crates of M-16 and M-60 ammunition. Sometimes it took awhile for my mind to get from flash to bang when a bomb went off, but suddenly, a few facts came together for me: None of us knew this guy. He was missing the nametag that all base camp people were required to wear, and he was in a real hurry to leave the armory when we showed up. Then, an hour later, he was in the middle of a firefight for a truckload of American ammunition. Those facts plus the discovery of a satchel full of American money, which was illegal to have in Vietnam, clinched it for us; our beer run guys had stumbled onto a black market dealer in the process of selling our ammunition to the enemy.

There wasn't a lot of discussion about bustin' a cap, or several caps, in this guy's ass right then. There seemed to be a common consensus about that. The argument was really about who would get to do it, what to do with the body, and the chances of getting away with it. The only thing that saved his life was the arrival of a jeep with an MP lieutenant and two PFCs. The lieutenant made it clear he wasn't going to allow anyone to shoot the REMF. Then he called his captain to report the situation and to request a squad of men for back up. His report guaranteed that someone else besides those present knew about the situation. So, we knew we couldn't shoot the REMF.

Most of us, me included, were pissed about the prospect of the REMF living long enough for a trial and jail. But then, the lieutenant gave us orders that cheered up everyone except the REMF. The lieutenant said the building we had been shooting at was a suspected black market warehouse, and he ordered it searched. Some of the guys kicked in the doors. They found uniforms, rations, various kinds of equipment, some M-16s, and happily, a lot of beer on ice. The lieutenant told us to take the beer. He also said he needed our help to secure the prisoner. He and his men all had handcuffs, but he asked us to see if we could find a roll of barbed wire in the warehouse. Somebody got one for him, and he had his men give the REMF a body-wrap in barbed wire from chest to knees. After that, the MPs body-slammed the REMF onto the lowered tailgate of a truck for the drive back to the MP headquarters.

While we were busy loading our truck with cold beer, a squad of MPs came out to secure the warehouse and its contents, and the lieutenant made the final prep for our little convoy's return to the base camp. He told one of his privates to drive the truck with the REMF on the tailgate back for him. The private said, "Sir, I don't know how to drive a stick shift." The lieutenant just smiled and said, "I know that."

It took four or five tries for the MP private to get the hang of making a smooth start with the truck. Every time he failed, the truck lurched forward, and the REMF would roll off the tailgate into the street. Sometimes he landed in the dust, but he also got dropped in a couple of puddles that smelled suspiciously like sewage. Every time he fell, someone from one of the following trucks would get out and redeposit him on the tailgate as roughly as possible for the next leg of his trip. Eventually, the private got the hang of starting off, but his gear shifting was not smooth. He also hit a lot of pot holes. So, he lost his passenger a couple more times while he worked on those skills.

When our beer truck and the rescue trucks got back to the landing zone First Sergeant White, the battalion sergeant major, and several trucks of ammunition were there. Everyone took what he needed and then we spent most of the rest of the night trying to drink a truckload of beer.

VIETNAMIZATION, KENT STATE, AND JACKSON STATE UNIVERSITIES

At 6:00 a.m. on May 1, 1st Battalion, 22nd Infantry lifted off from base camp, but we landed on LZ Jackson Hole instead of Cambodia. Most of us were severely hung over, so we appreciated the stay at Jackson Hole until other units of the III Corps Mobile Force landed at their staging areas on LZ Meredith and LZ Oasis. While we waited, we spent more time on target practice. We also got a number of new men in B Company who had just been transferred from the 1st Infantry Division (nicknamed the Big Red One). The new guys were a surprise. We had heard their division had left Vietnam as part of the Vietnamization program. Every one of them we talked to said they were transferred to our unit because they had not done a full tour of duty. They estimated that only about half their division was going home and the rest were on the way to Cambodia with other units.

We also spent a lot of time reading mail from home and rather than calming us, it escalated our pre-combat tension. Almost every letter had some mention of anti-war protests over the expansion of the war into Cambodia and the deaths of student protesters. The four Kent State University students who were shot by the Ohio National Guard were mentioned most prominently. There were also some letters from Mississippi that said an unknown number of students at Jackson State University had also been killed, but most of the media attention was on the four White kids at Kent State. There were even a few issues of *Time, Newsweek,* and *Life* magazines with pictures making the rounds between bunkers.

The controversy over the invasion and protesters spilled over onto the firebase. Lifers felt invading Cambodia was a strategic necessity. Conscripts saw it as an unnecessary risk of lives. There were also a lot of heated discussions about whether student protesters, who may or may not have thrown some rocks at the guardsmen, deserved to get shot. Again, the opinions on that matter split fairly predictably along the lines of Lifers and draftees. The Lifers felt the protesters got what they deserved for their lack of patriotism. Most of the draftees pointed out that rocks were no threat to helmeted men with rifles, and that it was really an un-American thing to shoot people because their idea of patriotism differed from yours. A few of the arguments got physical. I heard that weapons were pointed and rounds chambered, but I didn't see any of that happen.

THE INTELLIGENCE BRIEFING FOR BINH TAY I

The Command Group for III Corps Mobile Task used the week we spent at Jackson Hole developing intelligence and creating an operations order for our part of the invasion. It was called Operation *Binh Tay I*. In the middle of the afternoon of May 6 all the officers went to the TOC for a briefing. An hour or so later, the officers gathered all the NCOs and enlisted men together. We were told we would lift off for Cambodia the next day, and what we were supposed to do when we got there.

Our task force was to make combat assaults into Cambodia to find and destroy two areas called Base Areas 702 and 707. Our artillery support was based on some hills due west of Kontum, about twelve kilometers from Cambodia. We, of course, were going farther. Our combat assaults would take us as deep as twenty kilometers past the border.[13] Instead of the usual emphasis on high body count they said our primary mission was the destruction of enemy facilities and the capture or destruction of supplies. Actually, few of us enlisted men saw any real difference between this mission and search-and-destroy jobs in Vietnam. We had already been in a base area and fought the enemy for his supplies and secure locations, and nobody really believed they would just hand things over without a fight.

For the enlisted men, the important part of our briefing was to let us know how many of the enemy to expect when we landed. There were a lot of "Oh Shits" and "What the Fucks" when we heard there would be an estimated 27,000 NVA in the area assigned to III Mobile Task Force. The news didn't get much better as the number of enemy expected in each battalion's assigned area was discussed. Our battalion had about 400 fighting men. The intelligence people said we would face three major units with about 800 men. The first was the B-3 Headquarters Front with 300 men. The second was the 300 men from the 24th NVA Regimental Headquarters Group. The last group was the 260 men of the 24th Regiment's front line troops.[14] One of the new guys from the Big Red One said out loud that we should be okay because it sounded like two-thirds of these people were NVA REMFs. Lieutenant TJ told him what the rest of us knew: the NVA didn't have any REMFs. The term "Headquarters" in their unit names meant they had assigned the best troops they had to protect their commanders.

After the company-level briefing, the NCOs and platoon leaders huddled with the men to make sure everybody in every squad knew what to do, to check equipment, and to announce the order of lifts going into the landing zone. I already knew what was going to happen. Lieutenant TJ, the company commander, told LT Mack that it was second platoon's turn to be first. LT Mack told me it was my squad's turn to be on the first bird. The good news, he said, was that from the aerial photos we had, the landing zone looked big enough for the entire platoon to go in at one time.

PSYCHOLOGICAL PREPARATION FOR THE INVASION

For the first six weeks I spent in Vietnam, it seemed like I was afraid all day, every day. Then, I became angry and fatalistic. I didn't really think I would get home alive, but I was determined to stay alive as long as I could. Then, when I was still alive in the spring of 1970, I had begun to hope I might see home again. In fact, I even started making plans through the mail to re-enter classes at Ohio University at the end of June when the summer quarter started. So by early May, when it was time to go to Cambodia, I was a short timer.

My assignment to the first lift of birds from my battalion to land in Cambodia set me back to my angry, fatalistic stage. That night, while we sat around the bunkers, some of my friends said they would ask LT Mack to let me come in later. I told them "fuck it, it don't mean nothin' if I go on the first lift or the last, so don't bother." I knew from experience you could still get killed riding in one of the late birds because the enemy had practiced shooting at the first ones and had the range, speed, and windage correct.

I was back at my fatalistic stage again, but with one major difference: I was going to make sure I did what my dad told me when three White guys jumped me in a locker room in ninth grade. I lost that fight, and my face and body looked like it. When I got home, Dad ignored my black eye and swollen mouth and all the rest. He looked at my hands. He pointed out that there were no serious scuffs on my knuckles, and no swelling at all. Then he said, "Son, even if you lose, you have to let 'em know it's gonna cost a lot to get you down."

I spent most of a sleepless night getting ready to make my death as expensive as I could. I collected ten extra magazines to add to my usual load of twenty. I emptied all thirty magazines, lubricated the insides, and put eighteen rounds in each one. That was the recommended method to prevent jamming. Then I set my arsenal of 540 rounds aside and field stripped and cleaned every part of my rifle twice with a toothbrush and Q-tips.

I set the rifle aside and hunted up ten grenades instead of my usual four. I broke half the safety pin off all of them for an easier release and throw. Then, out of pure meanness, I went back to the munitions bunker and picked up a "Willie Pete." A Willie Pete was a white phosphorous grenade. They were explosive chemical devices that were too heavy to throw far. A big man could throw one about twenty-five meters. When they exploded, they created a forty-meter-wide circle of burning phosphorous with a temperature of 1,000 degrees Fahrenheit. That was why most Grunts wouldn't carry them. Engineers used them to destroy enemy equipment and supply dumps. Grunts, if they had one, dropped them into enemy bunkers or used them as booby traps. After I packed up my arsenal, I spent a long time talking with friends while I sharpened my fighting knife with the staghorn handle. We were all scared. Some admitted it, and some didn't. I wasn't the only one who thought he would be dead soon. I didn't bother to write home.

8.

The Cambodian Invasion

May 7 to May 15, 1970

COMBAT ASSAULT INTO CAMBODIA

The 1st Battalion, 22nd Infantry lifted off from LZ Jackson Hole for Cambodia in the middle of the afternoon on May 7, 1970. Col. George Webb, the acting chief of staff for the II FORCEV, wrote a report on what we did there called, "The Commander's Evaluation Report—Cambodian Operations." I read it in the summer of 2003, and I was surprised by the brevity of information about what happened to us that day. The colonel wrote, "Immediately upon landing, 1/22 made contact with a reinforced platoon in bunkers. Killed 4 NVA. Captured 2 weapons."[1]

Maybe the colonel's terseness was because he was separated from our landing by both time and space. He wrote the report at the end of June, and as the acting chief of staff for the II FFORCEV, he was not in Cambodia. He was in the command post in the Central Highlands Special Forces camp at New Plei Djerang. That probably explains why his report makes it seem like the four hundred men of our battalion dropped on a clearing with thirty or forty NVA, shot four of the outnumbered enemy, and took two of their weapons home as souvenirs. It has often been said that truth, like beauty, is in the eye of the beholder.

Since I beheld this action as a participant that day, my truth about it is different from the colonel's. This is how I remember it.

At midmorning, we formed lift groups and sat in the sun waiting for the troop slicks (UH-1 helicopters) to arrive. They showed up around 1:00 p.m. and landed in groups of four. As each lift landed, the men assigned to it swung on their packs, locked and loaded their weapons, and sat in the doorway. My friends Greg Bodell and Richie Beunzel gave me the "safe" seat, in the middle. It was "safe" because it was equidistant from the door gunner and the pilot who were always prime targets on hot landing zones. Cecil Dykes, Jim Henderson, and Jim Hinzo sat in the doorway on the other side. LT Mack sat on the floor in the middle because the platoon leader of the first unit always went in the first slick of the first lift. The slick lifted off, and I remember feeling sleepy, scared, and angry all at the same time.

There were about a hundred slicks in our part of the invasion. They landed in four-ship lifts, picked up the infantrymen, and then orbited Jackson Hole until the entire battalion was airborne. Each lift was flanked by two Cobra gunships. We flew most of the way in the cool air, above small arms range at 1,500 feet over the triple canopy jungle. A kilometer from the landing zone, our Cobra escorts dove in ahead of us to strafe the wood line around the clearing. They gave it their full treatment of 2.75-inch rockets, 40-millimeter cannon, and six-barreled machineguns. While they were doing that, our four-ship lift took one turn over the landing zone to go in facing the wind so the pilots would have better lift and maneuverability. Then we started the descent.

We dove in nose down and tail up, to give us the most speed, and the ground came up so fast I thought we had been shot down. At about twenty feet off the ground, the nose came up, the tail rotor dropped, and the slick began to shudder from the strain of converting a dive to a hover and from the hits we were taking from ground fire. I couldn't actually hear the shots being fired, but I knew we were taking ground fire when I saw some green flashes in the dust storm we were kicking up and heard a sound like hammers hitting the aircraft. I thought they must have been using the big 12.72-millimeter machineguns because when they hit, the rounds made fist-sized gray circles in the olive drab paint on the doorframe between Greg Bodell and the pilot.

The door gunners in all four slicks opened up with their M-60s to give us some protection while we were over the LZ. Then, when our ship came to a swaying hover four or five feet off the ground, the crew chief stopped firing his machinegun, turned in our direction, and screamed "un-ass this fucking bird right now!" We couldn't really hear what he said. We were sitting within three or four feet of two machineguns firing eight hundred rounds per minute, but we could read lips. Besides, all of us had been to this kind of dance before.

Bo, Richie, and I stood on the skids and jumped into the dust and noise at the same time. I was almost driven to my knees by the weight of my pack and ammunition, but I kept my feet moving in a bent-over run toward the jungle while I fired short bursts of automatic fire into the dust on the LZ. When our pilot pulled pitch to gain altitude and clear the LZ, he raised more dust and I lost sight of Bo and Richie. I was operating blind in a suffocating dust storm, and after a few steps toward the jungle, I tripped on something and fell flat on my face. I knew the middle of a hot landing zone was the wrong place to stop because it was the tactical equivalent of lying down in the killing zone of an ambush. I fired a few more shots into the trees, and I was about to get up and start running again when my pack began to jerk around on my back. At first, I thought maybe Bo or Richie was trying to get me on my feet and moving. Then it came to me that none of the jerks were an upward motion of someone trying to pick me up. The second time my pack started jerking, it felt like someone was pulling me backwards and to the left. No doubt about it, somebody was shooting into the top and right side of my pack.

I pulled the quick release on my shoulder straps and flipped my pack on its side in front of me for cover. Then, I rolled on my left side and pulled two grenades out of the cargo pocket of my pants. We always threw them two at a time because the enemy would pop up as soon as a grenade went off to catch us moving forward. When we threw two of them, they would usually pop up in time to catch the blast from the second one. I yelled, "fire in the hole" as loud as I could to warn Bo and Richie, and I used a short overhand toss like a basketball hook shot to throw them at the tree line. When the second grenade went off, I jumped over my pack and charged into the trees firing as fast as I could. I fell two more times, but I kept crawling and running until I got in the trees and behind some cover.

When I looked to the left and right, the rest of the men from my slick were in the bushes with me and we advanced on line, moving from one piece of cover to the next, panting, sweating, cursing, and shooting at the same time. The second time I moved, I rolled over a log and braced myself on one knee next to a tree trunk. I saw some bushes moving about twenty feet away, so I emptied a whole magazine into them. I felt something soft under my right knee, and I looked down to see I was kneeling on a forearm with a hand that held an AK-47. The rest of the body was a few feet away, next to another dead man. The other dead man had a hole the size of a softball in his chest and only half a head. While I changed magazines, I wondered whether these guys had caught the blast from my second grenade, or gotten torn apart by the Cobras when they prepped the landing zone. Two seconds later, I had a round chambered and I thought, "Fuck 'em. How they croaked don't mean nothin', but I should send some more of 'em to Hell before I join 'em."

The first lift kept up its fire and maneuvered on our side of the LZ until a dust cloud enveloped us from behind. The dust storm was the signal that the second lift had landed, and we had help. But then, we had to be careful they didn't start shooting into the trees where we were. I looked back to see how close they were, and I was relieved to see them all standing upright and not firing. I knew then I had survived what was probably my first three minutes in Cambodia and that the enemy had withdrawn from the landing zone.

In no time at all, we had the entire battalion on the ground, and each company set off toward its assigned area of operation. B Company had orders to go due west, and since the second platoon was already on that side of the LZ, we led the company. Bodell and I were on point. We walked an azimuth through the jungle instead of a trail. The other two platoons spread out behind us to make a wedge-shaped formation. Within two hundred meters we knew we were in the right place. We found a thatched hut with ten hundred-pound sacks of rice.[2] Since we were still close to the landing zone, Lieutenant TJ ordered the third platoon to take the rice back so it could be hauled away and the rest of the company waited in place. Darkness comes early in the jungle, and by the time the third platoon got back to us it was too dark to travel safely or see very much, so Lieutenant TJ ordered a company-sized perimeter for the night.

We had expected heavy resistance when we landed. When that didn't happen we assumed we would get hit with mortars or a heavy ground attack because the enemy knew where we were. We took special precautions to counter those possibilities. We dug chest-deep foxholes as usual, and some of us cut branches for overhead cover and put sandbags on top of them just in case of a mortar attack. We also made each hole wide enough for three men instead of two, to add more firepower at each position. Then we put out a ring of trip flares fifty feet in the jungle and backed them up with a ring of the deadly Claymore mines ten feet behind the trip flares. No one put up a hootch behind the foxholes because no one felt safe enough to lie above ground to sleep. Instead, we stayed in the holes all night with someone holding the firing handle of the Claymores at all times. The first night in Cambodia passed uneventfully despite our expectations, but I doubt anyone got much sleep.

DESTROYING THE ENEMY AND HIS SUPPLIES

At dawn we got on with the main part of the mission: the capture and destruction of as much of the enemy's supplies and materiel as we could find. In essence, we were like burglars walking around in Nguyen's house trying to steal him blind without getting killed in the process. When we set out that morning to search our assigned area, we expected Lieutenant TJ to break up the company and send each platoon off by itself, but he didn't. I think even he was impressed with the idea of where we were and what we were doing. He might have even realized that a little tactical caution and large groups were the better part of valor and career advancement.

There was still no trail to follow, so we kept the platoons in wedge formations while we swept back and forth across the thousand-meter grid square assigned to us. My platoon was in the center, and Bodell and I took the point again. Within fifty meters we found three more huts. Inside these other huts we found forty sacks of rice, a fifty-pound sack of tobacco, a flintlock rifle, and ten swords.[3] This time, we didn't bother with the idea of back hauling anything. We set fire to all of it and moved on.

The enlisted men in the company were feeling pretty good. We were in our second day in Cambodia, and we had found two caches that would have been a major find in Vietnam within hours and meters of our landing zone. Also, there was the important fact that nobody in B Company was dead yet. On the other hand, Lieutenant TJ and the Lifers back in the TOC had other ideas about what constituted success. TJ had been on the radio to the TOC to explain our progress with the mission, and Colonel Webb let him know we were there to find depots, not caches. Since shit always rolled down hill, TJ called his NCOs together and told us the difference between finding a depot and a cache. A cache, he said, held the contents of a pickup truck. A depot held the contents of several boxcars. The message was clear: we needed to step up the production. There were in fact, a lot more camps and supplies to be found in the jungle. Some of them were easily discovered because they were on or near high-speed trails. Others were on narrow trails, reachable only by men on bicycles or foot. Then, there were many others that were well hidden and randomly scattered. Those were found only when the camouflaged entrance to a tunnel was discovered.

When I conducted the research for this book, I found a frank admission by Colonel Webb that we were basically unprepared for the subterranean part of our mission. I also found his solution to the problem. He swallowed what was probably a lot of Army pride and borrowed some naval high tech gear called Magnetic Anomaly Detection (MAD)units to help. MAD units were essentially very sensitive metal detectors suspended from a cable on a helicopter. Normally, they were used to hunt submarines. At sea, the MAD sensor was dipped by cable into the ocean and it broadcast sound waves through the water. Then the MAD technician in the helicopter analyzed the bounce-back, or echo, on his earphones and a screen that diagrammed the sound wave return to determine if it was rebounded from metal of any kind.

In theory, the MAD system sounded like a perfect tool for searching the triple canopy jungle for depots. In practice, it was not. The problem was the abundance of metal in Cambodia as opposed to its scarcity in the ocean where the MAD was designed to function. Sometimes it detected units of enemy who of course had metal on them. That was O.K. because we were there to destroy them, too. But, on other occasions, the MAD units found shrapnel from exploded artillery or bombs. So, after all was said and done only about 10 percent of the positive MAD readings were from depots.[4]

Even with a 10-percent efficiency from the MAD units and the hit and miss of searching the old-fashioned way with infantrymen just poking around in the jungle, II FFORCEV found a number of depots and as a whole, we made off with or destroyed a considerable amount of goods. We found the sanctuary called Base Area 702 and three depots inside it: Shakey's Hill, Rock Island East, and the City. We robbed them blind. We took 10,353 small arms like SKS carbines and AK-47 assault rifles. We also got 1,786 crew-served weapons like heavy machineguns and mortar tubes. There was so much ammunition we didn't count the rounds as was the custom in Vietnam. We weighed it. It came to 1,534.8 tons. We took 5,873.6 tons of their rice too.[5] Units from the Corps of Engineers dumped most of the find into cargo nets and hauled it away with either flying cranes or Chinook helicopters.

Once the II FFORCEV cleared out the majority of equipment and supplies from Base Area 702, the 1st Battalion, 22nd Infantry, with B Company in the lead, was ordered to move farther west to find and destroy Base Area 707. We found it about ten kilometers southwest of a town called Krek, and fifteen kilometers northeast of Base Area 354.[6] When the battalion came upon Base Area 707, B Company had its share in the discovery and seizure of enemy supplies. We found part of an NVA training camp and an underground hospital complex. We found the training camp as the result of a botched attempt by the enemy to draw us away from the area by attacking a patrol near the firebase we were building. We found the edge of the hospital because we were responding to the diversionary attack. Also, this was the time I returned to the war in the ground to explore the hospital.

A FAILED DIVERSION

B Company and the rest of the 1st Battalion, 22nd Infantry were about twenty kilometers west of Vietnam. So, we were beyond the range of our artillery support at New Plei Djerang.

To compensate, D Company, the mortar company of the battalion, and B Company were ordered to construct and secure Fire Support Base Jood so the mortars could fire in support of the troops in the area. B Company got this assignment because it had been the lead company of the combat assault. Because second platoon had been the first lift of that assault, we got the assignment of helping D Company build the base. The rest of the company was assigned to security patrols and searching for more of the enemy's supplies.

About midmorning of the first day of digging bunkers a burst of automatic weapon fire swept across the bunker to the left of mine. I was filling sandbags for the roof of my bunker so I dropped behind it and exchanged my shovel for my rifle. Before I could fire a shot, somebody got on the M-60 machinegun at the bunker to my right and started tearing up the jungle in very long bursts. I expected to see Jesse Johnson or Smoke Carter. Not! It was Carl Dover working the M-60 with a vengeance. He was lying prone on top of the bunker firing twenty or thirty rounds at a time. He was a small man, about my size, and the recoil from the machinegun drove him backwards off the edge of the bunker. When his lower body hit the ground, he should have stayed there and taken advantage of the lower profile. Instead, he climbed right back on top of the bunker and started all over again. For some reason, the very sight of Dover actually contributing in a firefight, and overdoing it too, was amazing and funny at the same time. With him, it was feast or famine, cowardice, or some kind of half-assed bravery. I just lay there on the ground and laughed while he worked on burning up the barrel of the M-60.

Some of the other people around me were laughing at Dover too, because the gun was knocking him all over the place. Then, in the middle of our entertainment, Tiny Pederson, our radioman, gave me the handset because Lieutenant TJ was calling. TJ had been with a squad searching the jungle on the north side of the firebase when the shooting started. (Yes, he was actually on patrol with only ten men inside an NVA base camp!) He said he was chasing the people who had just fired on us farther north. He said he was in a running firefight with at least two NVA, and he wanted me to help trap them. He wanted me to get another squad, leave the base on the east side, and move as fast as we could along a high-speed trail to the northwest so we could cut these guys off, pin them between us, and kill them. I was a little leery about using the trail with only a squad, so I had a quick conversation with LT Mack. He decided I should take the whole platoon with me, and he would coordinate the gunfire of one of the mortar tubes if we ran into more people than we expected.

Lieutenant TJ was our company commander, and he was popular with many of the men, even though I didn't think all that much of him. Also, since he was in the jungle, in a running firefight with a squad of our enlisted men, we all pretty much threw caution to the wind. The whole platoon grabbed weapons and gear and we sprinted along the trail to the northwest. After about 500 meters, I spread the platoon in a skirmish line in the jungle to wait for TJ's patrol to drive our prey to us. I took up a position in the middle of the line because the sound of the running firefight sounded like the enemy would show up near there. The trick of course was to kill these people without killing TJ or his people. I kept passing the word to use semi-automatic fire instead of rock and roll and that nobody was to fire without a clear target. In five minutes we heard and saw movement in the jungle.

The firefight only lasted about five seconds, and only four shots were fired. It was, in a sense, a classic example of battle sighting and combat marksmanship. I was staring over my open rifle sights at some bushes that had started moving when two NVA in khaki uniforms with AK-47s broke through them. They were sprinting side-by-side right at us. I saw them both clearly when they were about twenty meters away, but I was too slow about lining up a proper sight picture and getting on the trigger. Cecil Dykes, who told me he hunted for his family's food in

North Carolina, took the first one down with a single shot to the head. Dykes told me later it was just a snap shot. The man dropped straight down in the rag-doll style that meant instant death. For a few seconds after he fell, there was a reddish mist in the air from the explosive action of the high velocity bullet when it blew off the back of his head.

Jim Hinzo put the other man down with three quick shots from his M-16. I saw from the impacts on this second NVA's body that Hinzo's weapon rose steadily from the recoil but he held his line of fire dead center on the man. The first two rounds hit his diaphragm and sternum. They stopped him dead in his tracks and stood him up straight. The third shot hit him in the face and knocked him flat on his back.

INSIDE BASE AREA 707

We waited to see if anybody else would show up, but there were only those two men. Lieutenant TJ and his men arrived as Cecil and Jim stripped the weapons and ammunition from the dead men. TJ decided that instead of taking the high-speed trail back to Jood, we would move southwest through the jungle until we got back to our base. I wondered whether he was finally out his habit of using trails twice in a row or if he was just eager to search for more caches or depots, but in the end it didn't matter. We were taking a safe route back and that was enough for me. The squad from first platoon that he left the firebase with took the point, and we all headed back to Jood on a zigzag course to be sure we didn't miss anything important.

We were less than fifty meters past the point where TJ and his men had started chasing the two dead NVA, and a hundred meters from Jood when we came upon something that made me very glad I had brought the entire platoon instead of just one squad. It was an unpaved road that ran out of sight to the east and west of us. We called it a road because it was at least ten feet wide and there was an American-made two-and-a-half-ton truck parked on the side of it. We speculated later that since there were no roads that we knew of between Jood and Vietnam, that the truck had probably been stolen or sold by a black marketeer, dismantled, and brought to the jungle by elephants. We guessed that the road had been made so the truck could move supplies or people with ease through the base camp we were looking at on the south side of the road. There was no one in the truck, but on the southern side of the road, along the base of a small hill between our growing firebase and us, we could see a number of bunkers and large foxholes. Fortunately, they were empty.

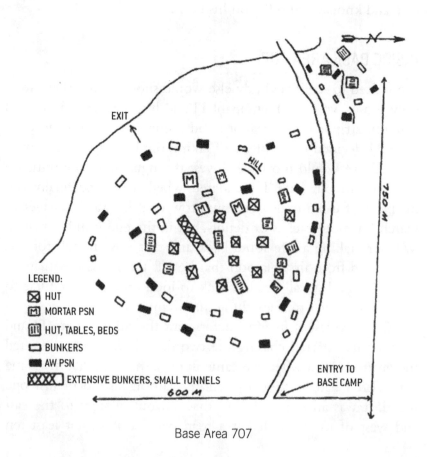

Base Area 707

Lieutenant TJ drew a map of the camp. I found a copy of it in the National Archives. It was appended to the report Colonel Webb filed for the II FFORCEV.

The road went a distance to the east and west so we figured we were on the edge of a really big camp. Lieutenant TJ called Jood and had the rest of the company come join us for security while we searched it. The camp was shaped like an isosceles triangle laid on its side with the junction of its two equal sides pointing to the west. The road ran for 750 meters on the north side, and it crossed a stream that formed the second side of the point. The base of the hill that LZ Jood was built on formed the third side. That side was about 600 meters long. The camp had a perimeter of camouflaged bunkers for automatic weapons crews and open foxholes for riflemen. There were also two pits for mortar crews and the imprint of the base plate and bipod legs for the enemy's heavy 82-millimeter mortars were still visible in the dirt. Inside the perimeter of fighting positions, there were a lot of large thatched huts with tables and beds and there were several tunnels.

BACK TO THE WAR IN THE GROUND

There was a trapdoor tunnel entrance in the corner of one of the large bunkers in the center of the camp. When the tunnels were discovered, Lieutenant TJ told me to go down and take a look. I had not been in a tunnel since February, but I agreed to do it. I pretty much expected to die in Cambodia, and I was determined to make my death as expensive for the enemy as possible. I figured that if I could deprive them of the ammunition and supplies that were likely to be in the tunnels, it would make things just that much harder for them. LT Mack, ever the optimist, did remind me that I was getting pretty short. He said that maybe I should take a pass on this tunnel and he would square it with TJ. I just told him, "Fuck it man, it don't mean nothin'. I'll probably be dead before dinner anyhow."

I dropped my helmet and bandoleers on the ground and started getting my tools ready for the job. I had everything I needed but a pistol. The battalion sergeant major had collected all the .45 automatics from enlisted men when a couple guys had shot themselves in the foot to get sent back to the rear. So Mack loaned me his. I stuffed it in my belt and stripped the rest of the things I needed off my web belt. I clipped an L-shaped flashlight with a low-light red beam to my shirt pocket, and put the lanyard from my compass with a phosphorescent dial around my neck. I stuffed a couple frag grenades in the cargo pockets of my pants, and then I strapped my big fighting knife onto my belt. Then, just before I dropped into the hole in the corner of the bunker, I went back and got the Willie Pete grenade I had been carrying out of meanness since I found out I was going to Cambodia. I was hoping for a chance to make another nasty booby trap.

In some ways, the tunnel in Cambodia was different from any I had seen in Vietnam. To start with, it was bigger. You still had to crawl along, but you didn't have to do it on your belly and my shoulders didn't touch both walls at the same time. This one also ran in a straight line for a long way, and it angled downward at a shallow angle with bracing in the walls and ceiling made of fresh-cut hardwood from the jungle. I could smell the sap, and when I touched the braces as I felt my way along, they were still sticky. This tunnel smelled different too. They all smelled awful because tunnel dwellers literally shit where they lived, and carried it out when they thought nobody was around. But, as I inched along questing with my hands and senses for what was down there, I also smelled death, and something else that was familiar, but I couldn't remember what it was. I also heard movement. It was not the furtive thump and scrape of a person. It was the fast, scratchy sound of feet and the squeaky voices of packs of rats.

My original compass reading had been southwest, but without the usual turns every five meters or so, I had to just guess how far I had gone in that direction. I was about a hundred meters along when I felt a sharp angle on both sides of the tunnel wall. I couldn't tell if I was at a junction with another tunnel or the entrance to a room of some kind because it was still pitch black. I stretched out on my belly to listen for a long time, and then I moved to the right around the corner in the tunnel. My compass reading said I had turned northeast.

I always tried to touch a tunnel's walls, floor, and ceiling before I moved, but as soon as I made the turn, I lost touch with the top and left side of the tunnel. I moved to the left for two arm lengths, and there was still no wall or ceiling to touch, so I figured I was in a room. That made me really nervous because it was distinctly possible that I was not alone. So, I very slowly backed around the corner and into the tunnel again. When I got just inside it, I pulled the pin on one of the frag grenades and left-handed it gently around the corner into the room, hoping it didn't hit anything and bounce back to me. Then I flopped backwards away from the corner and lay flat on my stomach with my feet toward the room and my arms wrapped around my head to protect my eardrums while I waited for three-second fuse to set off the grenade.

I had thrown a lot of grenades by that time, but they all exploded above ground, at relatively safe distances from me or in bunkers with the enemy. This time I was only a few feet away in an enclosed area. I was not prepared for the result of the explosion in a confined area. The sound and shock waves pounded up my body from foot to head with such force that for a split second, I thought I had killed myself. Dirt and debris flew into my clothes and up my nose with the painful velocity of wind-driven sand in a desert storm. I felt like my whole body was getting sandblasted. It also seemed like the concussion had driven me involuntarily down the tunnel a few feet, but I couldn't be sure. I was gasping and coughing so badly from the smoke and dust that I was sure anyone in the room who had survived the blast would know where I was, so I turned around and rolled back into the room and turned on the flashlight. I kept it at arm's length in my left hand and held the cocked .45 in my right hand while I looked for a target. I waved the red beam around, looking for corners first. I ignored what I thought would be the center of the room because anyone there would be dead already from concussion or shrapnel.

When I was sure I was alone, I sat up with my back against the wall and took my time squinting through the dust at what I had found. As I did so, it slowly dawned on me that I had found an underground operating room. The blast had turned over a long shiny metal table with wheels and some large light stands that looked like giant, round desk lamps. Later, when I was back above ground, I described what I had seen to our medic. He confirmed that I had found an operating table and surgical field lights. The table and lights were ten or twelve feet from me, and it was another ten or twelve feet from them to the far wall. Against that wall, just to the right of another tunnel entrance, was a large machine with a heavy power cord running from it into the other tunnel. The wall that formed a right angle to the one I was sitting against had a large metal frame with shattered glass on the ground below it, and more wires coming from the frame. The ceiling was high enough for me to stand up and it had what looked like large sheets of parachute silk nailed to support beams in the ceiling. I think they were there to keep dirt from the ceiling from falling on the operating table. I stood up and walked across the room for a closer look at the metal frame. It was a light screen for viewing X-ray film. The large machine on the other side of the room had a large flat plate on a moveable arm and I figured it was the X-ray machine. The floor of the room was littered with shiny surgical tools scattered about by the blast. I saw scalpels in several different sizes, some gruesome-looking bone saws, and several pairs of forceps, and some other tools I couldn't recognize.

The tunnel on the other side of the room was a short connecting passage to another room. The beam of my flashlight showed a lot of boxes stacked against the walls, and I went in and pulled some of them open. There were cardboard boxes full of rolls of adhesive tape, gauze, syringes, and sponges in various sizes. There were also boxes of pills with Chinese characters on the labels, and some wooden crates. I pried the lid off some of them, and they were full of glass bottles. Some of them had what smelled like alcohol and some smelled like the standard disinfectant you found in hospitals. When I opened a bottle of that, it dawned on me that the familiar odor I noticed on the way in was from this kind of disinfectant. I had not expected to find a hospital facility underground, so I guess that was why it took me so long identify its smell. There were even a few bottles that smelled like chloroform, and that confirmed the fact that this was probably an operating room instead of just an aid station.

You never knew how long you would be alone in a tunnel, and I decided that I should get out before somebody showed up to investigate the noise I had made. As I prepared to leave, I decided how I could make this trip into the tunnels really costly for the enemy. I wasn't sure if the X-ray machine was beyond repair, but I was sure I could use the Willie Pete grenade I had with me to make sure nobody could use any of the stuff I had found. I went into the storeroom and took a roll of adhesive tape and a box with a dozen rolls of gauze. Then, I knelt next to the X-ray machine and taped the white phosphorous grenade to one of the legs. I pressed down on the handle of the grenade and eased the pin out, straightening it as much as I could at the same time. When I got it out, I reinserted it in the second hole on the top of the device to keep the spring-loaded striker from flopping over and setting off the three-second fuse. Once I had it in, I gently unhooked the handle from the grenade. After that, I lined up several crates of alcohol in the tunnel to the storeroom to make sure the fire I was setting up with the incendiary grenade would spread there.

The final preparation for my role as an arsonist was to gently tie the end of one of the rolls of gauze to the ring on the grenade pin. After that, I started crawling out the same way I had come in, pushing the box of gauze rolls ahead of me as I left the hospital. I had no intention of setting myself on fire, so I kept the light on to make sure I didn't snag the gauze strips I was stringing together on the way out of the tunnel.

Keeping the light on also helped me understand why the tunnel smelled like death. Every so often, I came across holes of varying sizes in the side of the tunnel that had bones showing in them. They were human bones. I saw hands, femurs, and even skulls. They were the remains of people who had died, possibly in the operating room behind me, and been buried in the walls of the tunnels. They were visible because the rats in the tunnels had been digging them out for food. When I got close enough to see the light at the end of the tunnel, I pulled on the gauze rope and set fire to the whole stinking mess.

When I got out of the tunnel, I discovered that I had a nose-bleed and trouble hearing from the concussion of the grenade. While I sat on the ground using a canteen of water and my Lifer Scarf to wash the blood off my face, Mack and Richie Beunzel told me at higher than normal volume that someone in the third platoon had also found a tunnel entrance in the bottom of another bunker. They said the other tunnel rat must have come into the complex I had found from another angle. He reported finding a microscope, a sterilizer, boxes of surgical tools, cases with over a thousand bottles of different kinds of drugs, and a lot of syringes in plastic bags.[7] He said he got out of the tunnel when he saw a bright flash and smelled smoke. It must have been the incendiary I set off.

In summer 2003, I located Colonel Webb's accounting of the enemy losses from Base Area 707. In retrospect, they didn't lose much in the way of munitions. We only took four AK-47s, seven SKS carbines, eight French MAS rifles, three flintlock rifles, and two home-made rifles made from parts of several others. They also lost some ammunition, but not much. We took 1,576 rounds of small arms ammunition for the rifles, ten 60-millimeter mortar rounds, nineteen 82-millimeter rounds, two B-40 rockets, a satchel charge, and eleven Chicom grenades. My personal load of ammo was equal to about a third of the bullets we found. In fact, I had seen more firepower in one of our platoons up on the firebase.

However, there was also a lot of equipment that tended to confirm the idea that we had found a training camp: one hundred dummy grenades, fifty-one satchels with sticks instead of dynamite, and four human silhouette targets of men with round helmets and M-16 rifles. The absence of more weapons and people carrying them probably meant that the training personnel and whatever students they had had moved on and taken their guns with them, but judging from the amount of food left behind, they were going to be really hungry. According to Colonel Webb's report, 75,385 pounds of rice, 300 pounds of corn, 600 pounds of barley, 300 pounds of salt, 1,525 pounds of potatoes, and 330 pounds of cotton cloth were also found and destroyed.[8]

RESISTANCE AND BODY COUNTS

The raid into Base Areas 702 and 707 cost the enemy a lot of personnel too. However, it was hard to separate B Company's kills from the rest of the battalion's or the kills made by the II FFORCEV. One reason is that the original number of enemy we expected to face was badly underestimated. The first forecast of the opposition to the II FFORCEV was 27,000 men. Then, after the operation got started, documents were found, and prisoners were taken and interrogated, and the picture changed. The new estimate was 63,000, about two and a half times the original guess.[9]

Eventually, the intelligence specialists produced both narrative and statistical evaluations of the damage we did to enemy personnel. When I read the narrative section, I was struck again by the way that time and distance from the fighting seemed to inform the description of the resistance we faced. Colonel Webb, writing from the TOC that was an hour or more away by fast helicopter, wrote that we were giving the enemy hell and that their combat troops were working hard to avoid contact with us. Maybe he was influenced by the fact that we found so few weapons in Base Area 707. Maybe he got similar reports from other units in the field, too. Anyway, his intelligence estimate of our impact said that during the course of the operation, most of the main force combat elements avoided contact with us, and so the enemy had suffered a lot of losses among their rear service people. The figures he gave for those losses were a total of 7,807 killed in action and 909 taken prisoner. [10] I could be wrong, but nearly eight thousand dead men in a week didn't sound like the NVA were doing a good job of avoiding us.

Colonel Webb also commented on what he thought was the damaged morale situation for the enemy. According to him, 30 percent of the NVA in Subregion 2 (Eastern Cambodia) were agitating for a return back to North Vietnam. He buttressed that opinion with documentary and intelligence evidence of mutiny among the enemy's officers and enlisted men in Cambodia. For example, Webb alluded to COSVN documents captured in April 1970 that said that seven hundred men, the equivalent of nearly two battalions of our troops, had refused to fight. There were also reports of officers, including six battalion commanders and 4 company commanders, who also refused to fight. In fact, according to Webb, sometime around May 19, 1970, when Operation *Bin Tay I* was winding down, the commander of Battalion 2642 and eight officers at the battalion and company level left their units and went back to North Vietnam. [11]

There were also reports of the enemy losses that originated at the lower levels of II FFORCEV. In fact, some of those reports came directly from the field near contested landing zones, or from places like Firebase Jood out near the leading edge of the American penetration of Cambodia. Those reports did not describe an enemy trying to avoid contact. For example, Maj. Malcom Dixon, the adjutant for our battalion, wrote a report of our activities for the week of May 7 to 13 to be sent up the chain of command to Colonel Webb. Dixon's "Chronological Summary of Important Events," said that during that seven-day period, we had sixteen firefights, six initiated by the enemy and ten initiated by our side.[12] That number of firefights was similar to what we experienced when our battalion went through the NVA's Base Area 226. So the idea that the enemy was avoiding contact in either base area would not have occurred to those of us who were in those camps.

At the end of his chronology, Dixon also wrote that the 1st Battalion, 22nd Infantry had accounted for fifty-seven enemy dead during the week of fighting around Base Area 702. Our infantrymen killed twenty of them with small arms fire; eleven more died when we directed mortar fire onto their positions, and twenty-six more were killed by close air strikes from gunships we called in for support.[13] From our perspective, a body count of fifty-seven enemy dead in a week, no matter how we killed them, did not seem like the enemy was avoiding contact.

There were also American casualties on Operation *Binh Tay I.* Annex C to Colonel Webb's report was a detailed accounting of the American dead, wounded, and missing in action from the operation. When I read it in the summer of 2003, I had great difficulty rationalizing the numbers there with the statement in the narrative portion of his report that the enemy's main force combat units were working hard to avoid fighting with us. The plain truth of the matter is that there were a lot of Americans killed in Cambodia although 1st Battalion 22nd Infantry II FFORCEV had the fewest casualties of any of the units sent there. Three men in the artillery and mortar units assigned to support the invasion were killed in May, and eighty-five of them were wounded. The next month, six more of them were killed.

Amazingly, none of the infantrymen in II FFORCEV were killed or wounded in May, but many of the other units fared much worse. In fact, the numbers of American casualties for the overall operation did not reflect the light or hesitant resistance Colonel Webb alluded to. In May 1970, 189 Americans were killed in Cambodia and 1,376 were wounded. In June, as most of the American units were moved back to Vietnam, 95 more died and 963 were wounded.[14] To me, those numbers don't fit Colonel Webb's narrative statement that enemy reaction to the invasion was "light in intensity and low in volume."[15] That might have been true from Webb's perspective in the safety of his bunker in New Plei Djerang, but for us, the bottom line was if a personnel clerk or a doctor shot you in the head, you were just as dead as if a front-line NVA infantry marksman had shot you.

NIGHT FIGHTING INSIDE THE WIRE

Leaving aside for the moment the controversy about whom we fought and how hard they fought us, our commanders felt that we had bought about six months' time for the ARVN to adjust to the withdrawals of our troops in the Vietnamization plan. And surprisingly, the diplomatic mission of Lowenstein and Moose agreed with the Army.[16] They visited some of the caches that had been unearthed and saw piles of Soviet and Chinese weapons, Chinese and Czech ammunition, East German medicine, Japanese and Chinese textiles, and Cambodian rice. The diplomats and MACV also thought the effects of the invasion would be felt from southern II Corps all the way south through III and IV Corps areas too.[17] It was with those predicted successes in mind that orders were given for American troops to leave Cambodia.

Moving the II FFORCEV back to Vietnam took about three weeks, and the units farthest west left first. In many cases, a last heavy strike by air cavalry, artillery, Air Force close air units, and even *Arc Light* missions by B-52 bombers preceded the withdrawal.

The vicinity around Base Area 707 where the 1st Battalion, 22nd Infantry was working, was beyond the effective range of the artillery, and we lacked the helicopter gunships the Air Cavalry units had to finish destroying the base, so our area was scheduled for an *Arc Light* mission.[18] That was another reason we left Cambodia ahead of some of the other units.

In 1990, Texas Tech University's Vietnam Oral History Project interviewed several veterans of the Cambodian invasion. One of them was Donald McBane. McBane was with D Company, the mortar support unit on Firebase Jood, and he talked briefly about that last night the 1st Battalion, 22nd Infantry spent in Cambodia. As I read his comments, I noticed that our military lives had taken similar paths, placing us in close proximity to each other, but I could not say with certainty that I ever saw or talked to him. We attended the NCO Academy at Fort Benning at the same time, but he was released before graduation because he was diagnosed with Bell's Palsy. Bell's Palsy is an eye affliction that prevents the victim from accurately sighting a rifle. Yet, like me with my chronic back problem, McBane too was sent to Vietnam and eventually ended up in combat. He started out driving jeeps and trucks, and it was the truck driving that first brought us to the same place in Vietnam. I guarded the water point at LZ Beaver, and McBane was one of the truck drivers who drove tank trucks of clean water to the top of LZ Beaver. We probably saw each other, but had no meaningful contact or memory of each other. Grunts and truck drivers rarely socialized.

McBane's interview was also another striking example of how time and place affect the telling of what happened. He came to Jood in one of the last lifts for the battalion and served as the pit boss for one of D Company's mortar crews. In his interview, he confirmed the fact that our battalion had landed near a medical facility with X-ray and surgical capabilities, and he also knew there was a training facility for NVA troops. But since he was never off the firebase, his description of what happened in the jungle was brief and devoid of the details that I recalled on those subjects.

McBane recalled that sappers got inside our perimeter wire under covering fire from mortars and rocket-propelled grenades. He even told the interviewer that B Company was on the western side of the firebase where the sappers attacked. He also said he heard we had some people killed over there.[19] People did indeed die that night. Three Americans and six enemy that I know of died that night. I killed three of them myself, and almost died doing it.

Just before sundown on that last night, we got the word that we were leaving for Vietnam in the morning. Some of my optimism about going home alive returned. I spent some time inside a bunker with Richie, Bodell, and about half the other men in my squad making plans for going back to the World, as we called home. I even filled out a dormitory registration form for a space at Ohio University. Larry Black, a brother from Texas who always joked that he was going to marry my sister, pulled me aside. Larry said he still expected to be my brother-in-law so I should stay focused on staying alive for another three weeks. I laughed him off and decided to spend the night in a foxhole outside the sweltering heat in the bunker. I was in the foxhole when the sapper attack, most likely conducted by members of the 24th NVA Regiment's front line troops, struck our perimeter.

They came at us in two phases. The first one was a standoff attack with mortars and rocket-propelled grenades. The intent was to drive us into bunkers away from the hail of shrapnel. The second phase was a ground attack through the barbed wire perimeter in front of the bunkers. The lead elements of the ground attack were three-man teams of sappers. In each team, two men provided covering fire from AK-47s and the third one cut through the rolls of concertina barbed wire. When they got inside the wire, one of them would crawl to the nearest bunker and drop a short-fused canvas satchel full of explosives into a window or doorway. Then, all three of them would create a diversion by trying to do as much damage as they could to other bunkers or personnel on the base before they were killed, captured, or joined by the larger numbers of massed infantry who would try to exploit the holes in the perimeter and overrun as much of the base as they could.

When the first mortar shells landed, I decided to stay in the foxhole in the middle of the one-hundred-foot gap between the bunkers. Fifty feet is a long way to go when the air is full of white-hot metal. McBane's men and the rest of D Company manned their mortar tubes and alternated between firing their own explosive shells on pre-planned points of possible attack and sending up flares that exploded in the air and drifted down on small parachutes to light up the perimeter. The flares were swinging in the breeze, casting shadows and light alternately, but I did see two sapper teams, crawling one behind the other, headed for the bunker to my left.

The first team was nearly through the last of the wire, so I engaged them first, as did Larry, Richie, and the rest of the men in the bunker. Shooting by flare light while mortar shells and rockets were exploding was scary and difficult. I was worried about getting hit in the head by shrapnel and trying to shoot accurately in a visual situation that was like being in a dark room with a strobe light. We all did the best we could, but all three men in the first sapper team got inside the wire even though I think they were all wounded. Then, for some reason, they all made a fatal mistake. They stood up and charged right at the bunker. A hailstorm of M-16 bullets dropped them in a pile less than ten yards from the front of the bunker. I knew what was coming next and I ducked into my hole just before their satchel charge went off.

I tried not to think about the body parts falling around me and got my head up to look for the other team in the dust and smoke from the explosion. They were inside the wire too. They were crawling to my right, moving up to the bunker on that side of me at an oblique angle that would take them toward the bunker's left wall where there was no firing port. That kept them out of the line of fire from either bunker and made a three-on-one firefight with me fifty feet away in the foxhole. I switched my weapon to automatic and put the last half of an eighteen-round magazine into the satchel man. I shot him first because he was closest to the bunker, and the biggest threat. I was also hoping that his satchel would go off and kill his partners, but no such luck. In fact, killing the satchel man gave away my position, and the other two turned on me and sprayed the ground around my hole with AK-47 fire. I was down inside the hole changing magazines. Then the flare above us went out and I took advantage of the darkness to make a fast low crawl to the shadows on the left side of the bunker to my right.

Under the circumstances, I knew better than to try and get inside. That would most likely get me killed by the men in the bunker. Instead, I lay next to the bunker wall, hidden in shadow, facing the direction I had come from. I was hoping the two sappers would crawl toward the foxhole and give me a chance to shoot them in the back or side when they moved on my empty foxhole. A mortar shell exploded, and I saw that they had showed up just about where I expected, crawling side by side toward the hole I had just left. The one closest to me emptied his weapon at the hole to cover his partner's advance, and then he rolled on his right side to change magazines. He was looking right at me when I chopped his rifle, chest, and face apart with a blast of full automatic fire from twenty feet away. Another flare lit up the area and the last sapper and I squinted against the glare and we started to shoot at each other from a distance of about twenty-five feet. The brightness of the flare and panic ruined my aim and his too. I shot up the ground around him, and I could hear the heavy 7.62-millimeter slugs from his weapon tearing holes in the side of the bunker's sandbags to my left. Then, my magazine ran out. I had just shot a man to pieces while he reloaded, and all I could think of at the time was, "Fuck it Dad, I made them pay as much as I could." Then, the third sapper jumped up and charged me with the bayonet on the end of his AK-47 because he was out of ammunition too.

At any other time, I would have simply shot him with my .45, but the sergeant major had collected them from all the enlisted men. That left me with an empty plastic rifle with no bayonet to fight a man with a wooden rifle tipped with a foot-long blade. I jumped to my feet and threw my helmet at him to distract him. I needed time to get to my combat knife with the staghorn handle and nine-inch blade. Once I had it in my hand, I closed in on the sapper while I did the mental things Sergeants Terry and Clay had told me to do to get ready. I called up the instant rage and cold calculating heart that Sergeant Terry told me I needed. Then, I spit my conscience and inhibitions out on the ground like Sergeant Clay told me to do. By the time I had closed the twenty-foot gap between us, I was determined to kill him as savagely and quickly as I could. He, on the other hand, had the same fate in mind for me, and he came at me hard and fast in a screaming rage.

He was a conventional right-handed bayonet fighter who held his weapon with his right hand behind the trigger guard at the rear of the weapon and his left hand on the front hand guard just behind the bayonet. I faced him in the Asian knife-fighting mode with my knife blade pointing down in my right hand and the cutting edge facing him. I took two steps to the right as he bore down on me to make sure he had no chance for a butt stroke to the head. He countered with a short step forward with his left foot to get closer. That step telegraphed to me that he was a stabber first and clubber second, so I was ready. He lunged forward and tried for the nearly instant kill of a stab through my throat and vertebrae in my neck. I slammed my left forearm and the flat of my knife that was held against the inside of my right forearm against his bayonet and the barrel of his weapon. That move forced the point of his blade a couple inches to the left of my neck and over my left shoulder. It also put his left hand just inches from the cutting edge of my knife. I jerked the blade up, slashing at the back of his left hand and wrist. The blade was razor sharp, and it cut him to the bone, severing most of the ligaments he needed to operate that hand.

The sapper gave out a short, sharp shriek of pain and frustration and his useless left hand lost its grip on the front of the rifle. I was already inside his guard then, and I stepped in chest-to-chest with him and trapped his right arm under my left one the way wrestlers do. He couldn't hold onto or use the rifle effectively with one hand, so he dropped it and karate chopped me on the right side of my neck with his bloody left hand. If he were stronger, he could have ruptured my jugular vein or carotid artery and I would have died of a stroke within seconds. He didn't get enough force behind the blow and before he could strike again, I jabbed him in the eye with the pommel of my knife. After that, we struggled, face to face, for a second or two, each seeking the balance, leverage, and position to bring the other one down.

He gave up on the karate chops and went for a killing blow to my right temple with his left elbow. He hit me two hard blows but I ducked my head and hunched up my right shoulder like a fighter in a clinch and his blows bounced off my shoulder and head with no real damage. Then I raised my head up, looked him in the eyes and stabbed him in the side just above his right hip. His eyes went wide with shock and rage, and he made a deep throated growling sound. We were so close I could smell the rotten fish of nouc nam on his breath and I thought he would try to bite my face or throat because we were that close, and teeth were all he had left. Instead, he gritted his teeth and spit in my face.

Years later, in therapy, I understood that spitting in my face was probably a dying man's expression of courageous contempt. Yet at that time, I responded as I had been trained. I screamed, "No mercy, motherfucker" and jerked the blade in his side across his belly to his navel. There was a horrible stench as his belly and bowels emptied shit and blood over the both of us. He also started making a sound I had never heard a human being make before. He offered no resistance when I grabbed the back of his collar and jerked it while I leg hooked him and put him on his back. I took the knife out of his belly, pushed the side of his face into the ground and cut through both his carotid artery and jugular vein to stop the inhuman sound he was making. He didn't have a lot of blood left, and his brain emptied out in a few seconds worth of ghastly spurts that struck my chin and chest. It took a lot longer for him to stop that sound. I heard it in my nightmares until the mid-1980s.

While I was busy disemboweling the sapper, I had ignored the shrapnel flying about, and I am still amazed neither of us was struck by it. I did, however, have enough sense to stay on the ground once I got him down and dead. I crawled back to get my rifle and picked up my helmet too, as I hustled back to my hole between the bunkers. The heavy phase of the ground attack never developed, and I spent the rest of the night alone in my foxhole.

The three or four hours until dawn felt like the longest week of my life. I was shaking from adrenaline overload and fear. I was glad to have survived the bayonet attack, but terrified that another sapper team might have seen what I did and was coming to avenge the man I had killed. I was also nauseated. I had blood and shit all over me, and there was nothing I could do about it until dawn. When the sun finally did come up, I went to one of the water tanks that had been flown to the base and washed the blood off my hands and face. Then I looked under a poncho that covered a dead guy from one of the mortar pits. His clothes were less bloody than mine and they didn't have shit all over them, so I stripped my old clothes off and put his on. Then I went back and sat in my hole by myself until the middle of the afternoon when the helicopters came to take us back to Vietnam.

9. ✳

Joining the Vietnam Veteran's Class of 1970

LEAVING CAMBODIA

It was midmorning on May 15 when the helicopters began to land at LZ Jood to withdraw the 1st Battalion, 22nd Infantry from Cambodia. Happily for the men of B Company, the usual policy of first men in, first men out of an LZ put second platoon in the first lift to leave that miserable place. I was the acting platoon sergeant, so when the choppers got close, I popped a yellow smoke grenade on the landing pad to mark the wind direction and ground-guided the first lift of six choppers to the ground. They clattered in and raised a huge dust storm. We waded through it, flopped down in the doorway, and they lifted off.

There was a shortage of Cobra gunships to escort the slicks back to Vietnam, so we had to circle the firebase until three lifts of six slicks were loaded up and ready to be escorted by two gunships. When we passed over our side of the perimeter we saw the damage from the sapper attack. An obvious damage site was the base commander's conex. They were pretty nice places to live until an attack happened. They were big steel boxes that had bunks with real mattresses. They had a gasoline generator to power electric lights and air conditioning, too. But, its high profile and the noise of the generator made it an obvious target for sapper attacks. From the doorway of the chopper, we saw signs of serious wear and tear on the colonel's house. There were a couple big dents, probably from satchel charges, and there were also a lot of fist-sized dents with shiny centers and long bright gashes in its surface. Those were the results of bullet strikes and shrapnel that had bounced off its sides the night before.

There were also some black rubber body bags for the American KIAs from the mortar pits on the western side of the perimeter. I counted three of them before a Medevac helicopter with the big red cross on a white background came in and obscured the body removal scene in another dust storm. The sight of the body bags set me to wondering for a moment about who the dead man was that I had stripped for his clothes because they were less bloody than mine. Those thoughts were interrupted when Cecil Dykes nudged me in the side and said, "Hey Gill, check 'em out." He was pointing at three bodies in the dirt between two of our platoon's bunkers. They lay in contorted positions on the orange dirt and there was dark stain around all of them from where they had bled out and died in the night. Cecil had spent the night inside his bunker and had no idea who had killed them. I looked at them briefly and pulled my emotional Teflon more closely around my heart. Then I spit out the door at them and said, "Fuck 'em, Cecil, they're just dead Gooks, they don't mean nothin'." Then I leaned back and tried to sleep on the ride back to Pleiku, but I kept hearing a strange, inhuman sound.

About three hours after we lifted off from LZ Jood, we were back in our barracks at the 4th Division base camp. The barracks had shoulder-high wooden sides topped by a screened-in section that went up to the corrugated aluminum roof for ventilation. There were no doors or furniture, so we just sat on the concrete floor, or packs, or our air mattresses when they didn't have holes in them. Mine was full of holes from the landing in Cambodia, so I just sat cross-legged on the concrete with my back against the wall. I knew I was a short timer, but I also knew I would have to go back to the jungle at least one more time. So I automatically went through the necessary weapons maintenance we always did on stand downs. I cleaned up my rifle and refilled all my magazines. Then I decided to clean and re-sharpen my knife. The top of the sheath and the grooves in the handle were clotted with blood. I scrubbed most of it away with a toothbrush I kept for weapons. Then I threw the brush and cleaning rags in the half oil drum we used for a toilet.

While we tended to our weapons, the supply clerks brought piles of clean shirts and pants and almost enough clean socks to go around. Army boxer shorts were known for chafing the inside of your thighs in the heat, so they never brought us any underwear. I pulled a clean set of jungle fatigues off the pile and headed off for the usual cold-water shower from the big tank suspended over a "shower building." The showers also had screens around the upper third of the walls and there were twenty shower nozzles for the one hundred and twenty men in the company. The building was next to a dirt road traveled frequently by supply trucks so you could end up covered in mud if one came by and raised a dust cloud before you got dried off. I hadn't had a bath in a month and after the killing in Cambodia, I literally smelled shitty. I was really feeling and smelling the need to get clean again. So, I headed off for a shower-mud bath.

When I reached the showers, I got a surprise. There was a new building with four solid walls and a water heater! It had a sign on it that said, "E-6 and UP." It was the good old Army caste system at work again, and it meant that NCOs with the rank of staff sergeant and above plus officers of any rank were allowed the luxury of a hot-water shower. I had been promoted to staff sergeant (E-6) in February, and I hadn't had a hot shower since I left Fort Lewis Washington, ten months before. So I took my time and really enjoyed myself. After that, we all went to the mess tent and had a hot meal. This was a big treat because we usually ate

C-Rations, many them canned in 1948, or dehydrated meals that were shrunken into hard, barely digestible pieces in 1965. After that, we drifted back to the barracks where we spent the rest of our two-day stand down getting drunk on the huge amount of beer delivered to the barracks, playing cards, and writing letters. I wrote to my family to say I was back in the base camp, and that things were probably going to be much better for me because I was out of Cambodia and due back in "the world" in about three and a half weeks. Looking back, the fact that I wrote a letter from Vietnam, during the war, to say things were looking good for me was a pretty telling quality of life comment. How many people write home from a war zone to say their life has taken a turn for the better?

THE LAST MISSION

In May 1970, I had been in combat for ten months, and every time I sat for a mission briefing or took a patrol order in the field, I always hoped and predicted that things would be easy. I was wrong every damned time. So, when newly promoted Captain TJ gathered all his NCOs at one end of the barracks for the mission briefing I had no illusions. I just sat on the floor in the corner of the room and took a few notes and tried to focus on what I had to do to stay alive for another three weeks.

Operation *Putnam Paragon* had been cut short by the Cambodian escapade, and we were sent back to finish that job. As a mission, *Putnam Paragon* was nothing new, just another search-and-destroy mission: find out where the NVA and Viet Cong had moved Base Area 226, wreck it, and kill as many of them as we could in the process. The battalion intelligence people had tentatively located this base in the mountains of Binh Dinh Province, about thirty kilometers northeast of An Khe.[1] We had found this base in February and March. We damaged it while the enemy fought a disciplined rear guard action while they moved as much of their supplies and people as they could to a new location. I figured the new base must be a pretty big one because all three battalions of the 4th Division's 2nd Brigade were assigned to the hunt.[2]

My guess about the size of the place was confirmed when we got to the who and how many part of the briefing. The intelligence estimate said there were twenty different enemy units with 5,254 personnel confirmed. Included in that total were six battalions of NVA, averaging 300 men each. There was also supposed to be an anti-aircraft battalion of 250 men armed with the lethal 51-caliber heavy machineguns that had wreaked havoc with our helicopters. And, finally, there was even the confirmation that the 400th Sapper Battalion was lurking about.[3] It had only been four days since my last encounter with sappers, and another go around with them was right down there with getting diarrhea on my list of things to do.

The execution section of the briefing called for the 1st Battalion, 22nd Infantry, to lead the way in, and to be joined by the other units in a couple days. That was cause for some mumbling because we had been first into the LZ in Cambodia. Then, Captain TJ hit us with the good part. He said that B Company was first into the LZ again. When the cussin', moanin', and groanin' subsided, he explained that since he was the newest captain in the battalion, he was first up in the rotation. I wasn't buying it. He was a company commander when we went to Cambodia, and rotations went by unit not unit commander. I, and quite a few others, all thought he had more than likely volunteered for this and we had to go with him. I just retreated into my "Fuck it, it don't mean nothin' " attitude, and told myself I'd already made forty-six combat assaults, I should be able to get through just one more. The only good news was Captain TJ was riding with the third platoon on the first lift because second platoon had been first into Cambodia.

Early on the morning of May 18, a convoy of deuce and a half trucks took us to the landing pad. As usual, we were hung over, so the ride to the pad was quiet, and everyone seemed to be working on automatic. We climbed off the trucks and onto the choppers. The pilots took us to work. At 1,500 feet altitude, the air was cold, even though it was the hot, dry season again in Vietnam. The LZ was cold too; nobody home.

Captain TJ took the "Third Herd," and went immediately to work looking for the enemy. The rest of the company got busy building a firebase called Chippewa. It took two days of heavy labor in the hot sun. We blasted down the really big trees with blocks of C-4 explosives. We chopped the smaller ones away with machetes, and dug out bunkers in teams of three with picks and shovels. By the time we got logs and sandbags on top of the bunkers, most of the men were glad to get off the hill and start looking for somebody to shoot. Three days after we landed, the other two battalions were air lifted into the area. They built Firebase Warrior, and then we all got down to the familiar business of search and destroy.[4]

It took two days to find the enemy. Our first platoon found them closer to LZ Challenge than our to base at Chippewa. My squad and I had just finished a security sweep. I was into the short timer habit of sitting inside a bunker as much as possible, and so I heard the shooting start on Tiny Pederson's radio. Someone in the first platoon, probably the point element, saw two NVA about thirty-five meters off the trail and opened fire. I heard the enemy return a long burst of fire on the radio and in real time too as the echoes bounced around in the valley. The two NVA disappeared into the jungle. No blood was drawn on either side, and no bunkers, foxholes, caches or anything of that nature turned up. Challenge was on the edge of the area assigned to the Second Battalion, 35th Infantry, another of the units in our operation, and Captain TJ, who also heard the firefight on the radio, wanted to know why first platoon was so far away. He ordered them to make tracks back to our area of operations right away.[5]

For the rest of the month of May, we patrolled our assigned area around LZ Chippewa, and as usual, I had gotten my prediction wrong about the kind of action I was getting into. But this time being wrong was a good thing. In that ten- or twelve-day period, our entire brigade, approximately 1,200 men, managed to locate and kill only nine enemy and capture three more. The movers and shakers back at battalion and brigade headquarters weren't very pleased with our production, but I, on the other hand, was practically ecstatic. I was a short timer with less than a month to go, so spending nearly two weeks in the jungle without seeing one enemy or getting shot at was just great. It was kind of like going on a camping trip, but with rifles, just in case something happened. I was starting to believe again that I might get home alive.

When it dawned on the Lifers that there was no one around to kill, all three battalions were ordered to their firebases, picked up, and dropped on new sites to start searching again. The 1st Battalion, 12th Regiment's men were sent to build a new base called LZ Kiowa, twenty-five kilometers northwest of An Khe.[6] The 2nd Battalion, 35th Regiment's men were pulled off LZ Challenge, and sent to build Firebase Warrior, eighteen kilometers northeast of An Khe. In fact, before the operation was over, the brigade built or occupied eight firebases and tramped around in the jungle near them in search of the enemy. My battalion, the 1st Battalion, 22nd Infantry ended up thirty-six kilometers due north of An Khe on an old firebase called Niagara.[7] The rest of the brigade was scattered into other bases called Baxter, Cheyenne, Lance, Armageddon, Ute, Terrace, and Welch.[8]

Firebase Niagara was on a hill on the edge of the Central Highlands Plateau, and there was a waterfall on one side that plunged off the plateau and ran along the base of the hill. It was a picturesque place we could have enjoyed if we weren't trying to find someone to kill. Niagara was the last firebase I worked from, and as soon as we got there contact with the enemy began to pick up in frequency, but there was nothing on the order of what the Lifers expected to happen until just after I left the field. The After Action Report for *Putnam Paragon* I read in the National Archives said that in early June there were sporadic contacts with enemy units of five to seven men, occasional sniper incidents, and an increase of ground-to-air fire on helicopters.[9]

Members of B Company in general, and my platoon especially, saw none of that action. In fact, the only action we had in the first week of June was no big deal, but it did show how much luck figured in getting home uninjured. It was my last day on point, and my platoon was on a trail when LT Mack called a rest break. He decided to take a new guy up the trail to post him for security while we ate lunch. As they went past me, Mack tripped the wire on a punji stake trap. It was a single, foot-long bamboo spike, tied to a sawed-off springy sapling secured parallel to the ground. When he sprung the trap, the sapling popped loose and the spike swung across the trail in a vicious arch. It should have stabbed him in the leg, but it passed in front of his right knee, and the sapling whacked him hard on the outside of the knee. [10]

Mack yelped in pain, staggered a step, and then realized how lucky he had been. The tip of the spike was black with shit meant to cause an infection, and it had passed in front of his kneecap without even breaking the skin. He did have a bruise but we both knew too that he probably would have been crippled for life if the poisoned spike had stabbed him in the side of his knee joint. I also thought of the fact that had he not called a halt and had I not decided to sit down where I did, I might have been crippled on my last day on point. I had never voiced the concern aloud to anyone, but I feared coming home maimed or crippled more than death. When you're dead, I reasoned, that's it. No more worries. When you're maimed, you have a lifetime of stares, rude and insensitive questions about the injury, and adjustments to make for the missing or malfunctioning parts. So, on my scale, I always figured dead was better than a having a hook for a hand, or God forbid, riding a wheelchair because I was dead or missing below the waist. It was those fears that made me ask LT Mack to let me walk where I wanted to in the formation for my last week, and he agreed.

LEAVING VIETNAM

The first major action of *Putnam Paragon* came on June 20, 1970, and it involved B Company. The company encountered a unit that they estimated to be a whole company of replacement troops moving through the area. Brand-new uniforms on all of them was one reason they were tagged as new recruits. Their lack of skill in the ensuing two-hour firefight was another reason. When it was over, thirty-one of them were dead, and two were wounded and captured. An experienced enemy unit would never have fought that long or left that many dead on the field to be counted. Experienced fighters would have acquitted themselves better against B Company too. Not one man in B Company was wounded in that firefight. Besides losing a third of their men, there was one final indignity imposed on that NVA company. The area of the firefight was converged upon and searched by the other battalions on the operation, and between them, the other two units found and hauled away a three-ton cache of rice. [11]

The firefight on June 20 was a pretty good job for B Company, but I missed it. I only got to read about it twice. The first time was in letters from Jim Hinzo and Cat Ackzinski in late July 1970. The second time was in September 2003 in the National Archives in Maryland. I missed that action because I had begun the multi-stage process of going back to America on the morning of June 13.

I spent my last week or so in the field on the search-and-destroy mission my unit had been assigned, but it was more search than destroy. In fact, the only action I saw before I left the field was when Richie Beunzel put the field radio down too close to the firing device for a Claymore mine one evening. The static charge from the radio set off the mine about ten feet from where I was sleeping. The back blast knocked me out. When I came around, I had a nosebleed and trouble hearing and moving for about an hour, but that was the last action I saw in the field in Vietnam.

June 13, 1970, was the last night I spent in the jungle. My company was still working the jungle around LZ Niagara, and we stopped on a hillside for the night. Sergeant First Class Jim Coontz, a man we considered really old at forty, had come out to serve as our platoon sergeant. Sleeping on the hillside was his idea. He had been to Vietnam before, and he said sleeping on hilltops was too predictable and made you a good target for a mortar attack because any VC rookie could hit the top of a hill. A lot of the guys didn't like it because after they had dug out a fighting position for the night, they would either have to dig out a level place to sleep, or spend the night with their back against a tree to keep from sliding away. I didn't care because I knew I wasn't going to sleep that night. I spent the whole time moving from one foxhole to the other talking with my best friends in whispers, promising to write letters, and taking orders for special things to send to them when I got back to the world.

When the sun came up, I gave away the peaches and pound cake in my C-Rations, all my ammunition except for two magazines, and I even parted with my extra socks. Then, we used some blocks of C-4 to blast down a couple big trees, and my friends cut down a couple smaller ones so a chopper could hover over the hillside while Alberto Negron and Richie Beunzel boosted me into it. Greg Bodell tossed my pack up to me, and then Cat Ackzinski threw me a bag of miniature smoke grenades. He told me to amuse myself by throwing them out the door on the platoon while the chopper eased up through the hole in the trees. The last I saw of them was when they were standing in the jungle waving to me while little streams of yellow and green smoke swirled around them.

The first stage of going home was a stop in Pleiku, the division base camp, to get "processed" for the trip home. This was where I was supposed to turn in all my equipment and get cleaned up for the move to Cam Ranh Bay. I sat on the floor of an empty barracks and cleaned my weapon for the last time, dumped all the dirt and dead insects out of my pack, and gave everything to one of the clerks at the company armory. He gave me a complete set of clean clothes, including a T-shirt and boxer shorts, and then he threw in a towel and a bar of soap. I headed off, acutely aware that I was unarmed for the first time in almost a year, to get my second hot shower in almost eleven months. I was soaping up for the third time and wondering if I could get used to wearing underwear again when the man under the nozzle across from me asked my name and rank. I said "Gillam, Staff Sergeant." He said, "you gotta get out of here." He said the shower building, which was empty except for the two of us at the time, was being used by too many people, so the battalion sergeant major had raised the rank requirement to master sergeant for enlisted men to have a hot shower.

I looked at this guy, and I knew him immediately for what he was: a base camp commando, a REMF. He was just too round and soft and pink to be anything else. I went from mellowed out about getting clean to really pissed off and nasty in a heartbeat. I stepped into the spray of his shower with him and got right up in his face. I said, "Look Motherfucker, I haven't had a bath in almost a month. I have had one Goddammed hot shower since last fall. I am finishing this one either before or after I kick your tubby ass, so let me know when you want it."

He did exactly what I expected. He went over to a bench, got dressed, and left me alone. I watched in disappointment while he put on his shirt, because I really wanted to hurt this petty asshole. I also noticed he had shiny captain's bars on one collar, and an emblem I couldn't quite make out on the other. That confirmed my guess that he was one of the clerks and jerks who hung out in base camp. No Grunt who wasn't suicidal would ever wear shiny rank on his clothes, and I knew whatever insignia he had on the other collar, it was not the crossed rifles of an infantryman. I said, "Fuck him, he don't mean nothin'," and then I soaped up one last time.

That same morning, while I was busy with mundane matters of base camp politics and the Army caste system, someone died in B Company. I never found out who it was, and I didn't even know the company had made contact until thirty-three years had passed. Again, I found out about it when I was sitting in the National Archives reading a few pages of the "Duty Officer's Log" that had been inserted into the "Chronological Summary of Significant Events" for Operation *Putnam Paragon*. There was a brief notation that on June 14, 1970, at 11:30 a.m., a man from an ambush patrol sent out by B Company's third platoon was shot fifteen times by two enemy armed with an AK-47 and an M-14 rifle. Ambushes require discipline, vigilance, patience, and luck. This guy ran out of all four at the same time. This man, identified for security purposes on the radio as "Line 54 on the Company Roster," had dysentery, and had gotten up from his ambush position to relieve himself. He was shot by two NVA who just happened to be near the trail when he squatted in the bushes.[12]

At about the same time Line 54 died lying in a puddle of his own watery shit, I had a second confrontation about the vital matter of whether I could have a hot shower or not. I was in the middle of using some new kind of shampoo called Head and Shoulders when the water in my shower stopped. I opened my eyes and saw that the sergeant major had my clean clothes tucked under his arm. He mentioned something about threatening a superior officer, the possibility of disciplinary action, and the fact that I could go get a cold shower over by the road. Then, he walked off with my clean clothes, leaving me month-old dirty clothes to put back on. I walked over to the cold-water showers, and took a shower with my clothes on so I wouldn't smell too bad when I finished. Pretty soon, though, I gave up. There were a lot of trucks going by and the dust they raised turned to mud on me. I walked to the company mess tent, soaking wet. I ignored the looks and comments from the cooks, and had my last meal in the Central Highlands. It was so tasteless I forgot what it was by the time I finished. Then, I spent most of the rest of my last day in the Central Highlands drinking beer. The only break I took was to stop at the company trains building to pick up my duffel bag and the SKS rifle I had left there since my first ambush in October 1969. There was another one from the firefight at the amphitheater in February, but somebody had stolen it.

Sometime that evening, Luis Ybarra, one of the men who went with me on the first ambush back in October 1969, came into the barracks. He was serving out his last days in Vietnam as a bunker guard. He brought me three things. The first thing was some news. He said the sergeant major had ordered Jim Lehman, another man from that first squad of mine, to type up an Article Fifteen proceeding to fine me for insubordination and threatening a superior officer. Luis said Lehman typed the Article Fifteen forms and my travel orders too. The sergeant major actually signed both. The travel orders were mixed in among a bunch of similar orders for men going home, and they got signed without too much attention. Then, according to Luis, Lehman "lost" the Article Fifteen forms. The second thing Ybarra gave me was the travel orders to get me to Cam Ranh Bay's Replacement Depot. The last thing he had for me was a bottle of Johnny Walker scotch. We drank it all and talked until dawn on June 15.

When it was light enough to see clearly, I went back to the hot shower building with my SKS carbine and fired the last three shots of my tour in Vietnam. They all went through the bottom of the hot water tank. Then, Luis put me in one of the company's jeeps and drove me to the division landing strip where I boarded a Chinook cargo helicopter bound for Cam Ranh Bay.

The ride to Cam Ranh was loud, hot, and boring. I sat amidships on a cargo net seat staring at the ground through the trap door opening the crew chief had opened for ventilation. When we landed, it was back to Army bureaucracy, and more "processing." "Processing" meant standing in lines, answering questions, getting your pay records and vaccinations updated, a quick physical, and getting a lot of meaningless things like a list of decorations and awards typed up and stapled to your DD-214 (personnel file). The last stop on the "bureaucrap" train left me standing self-consciously in front of a very pretty and neatly dressed female lieutenant's desk. She made a last check of what was in my big envelope against a checklist, and stuffed everything back in it. Finally, she looked me up and down and said, "Sergeant, you need a bath. The showers are just on the other side of the Post Exchange where you can get soap, razor, and deodorant." Her final humiliating orders to me were that after I had cleaned up, I should take special care not to lose my travel envelope and to stay near the short timer's barracks until early evening when the bus to the "Freedom Bird" would come to take us to the airport.

My flight was a night flight, and it was only early afternoon, so I had another tasteless meal while I reflected on the fact that a nice-looking woman had just told me I stunk, and that after I took a bath, I was to stay in my room and not to lose my note to go home. When I finished eating, I took another cold shower and put on deodorant for the first time in almost a year. Then I put my travel packet under my pillow and took a nap like a good little boy.

I had a nightmare that woke me up in a hyperventilating panic. I dreamt I had just gotten to Vietnam, and one of the sergeants assigned to process us in gathered the planeload of new troops together and said, "Welcome to Vietnam, I hope you all get home alive and well next year." When I woke up and looked around, I was in the same kind of barracks I had stayed in when I first got to Vietnam. So, for a few moments, it was rather difficult to tell reality from dream. To shake myself out of it, I grabbed the envelope with my personnel record and travel orders. When I got to the section in my DD-214 labeled Date of Separation from Active Duty, I saw that someone had typed in the next day, June 16, 1970. That's when it finally hit me: I was going to get home alive. No more rain, leeches, blistered shoulders, cuts, bruises, or combat assaults. No more dead NVA and Viet Cong to count. No more arguments about how many body parts constituted a dead enemy, and most important, no more live enemy trying to make me dead. Even better, in about twenty-four hours, I was getting out of the Army.

Once I was fully awake, I started to really believe I was going home. I even did something I hadn't done in a long time: I started to plan my life for weeks ahead. For a Grunt, a long-term plan was something that would happen in the next hour or two, so the idea of working on something like an invitation list to a party to be held the next week was pretty heady stuff. But hey, I told myself, normal people with a future that doesn't include sudden death can do stuff like that. In fact, I was starting to feel so normal, I went for a walk with no weapon, no operations order and not even a com check to make sure I could call for support should I run into trouble! I took myself back to the twenty-four-hour mess hall and had a bowl of chocolate ice cream. Then I bought a *Newsweek* magazine to read, and of course, I bought another bottle of scotch to start my homecoming celebration early.

I was right about returning home and trying to become what I called normal again, but just like all the other times I predicted what would happen to me in Vietnam, I still didn't get it right. I was not quite through with people trying to make me dead in sudden and unexpected ways. In fact, I was going to have two more near-death experiences before I finally got out of Vietnam. Professor Mona Phillips, a close friend of mine at Spelman College, has a habit of comparing things by saying, "it's the same, but it's different." That seemingly illogical description perfectly fits the first of my close calls while I waited to get out of Vietnam. Cam Ranh Bay was attacked the last night I was there, and that attack was the same as the first night I spent in Vietnam because it happened when I had no weapon to defend myself. It was different because it was not a mortar attack. It was one final confrontation with a sapper.

THE LAST CLOSE CALLS

When I got back to the barracks from my walk, it was dark and the place was half full with a lot of rowdy guys. I only knew one of them. He was the senior medic for our battalion. I had not seen him much since he got promoted from second platoon's medic to the chief medic's position on the battalion surgeon's staff. I thanked him again for saving me from amputations of some of my fingers and other help. Since he seemed to know more of the other men, I left him with them. They were clustered at one end of the barracks drinking and playing music and cards, all at high volume. They had pulled several bunks together in a rough circle at one end of the barracks for their party. Their duffel bags were piled in the middle of the floor. I had never been much of a card player, so I went to the far end of the barracks, drank some scotch, and took another nap.

I had another nightmare. This time it was the sapper I had killed in Cambodia. I had just cut his throat again when I heard the voices from the other end of the barracks. Their singing and carousing had turned into a lot of "what the hells," and "holy shits." I was about to sit up to see what was going on when the explosion went off. The concussion and shock wave roared through the barracks, driving debris from broken support posts, bunks, duffel bags, and me against the wall next to the doorway at my end of the barracks. I think I passed out for a bit, but when I came to I realized my double bunk had flipped over on its side. I was on the floor in the space between the bunks. Just as

I started to sit up, the heavy wooden frame supporting the sheet metal roof broke and the roof caved in. The whole pile of junk fell with a grinding, dusty crash and the only reason I wasn't crushed was most of the big pieces fell across the metal frame of the overturned bunks.

I got really panicky when I realized I was trapped. The heavy six-by-six support timbers and sheet metal from the roof were just inches above me, and it only took a second to realize I couldn't budge them. In front of me was the sturdy, solid lower wall of the barracks. And all around the sides of my little cave was a mountain of luggage, twisted bed frames, and other debris. I could hear shouting outside, and I tried to yell loud enough to make myself heard, but I couldn't be sure what was happening. I kept telling myself to be calm, that I would get out of this in a few minutes and still make my plane, but I was having trouble breathing. I thought at first it was just dust, and that it would settle down soon, but then I realized it was smoke; the wooden support timbers and the collapsed sides of the building were on fire. I tried a couple more times to raise the pile of debris on top of my space, but that was a no go. There was just too much of it, and the sheet metal was getting too hot to touch. As my panic mounted, I thought I could dig out through the luggage behind me, but the metal net that held up the mattress on the lower bunk frame was in the way. The net for the top bunk kept me from reaching the outside wall of the barracks. The only area of relatively free movement was at the end of the bunk where I could get at the debris piled in the space at the head of the bunks.

I tore frantically at that junk and shoved it behind me while my eyes and lungs started to burn in earnest from the smoke. When I uncovered a section of the wall near the doorway, the best I could manage was to get in a few kicks through the end of my little prison onto the wood next to the doorframe. I was banging as hard as I could at that task when cold water and ashes started to wash over my back and legs. I was wondering if I would die from smoke inhalation or drown when I heard voices on the other side of the wall. Someone was shouting to bring an axe because he could hear a survivor trying to get out. After a few seconds that seemed like years, an axe blade punched through the wall near my feet. I curled up in a fetal ball and let the axe man do his thing. I watched the hole get a little bigger, and I noticed that I could breathe a little better. Then, somebody ripped enough of the boards away that I could start backing out feet-first through the hole. In a second, I was grabbed by the ankles and hauled out of the burning building. Then, I got shoved into an ambulance with a lot of other people, and we went off to the hospital.

One of the other people in the ambulance was the medic I had just thanked for helping me. He had a shrapnel wound in his chest and his lungs were filling with blood. He was literally drowning in the back of the ambulance. I covered the hole with a piece of plastic as I had been taught to do in such cases, and tried to get him to lie on the side with the wound to keep his good lung clear. He said the wound was so big he didn't have a good lung. He knew he was going to drown and he asked me to hold him, so I did. He told me he had a daughter in New York who was in first grade. Then, he died.[13]

The hospital was part of the Cam Ranh Bay Convalescent Center, just south and east of the Replacement Center where all the short timers' barracks were. I spent the rest of the night in there where I ranted and raved, between hits on an oxygen mask, that I had a plane to catch. No one paid the slightest bit of attention. They were busy tending to concussions, fractures, and some hideous looking burns on one of the men from the card party at the other end of my barracks. A skinny Black guy wearing soot-stained, smoky-smelling jungle fatigues with a 1st Air Cavalry insignia on the shoulder of his uniform told me what happened. He said he had been with the card players, and that they noticed a Vietnamese, probably one of the thousands who worked every day on the base, was hanging around the doorway, looking in. He left when someone went to see what he was up to, but he came back in a few minutes. That was when he flung a satchel full of dynamite into their card game. Someone recognized it for what it was and tossed it away from them, toward the middle of the long barracks where it blew up and literally brought the house down.

The 1st Cav trooper also said the satchel charge in our barracks was just part of a larger attack on the base. And, like me, he was pretty agitated about not getting on the plane. Both of us kept asking MPs, doctors, medics, and anyone else who would listen, if they would at least get us some weapons until we could get out. They all pretty much ignored us, but eventually, we cornered one of two Air Policemen, the Air Force equivalent of an Army MP. He had an M-16 and a .45 automatic. I asked him for one of his weapons, and he actually laughed at me. He said to me, "Sarge, they're only a bunch of sappers, how tough do you think they can be"?

He never saw the right hook to the jaw that knocked him off his feet. Once I got him on the ground, I stepped inside the end of his rifle barrel so he couldn't shoot me and grabbed his right wrist. Then I kicked him in the armpit as hard as I could to dislocate his shoulder so I could get control of his weapon. He was either tougher than he looked, or I was more worn out than I thought. He was still holding onto the rifle, so I dropped a knee on his chest and punched him in the middle of his face. We were still wrestling over the weapon when the 1st Cav trooper, another AP, and two medics jumped me. They pulled me off him and slammed me face down on the floor. When I stopped struggling and screaming, they eased up a bit. They also told me that if I kept promising to rip the AP's throat out when they let me up, I wouldn't get on the plane. So, I promised not to kill him. Eventually, the two APs walked off together, and I heard the one I had knocked down still mumbling about "crazy fucking Grunts."

It was the middle of the afternoon on June 16 when I finally got on the plane to come home. During the morning, the survivors of the barracks had been taken under guard to retrieve their belongings, and to get a bath and clean clothes. I and the other Grunts were willing to go home dirty since we'd been filthy most of the last year, but no one was hearing that either. So, while we cleaned up again, our duffel bags were loaded onto a commercial jet, and then we were hustled off to stand inside a small compound made of sandbags piled head high and guarded by APs.

In a little while a loadmaster arrived and started calling off the names on the manifest for the "Freedom Bird." I could see right away this was going to be a problem. We had about a plane and a half worth of people, and only one plane. There had been two scheduled for the night before, but one of them had been damaged in the sapper attack. Some of us were going to get left in Vietnam for another day while another plane came in.

Names were called in groups of five, and we were supposed to jog from our holding area across several yards of asphalt and up the stairs into a cool air-conditioned plane. I was on the verge of a straight out anxiety attack because I could see no logic to how the names were called. Normal people would do it alphabetically, but Army people are not normal. I think they used a combination of the alphabet, rank, and the DEROS date (Date of Estimated Return from Overseas Service). Whatever they were up to, I finally heard my name called fourth in a group of five.

We were already on the stairs when there was a single rifle shot, and the man ahead of me dove full length onto the stairs. I was flat on the stairs too, hoping the sides of the ramp would offer some cover from whoever had fired at us. Then, I saw blood running down the stairs toward me. I moved up the stairs taking care to stay below the solid sides of the ramp for cover and got ready to roll the man over, but I could see it was useless. There was a hole in the back of his skull bigger than my thumb. I knew even before I rolled him over that he was as dead as you could get. One glance at him confirmed it; he had no face. While I stared at the corpse that had been a happy, homeward-bound, soon to be civilian only two seconds before, someone grabbed my arm and hustled me up into the plane.

While we waited for the rest of the plane to fill up, there was a lot of worried speculation going on. Some of us were guessing how many people would get left behind. Others were wondering if someone would try to make us get off the plane if there were some high-ranking people with no seats. That got me really tense because I was sitting in a row with two officers and a master sergeant. There was also a lot of talk about how the guy ahead of me had gotten shot. My thought was that it had been a sniper, but I heard more than one person who had been standing in the sandbag enclosure say that it was an accidental discharge by one of the MPs or APs dashing all over the place. According to that version, one of our protectors was running across the tarmac with a weapon at port arms in pursuit of a suspected sapper when he fell and his weapon discharged.

All the speculation stopped when the door slammed shut, the engines came on and we started to taxi toward our takeoff point. The takeoff was just like the landing in September 1969, only it went in reverse. The pilot did the shortest run possible and lifted off in the steepest climb he could so as not to give any enemy in the area with a B-40 rocket launcher a chance for a promotion. When we lifted off, there were all kinds of reactions. Some of us cheered and screamed. White guys started high-fiving anybody they could reach. The Brothers started dappin everybody they could reach, including the stewardesses who we finally noticed were aboard, and some just sat back and grinned. I think I did all of those things and then I started asking the stewardesses if they could get the pilots to fly a little faster.

We made two stops before we got to Fort Lewis, Washington, where I was discharged from the Army. The first stop was at Yokota Air Base in Japan where we topped off the tanks for the trans-Pacific flight to the Air Force base in Anchorage, Alaska. At Yokota, we got out for a stretch, looked around, and watched planeloads of troops going to Vietnam walk up the steps onto their planes and whatever fate awaited them. Some of the guys on our plane teased them, telling them how short they were before they were getting out of the Army. Some even had the bad taste to tease them about dying in Vietnam. I noticed that the ones who did that were the ones among us who looked well fed and had no suntans or thousand-yard stare.

I had my first readjustment to civilian life problem at Anchorage, Alaska. We were told we would be on the ground long enough for a phone call home, and there was a mad sprint to a line of phone booths. When I got inside, I didn't know how to use the phone. It had a push button keypad, and I had never seen one before. I stood there for a while with the receiver in my hand before I heard the guy behind me say, "push the buttons, dummy." I pushed the O, got an operator, and told her I wanted to make a long distance, collect call to the Gillam residence in Northfield, Ohio. She responded with a bored, rapid-fire nasal speech that I could dial that number direct by dialing one, the area code, and number. A lot of what she said was unintelligible, probably because she said it a thousand times a day. Also, I wasn't real sure what an area code was either. When I had left America, you just told the operator what city you wanted and they hooked you up. So, my response to her was to shout, "I dialed *you* direct bitch, so just get my fucking number!" She did. My Mom cried when I told her I was alive, well, and in Alaska. I told her I would call her again when I got to Washington and got a plane ticket for home, and then I had to hang up because the other guys who were slower sprinters were banging on the door to the phone booth.

The landing at Fort Lewis, Washington, was a lot smoother than the one in Cam Ranh Bay, and we all hurriedly deplaned, grabbed our duffel bags and personals off the pile on the ground at the rear of the plane and headed inside the terminal building. Surprisingly, there were rows of customs inspection tables, and officers and enlisted men alike pushed forward and dumped all their gear to be looked at. They made sure I had no ammunition for the SKS carbine I was carrying, and then I had to fill out a form to officially register my weapon as a war trophy. They confiscated a couple of AK-47s over the loud objections of their owners. The word was that there had been too much trouble with veterans and assault rifles. The customs officers also did random searches of cartons of cigarettes for contraband. They chose a pack from a carton at random and lit one of the smokes. I was really surprised to smell marijuana from a normal-looking pack of Salem cigarettes. The lieutenant who had had the special carton made up was surprised too when the MPs came and took him away in handcuffs.

It took another four hours of hurry up and wait before I finally got out of the Army. During that time, the Lifers and the unlucky draftees who were being sent to duty somewhere else were separated from the rest of us. The PFCs (Proud Fuckin' Civilians), as we called ourselves, were herded to an Army paymaster where we got our separation pay, and then to an airline ticket office where we got tickets on the first thing flying. I became a little angry when we were told to choose a ticket with a departure time of five or six hours from then. The extra time, they said, was for us to get a haircut, be fitted for a Class A uniform, stop at the Post Exchange and pay for the rank, unit insignia, awards, and decorations listed on our DD-214, and to have a steak dinner on the Army.

To save time, I stripped down to my underwear right in the middle of the PX and put on the Class A uniform. Since I didn't plan on wearing it more than once, I also skipped getting it altered by one of the hordes of tailors on duty. I kicked the jungle fatigues I had been wearing under the nearest clothing rack and hauled my duffel bag and rifle to the table set up to review DD-214s and pass out appropriate insignia and awards. I got the expected cloverleaf patch for the 4th Infantry Division and my staff sergeant stripes sewn on, but I was a bit surprised by the awards I had listed. I knew that I had earned a Combat Infantry Badge (CIB) for sixty consecutive days of combat, but I had no plans to become a Lifer so I never bothered to read the rest of the citations. The lieutenant at the table opened up a drawer and laid the ribbons for my uniform on the desktop as he read aloud from my file. He told me that I had been awarded two Bronze Stars, one for valor and one for service, a Vietnam Campaign Ribbon, a Cambodian Campaign Ribbon, and a Presidential Unit Citation. Then he told me to be sure to put the CIB on top of the row of ribbons. As I fumbled to get the ribbons secured to my jacket, I heard a loud argument at the next table. There was a guy there protesting the fact that auto mechanics who spent their entire tour of duty in a division base camp would not be allowed to wear a CIB.

About twenty-four hours after I stepped over a man with a hole in his head to claim my seat on the "Freedom Bird," I realized I could walk away from the Army and no one could stop me. I had gone to the PFCs mess hall for my steak dinner, but I couldn't eat it. You could order any kind you wanted, and as many as you wanted, but I was just too keyed up to eat. I just took my weapon and duffel bag and walked out the door, away from the Army. I went to the shuttle bus for the Seattle-Tacoma Airport. The bus wasn't scheduled to leave for another hour, so I hailed a cab and paid the cabby an extra twenty bucks to get me to the airport in a hurry.

STARTING THE SEARCH FOR NORMALITY

When I got to the Seattle-Tacoma Airport, I had my second readjustment to civilian life problem. I had an American Airlines ticket to Cleveland, Ohio, with an overnight layover in Chicago.

I got my boarding pass, checked my duffel bag, and headed off to board the plane. A big guy in a blue blazer with the American Airlines logo on it stepped right in front of me, and stopped me dead in my tracks when he put his hand flat on my chest and pushed me back a step or two. I said, "what's your fucking problem man, I got a plane to catch." He said to me, "Sarge, why don't you let me box that rifle up and ship it along with your duffel bag?" I stood there a second or two and realized that this guy had a shoulder holster with a large-caliber pistol. I could also see in my peripheral vision that he had a couple friends on either side of me. I assumed they were armed, too. Then it dawned on me that I didn't have to, and wouldn't be allowed to carry a rifle anymore. I was equal parts pleased and embarrassed as I accepted the claim ticket for my rifle and headed off to the boarding gate.

I had my third, and more serious readjustment to civilian life problem in Chicago. The flight to Chicago was uneventful, but I knew something was not quite right. I shared a row with a man and a woman. They asked the attractive Black stewardess in our section for other seats. She got a Marine lance corporal with a cast on his forearm to move up to my row. Since they were White, I thought it was a racial thing. Then I heard the woman say from her new seat behind me that she wished the Army would make all their killers ride home on their own planes. The man with her told her to be quiet because we might hear her. I turned around and told them loudly that I did hear her. I also called her a bitch and told them both to kiss my ass. Then the Marine and I drank beer and talked loudly about Vietnam until we got to Chicago. That was where the serious problem occurred.

The Marine was on the way to the Naval Clinic at the Great Lakes Naval Center in Chicago to get an X-ray and have his cast removed. I was planning to find a good restaurant and maybe a good nightclub instead of a hotel for the night. Neither of us knew much about Chicago, so I asked the stewardess, who was passing by, for suggestions. She named a couple places, and

I offered to take her with me to start my civilian celebration. She declined. I got really bold and asked her if I could kiss her to thank her for the service on the plane and the club suggestions. I was really surprised when she said yes. The lance corporal and I were laughing about that as we went looking for a cab and we bumped into two guys near the exit. I was about to say "excuse me" when one of them said, "watch where you're goin' asshole." The other one stepped up and said, "hey, how many kids did you kill?"

While I was trying to process what was happening, the first guy knocked me off my feet with a pretty good hook shot. The lance corporal stepped in and slugged him with his cast. I got up and took on the other one. The lance corporal demolished the cast on his guy. I punched the other one in the throat. He went down and I was using my foot to break as many of his ribs as I could when two Chicago cops broke up the action. We all got cuffed and marched out the door. One of the cops was a veteran, and he let me and the Marine go on our way. We went clubbin' until around five in the morning. I tried to get a cab back to the airport, but none of them would stop for me. A prostitute told me they wouldn't stop because I was in uniform, so I gave her twenty bucks and stood in the shadows. She showed her legs, a cab stopped, and I hopped in it for the ride to the airport.

I got to Cleveland Hopkins Airport early on a Sunday morning, and my mother, father, and youngest sister Linda were there to meet me. There was a lot of hugging, crying, and such, and then they packed me off to church. I wasn't at all happy about that part. Given the treatment I had had while traveling in uniform, I preferred to just go home and change. Also, nothing I saw or did in Vietnam had convinced me to trust in God, but Mom was adamant. So, I went into a self-induced coma for the duration of the services. Then I stood around in front of the church and tried to answer all the silly questions with as much civility as I could. It didn't work. About the twentieth time someone asked me if I was glad to be home, I said, "Fuckin-A right!"

Things got quiet, and that group of well-wishers moved on. Then, people started talking to my family like I wasn't there. They were saying inane things like, "He looks good considering." While I was trying to work out what "considering" meant, somebody even asked my mother, "Do you think he really killed anybody"? Somebody else asked, "don't you think he should have made a confession?" I was getting really pissed at the indirect conversation, and so when somebody asked my dad if I had learned anything valuable while I was away, I spoke up again. I told them yes, I did. I learned that you don't have to fuckin' die to go to Hell. Then I walked across the parking lot and sat in the car.

10.

Epilogue

A week after I got home, Peg and Gene Mullen, the parents of Michael Mullen, came to my family's home. I had trained with Mike at the NCO Academy and shared a room with him in the barracks at Fort McClellan in the summer before we went to Vietnam. They told my parents Mike had been killed on February 18, my birthday. I missed the visit; I had already left for college. I still regret that I never had the courage to contact them, but I just didn't know what to say. That was the period when I was trying to cope with the strange situation in which I was losing *friendships* instead of friends because of the war. My friends weren't dying in combat anymore, but *friendships* I had before I was drafted, or new ones I tried to make when I came home, were dying. That was because of the difficulty I had making the transition from hunting and killing people to pretending to be a normal college student. I know now some of the trouble was because I got home in midsummer of 1970 while the protests over the Cambodian invasion and the killings at Kent State and Jackson State Universities were still fresh in people's minds. Soldiers were unpopular in some quarters. Then, too, I had a number of incidents where people's rudeness and stereotypes about violent veterans caused embarrassment for me, and sometimes pain for them.

One of those incidents happened in Athens, Ohio, about two weeks after I returned to Ohio University. The school had closed briefly due to protests about Cambodia, and some of the people there knew I had been in Cambodia and also in Vietnam. Bob De Gaetano, my roommate from freshman year, was there as a graduate student, and he refused to talk to me. Also, the Fourth of July was approaching, and a lot of people had fireworks. One evening, some of them amused themselves by dropping some behind me as my date and I left a movie theater. To me, they sounded a lot like AK-47s, and since I had lived on reflexes for most of a year, I found myself face down on the sidewalk next to my date. She was too embarrassed to be seen with me anymore in her group of friends, but too polite to say so.

I didn't see her again until after the Fourth of July. That next date was when I moved from embarrassing people to hurting them. Instead of going out where there was a chance I would end up groveling on the sidewalk again, she invited me to play pool in the basement of her father's house. That entertainment and my friendship with her both ended because of the insensitive expectations of her seventeen-year-old brother. She told him I had been in Vietnam and he said, "Cool. Teach me how to kill with my hands." I told him I didn't do that kind of stuff anymore and turned my back on him. I was more interested in checking out his sister's legs in her mini skirt while she leaned over the table than in teaching personal combat. But, this guy was determined to make me teach him how to kill, so he grabbed me by the throat from behind and punched me in the kidney at the same time.

I taught him some things, but I stopped short of killing him. I swung my elbow back and broke his nose. His sister ran upstairs screaming to her father that I was having a flashback in the basement. It was no flashback. I was just sick of people's insensitivity and rudeness. Also, I was in a lot of pain from the blow to my kidney. I used a pool cue and took out my anger on her brother's face and body. I did enough damage that when her father came downstairs, he was more concerned with his son than me, so I got out of the house without hurting him, too. Still, though, my reputation in small-town Athens, Ohio, as a nutty veteran was pretty much set. Dates became few and far between. I also passed blood clots in my urine for two weeks.

I had some long-term adjustment problems too. Basically, they stemmed from the fact that the seven-day period beginning with February 18, 1970, had been a bad time in Vietnam for me. For a long time, I tried hard to forget that week. It hasn't been easy. My birthday is February 18. Every year when that day comes around, I try to ignore the low points of that week. It started off when I shot a man in the chest and he was dragged off to die. The next day, I had a firefight inside an NVA base camp area. I got shot, hit by grenade shrapnel, and left behind to cover the cowardly flight of my machinegun team. Two days later, one of my best friends took three bullets in the chest while we sat shoulder to shoulder. He died. Another one was gutshot and had his arm broken. Then when I got home I found out my roommate from the summer before Vietnam had been killed on my birthday by our own artillery. It was a long time before birthdays became a happy time for me again.

When I got back from Vietnam, the friends I had from early college were graduates, professionals, and had families. I wanted those same things because I saw them as symbols of normality, and I wanted to put my life back like it was before I got drafted. I set myself up with a personal five-point operations order to get them. I finished a year and a half of college in twelve months. I got straight As. I also married the woman I had been engaged to when I was drafted. It was a big mistake, but she was one of the few people besides my brother who I had a comfortable frame of social reference with. My first meaningful employment was a demanding, but satisfying stint in the world of federal programs. The city of Cleveland, Ohio, hired me as the director of the Veteran's Education and Training Service (VETS). It was funded jointly by the city and the U.S. Conference of Mayors/National League of Cities (NLC/USCM). The VETS program was an auxiliary of sorts to the Veteran's Administration that found itself swamped, especially in large cities, with Vietnam veterans who had more problems and different problems than the VA was used to coping with. I hired a staff of male and female Vietnam vets and we turned the Cleveland program into a national model.

After three years as a "normal" person, I had a professional and marital burn out. As director of one of the VETS model programs, I also worked part time as a field representative for the NLC/USCM. That meant I was essentially a fixer for programs across the country that had start up problems or issues with their funding contracts. I kept a suitcase in my car, and the airlines people knew me by sight. It was a time when it was normal for me to come home three weeks late from work. My marriage foundered on the rocks of travel, stress, and my wife's infidelity. The House Veteran's Affairs Committee invited me to testify in hearings about a bill to improve educational benefits for Vietnam veterans. I finished the work and came home early. When I got home my wife was upstairs, in bed with her lover.

I buried myself in work for a while, but the case load and the misery it held finally overwhelmed me. An infantry veteran with a 110 percent disability came to the office. He had brain damage from a grenade that brought on unpredictable catatonic states. All we had to do was find him a job where it didn't matter if he "zoned out" for a minute or an hour, and figure out how to get him there. He couldn't drive, and often, he would "zone back in" on a bus with no idea where he was. Two days after we started working with that man, a hysterical veteran's wife asked me to help her. Her husband had lung cancer and a VA surgeon had mistakenly removed his best lung. I cried with the two of them in the hospital. Then I went to the mayor's office for a meeting about continued funding for VETS. Once the funding was set for another eighteen months, I borrowed some stationery from the mayor's secretary, wrote a letter of resignation, effective immediately, and walked out.

A month later, I was hired by Case Western Reserve University as an Associate Director of Student Services. I stayed at CWRU for a little over three years. I was in charge of a federal program called the Upward Bound Program. Basically, we recruited bright underachievers from local schools, patched the holes in their education, and sent them on to college with a scholarship. I married Connie, my present wife, in 1974. By 1975, I also got the kids I had always wanted. I had about 150 teenagers in my program. Connie and I also had our first child, Damon. By the time he started preschool, he had hordes of unofficial siblings.

As my colleague Mona Phillips would say, the VETS and Upward Bound Programs were the same but different: the clientele were different, and you couldn't save everybody. Most of our students finished the program and went off to college. There were two of them who didn't and it broke my heart. One of the girls was a victim of incest. My wife and I took her home for a short time, and then relatives in Chicago took her in. She never finished high school. I lost one of the boys too. I took him to a dramatic competition in Michigan. He won a full scholarship to the school of his choice as a drama major. The day after we got home, he was shot dead by a mugger who attacked his mother at a bus stop in Cleveland.

One of the benefits at CWRU was a free class each semester. The first course I took was ancient Chinese history. The second was Mandarin. I discovered a facility for Mandarin and the language made the history more vivid and enjoyable. I resigned from Upward Bound and became a full-time student. Seven years later, I had an M.A. from CWRU, a Ph. D. from The Ohio State University, and Jessica, the first of two daughters.

I taught one semester at Ohio Wesleyan University in Delaware, Ohio. Then I moved to Atlanta, Georgia, in 1985 when Spelman College hired me and Emory University hired my wife. Whitney, the last of our children, was born in Atlanta, shortly after we moved here. The years here have been pretty good. My children are grown and I have grandchildren, and will retire soon. I went into therapy when my mother and brother died, and I rarely hear from the noisy dead man in Cambodia.

Appendix

2nd Platoon, B Company, First Battalion, 22nd Infantry

Where Are They Now?

Most formal military histories of infantry units focus on what are known as "maneuver-sized units." The smallest of those units are battalions, groups of roughly 400 soldiers commanded by at least a lieutenant colonel. Those histories provide the "big picture" of wars and battles. The Vietnam War, however, was fought mostly with small units: companies, platoons, and squads. A company was composed of four platoons. Normally, each platoon was supposed to have had forty three men: one officer, one platoon sergeant, and four squads of ten men. Each squad was led by a sergeant. These were the men who lived in the "small picture" of the war. This book is the history of how the small picture of the second platoon of B Company fit into the larger picture of the Vietnam War in the year after the Tet Offensive.

The second platoon never fielded forty three men while I served with it. The most we managed was twenty-nine because of rotation back to America, R and R, illness, injury, and death. We fought through our small picture part of the war while our numbers grew and shrank because of those factors. The life we led was tribal. We had leaders, followers, favorites, and pariahs, but for the most part, we tried to keep ourselves and our tribe members alive.

The nature of the Vietnam Only Army broke the tribe apart piece by piece as our DEROS dates came due, and forty years has passed since I last saw them. Time and circumstances of civilian life have diminished our tribe even further. The information below is what I remember best about them while they were in the second platoon and what I have been able to verify about them since they left Vietnam.

Ackzinski, Joseph "Cat" Ackzinski was an NCO Academy graduate, an Army Ranger, and a squad leader in our platoon. He was both funny and fearless. He was also one of my best friends. Cat left the Army in 1971 and had decades of readjustment problems. He drowned in the spring of 2008 when he fell off his houseboat in the bay of Baltimore, Maryland.

Bennet, Edward Ed was the radio operator for second squad when I was first assigned to be the squad leader. Later, he worked for LT Mack, the platoon leader. He played guitar, sang country western songs, and was Bob Frost's best friend. He died in November 1999.

Black, Larry Larry was a Texan and served in the second squad. He was famous for being late for everything and getting lost on patrols. He also was the barber for all the African-Americans in the platoon. Larry promised to come to Ohio and marry my sister because he loved the cookies she sent to us. Larry died in Galveston, Texas, in February 1992.

Bodell, Gregory Greg, "Tigerman," "Bo" was the first man I met in B Company. He was run over by a Tiger and had many stitches on his head from the event. He was also a very good point man who taught me how to be a mediocre one. He walked my slack, and I walked his for most of the time I was in Vietnam. We took R and R in Hong Kong together. Bo worked as a civilian employee on an army base in California after he left the Army. He died of a heart attack in 1997.

Bostwick, Robert "Stretch" was in the third squad for most of the time I was in Vietnam. He was a laid-back Californian and the tallest man I ever saw in the army. He also had a love of monkeys that hung around firebases. Stretch died of cancer June 1997.

Brick, Albert Al carried the M-79 in the first squad. He was shot in the head in June 1970 by a sniper. Al survived and spent a year and a half in hospitals and recuperation. After graduate school, where he met his wife in Argentina, Al became an event organizer in Columbus, Ohio. He is retired now and he and his wife spend time between Ohio, Venezuela, and Europe.

Beunzel, Richard "Richie" was an NCO Academy graduate and one of our squad leaders. He was one of my best friends and helped care for Bob Frost and Jose Rocha when they were wounded. Richie was promoted to staff sergeant on the spot by the battalion commander for valor in battle in June 1970. Richie went home to King of Prussia, Pennsylvania, got married, and has a daughter.

Burke, Larry Larry was a grenadier and rifleman in third squad. Larry died in April 1999.

Carter, Jimmy "Smoke" was Jesse Johnson's assistant gunner in the machinegun team when I got to Vietnam. Smoke was from South Carolina and had the voice of Louis Armstrong and the patience of Job. He was promoted to specialist fourth class just before we went to Cambodia and took charge of his own gun team. Smoke stayed in Vietnam when his time was up, and stayed in the Army too. He said both were better than where he lived in South Carolina. The last I heard, Smoke was a first sergeant and nearing retirement.

Frost, Robert "Bob," "Rawhide," was a real-life Oklahoma cowboy. He was the perfect point man, excellent shot, and personified what it meant to "cowboy up" when toughness was needed. He was one of my best friends and we were sitting together when he got shot in the chest. He fought until he couldn't go any more, and he died that day.

Golladay, Fred   Fred was at the NCO Academy with me in the spring of 1969. Fred was one of the original G Men in chapter two of this book. He was discharged from the academy and sent to Vietnam in May 1969. He served in third platoon of B Company. Fred returned to Arizona after discharge in the summer of 1970 and had a rocky readjustment. He is now married, for the second time, this time happily. He also received the Purple Heart he earned in Vietnam in a special ceremony conducted by his Congresswoman in the summer of 2009.

Henderson, James   Jim served in the second squad as a grenadier. We were often hootch mates. Jim left the Army in 1970, and now lives in Texas with his wife. They have two daughters, and Jim has helped maintain the website for the 1/22 for a number of years. He was the first person from B Company to contact me since 1970.

Hinzo, James   "Jimmy" Hinzo was an Apache. He was also a drummer in a band, a high energy, fun person, who could never be still. He was also a very good shot. Jim died in June 1999 in Arizona.

Johnson, Jesse   Jesse was the best M-60 gunner in the company. Jesse was promoted to sergeant by the battalion commander when he took down an entire squad of NVA by himself. He challenged me early for my cowardice and kept me alive because he walked my slack often. I have been grateful for both those things for a long time. Jesse went home to the San Joaquin Valley after Vietnam. He died in 1999.

Joseph, Jerome   Jerome served with the second squad. He was a newlywed when he came to Vietnam, and Bo took him under his wing. They both moved to California after the Army and worked on the same post as civilian employees. Jerome also died in 1997.

Killian, James "Killer" carried an M-79 grenade launcher and served as an ammunition bearer for Jesse Johnson's M-60 machinegun team. He survived Vietnam and moved to Connecticut.

MacKowan, William "LT Mack." Mack was the platoon leader who served with us for most of the time I was in Vietnam. He didn't tell us he was an officer until he was sure he knew what to do in the field. We were all very surprised when he started giving us orders. I also liked him despite the fact that he was an officer. Mack went home to North Carolina, and married Debbie, his fiancée. I heard he worked for Mohawk Carpet Manufacturers and traveled to China frequently on business for them.

Negron, Alberto "Berto" was a quiet, taciturn Puerto Rican and member of the second squad. He helped me a lot in my first month, and he was also the one who boosted me into the helicopter when I left the field.

Pederson, Robert "Tiny" Pederson was the biggest man in the company. He served as my radio man after Ed Bennet started as LT Mack's radio man. He stayed with me for almost his whole tour and we were regular hootch mates. He was the perfect radio man, and perfect friend and a good soldier even though he hated carrying his rifle. Bob lives in Connecticut with his wife of over thirty years, three daughters, and three granddaughters. He retired from a job as a supervisor of a state program for children with disabilities last year.

Roberts, Glen Glen served with the first squad, and also the third squad as a rifleman. He went back to the Cleveland, Ohio, area after the army and is now retired.

Tijerino, Gilbert "Lieutenant TJ" was a first lieutenant, and company executive officer when I got to Vietnam. He volunteered to return to the field and eventually became our company commander. I was never easy with Lieutenant TJ because of my prejudices against officers, Lifers, and West Point graduates. I was interested in getting home alive. He seemed to be focused on winning the war. In retrospect, I think he did the best and most aggressive job he could. TJ did a second tour in Vietnam as a gunner on a Cobra gunship. He retired as a major. He and his wife live in Texas near Jim Henderson and his wife, and they are all close friends.

Ybarra, Louis "Louie" was in the second squad when I came to Vietnam. He stayed in the jungle for most of the year, but he finished his tour as a bunker guard in the division base camp. He saved my life on the first ambush I led. He also brought me scotch to drink my last night in Pleiku. Louie was another of the few married men in the company. He and his wife are still married and they live Los Angeles County. Louie spent most of his post-Army life as a mechanic and inspector of aircraft for McDonnell Douglas/Boeing Aircraft. He worked on all the F series fighter planes since 1970 when he left the Army. He is retired now and has two daughters and three grandchildren.

Notes

Endnotes for Chapter One

1. Interview by the author, with translation assistance of Professor Keith Taylor of Princeton University, January 15, 1991.

2. Seminar notes, Ministry of Education, Ho Chi Minh City, January 16, 1991; Tran Van Tra, "Tet: The 1968 General Offensive and General Uprising," in *The Vietnam War: Vietnamese and American Perspectives,* ed. Jayne S. Werner and Luu Doan Huynh (New York: Armonk, 1993), 40. Hereafter cited as Tran, "Tet: The 1968 General Offensive and Uprising."

3. Seminar notes, January 16, 1991; Tran, "Tet: The 1968 General Offensive and Uprising," 49, 51.

4. Tran, "Tet: The 1968 General Offensive and Uprising," 51; James Olson and Randy Roberts, *Where the Domino Fell: America and Vietnam, 1945–1995* (New York: St. Martin's, 1996), 185. Hereafter cited as Olson and Roberts, *Where the Domino Fell.*

5. Tran Van Tra, *Vietnam: History of the Bulwark B2 Theatre,* vol. 5, *Concluding the 30-Years War* (Washington, D.C.: Joint Publications Research Service, 1983), 35–36.

6. Seminar Notes, January 16, 1991; Tran, "Tet: The 1968 General Offensive and Uprising," 49, 51.

7. Ronald Spector, *After Tet: The Bloodiest Year in Vietnam* (New York: Free Press, 1992), Appendix 1. Hereafter cited as Spector, *The Bloodiest Year.*

8. Spector, *The Bloodiest Year,* xvi.

9. Joseph Alsop, "Khe Sanh, Major Turning Point," *The Washington Post,* January 31, 1968; "U.S. Recaptures Embassy in Saigon in 6 Hour Siege," *Baltimore Sun,* January 31, 1968.

10. Olson and Roberts, *Where the Domino Fell,* 185.

11. Olson and Roberts, *Where the Domino Fell,* 188.

12. Ibid.

13. Olson and Roberts, *Where the Domino Fell,* 170–71; William S. Turley, "Tactical Defeat, Strategic Victory for Hanoi," in *Major Problems in the History of the Vietnam War,* ed. Robert J. McMahon (Lexington, MA: D. C. Heath, 1995), 376–77. Hereafter cited as Turley, "Tactical Defeat, Strategic Victory for Hanoi."

14. Clark M. Clifford, "A Vietnam Reappraisal: The Personal History of One Man's View and How it Evolved," *Foreign Affairs,* July 1969, 609–13.

15. Charles Mohr, "Departure of Westmoreland May Spur Shift in Strategy," *New York Times,* March 24, 1968.

16. "Johnson Calls for Negotiations," document in Robert J. McMahon, ed., *Major Problems in the History of the Vietnam War,* 356–61.

17. Tran Van Tra, *Vietnam,* 35–36; and Tran Van Tra, "Tet: The 1968 General Offensive and General Uprising," 37–65.

18. George D. Moss, *Vietnam: An American Ordeal* (Upper Saddle River, NJ: Prentice Hall, 2002), 478.

Endnotes for Chapter Two

1. Rod Powers, "Army Enlisted Job Descriptions and Qualifications" *www.usmilitary.about.com:* Accessed November 25, 2009.

2. Spector, *After Tet,* 35.

3. "The M-16: What Went Wrong?" Transcript from ABC Television Program, Broadcast January 6, 1968, 1. Hereafter cited as ABC, "M-16: What Went Wrong?"

4. *Investigating Subcommittee of the Committee on Armed Services of the U.S. Senate, 19th Congress, First Session, April 5, 1967* (Washington, D.C.: U.S. Government Printing Office, 1968), 3, 7, 11. Hereafter cited as *Senate Hearings on M-16.*

5. "Army Rejects M-16 Rifles," and "M-16 A1," *New York Times,* August 28, 1968.

6. Major Thomas Johnson, "The AK-47," *Army,* June 1970, 40–45.

7. Ibid.

8. Ibid.

9. ABC, "M-16: What Went Wrong?" 10.

10. Huong Duy and Ngoc Doanh, *Quan Doi Nhan Dan,* October 23, 1970, "Practical Military Matters: Using the Weapon of the Enemy Against the

Enemy, The M-16 Rifle," Vietnam Virtual Archives. *http://ttu.edu*. Accessed December 16, 2009.

11. Walt Rostow, Memorandum to President Johnson, February 13, 1968, "Information on Republic of Vietnam Armed Forces," p.1, National Archives and Records Center II, College Park, Maryland; ABC Transcript, "M-16: What Went Wrong?" 2; Captain William Smith, "The M-16 is a Good Rifle Says a Veteran of 82 Patrols," *American Rifleman*, January 1969, 24; Major Thomas Johnson, "The AK-47," *Army*, June 1970, 40–45.

12. In 1972, I was the director of a program called the Veteran's Education and Training Service in Cleveland, Ohio. A local T.V. station gave us some news coverage. Bobby saw the news and came to my office.

13. Spector, *After Tet*, 33–35.

14. "The Ho Chi Minh Trail," Vietnam Virtual Archives, Douglas Pike Collection, p. 1. Hereafter cited as Pike, "The Ho Chi Minh Trail." Douglas Pike, *The VC Strategy of Terror* (Washington D.C.: Indo China Archive, 1970), 45–49; "History of the PLAF-PAVN Sapper Unit," History of the Vietnam War on Microfilm, Ann Arbor, Michigan, 2, 8, 11; Vietnam Virtual Archives, "Operation *Putnam Panther*, Operations Report, Lessons Learned, February 30–April 30, 1969," 25, 1; and, "*Putnam Panther* Operations Report, Lessons Learned, Intelligence Report, January 31 to April 30, 1969," 5, and 8–9.

15. "*Putnam Panther*, Operations Report, Lessons Learned, February 30–April 30, 1969," 1; "Operations Report, Lessons Learned, *Putnam Panther*, Intelligence Report, January 31 to April 30, 1969," 11, Vietnam Virtual Archives. "Operation *Putnam Panther*, Operations Report, Lessons Learned, Intelligence Report, January 31 to April 30, 1969," 11, and 2, Vietnam Virtual Archives; Michael Kelley, *Where We Were in Vietnam* (Central Point, OR: Hellgate Press, 2002), 5-280; "Operation *Putnam Panther*, Combat After Action Report," February 1 to June 16, 1969," 3, "Operation Report, 2nd Brigade, 4th Infantry Division, Lessons Learned, February 30-April 30, 1969," 2, Vietnam Virtual Archives. Associated Press Report, Saigon, March 26, 1969, "GIs Hurl Back Big Assault," and Kelley, *Where We Were*, 5-418.

16. "Operation *Putnam Panther*, Combat After Action Report," February 1–June 16, 1969," pp. 8–9.

Endnotes for Chapter 3

1. Major J. F. Harris, "Lessons Learned, Bulletin Number 76, Vietnamization 1969," Vietnam Virtual Archives, and the Army War College, 1. Hereafter cited as Harris, "Vietnamization, 1969."

2. "Beginning of the End," *Newsweek*, July 21, 1969, 14.

3. Harris, "Vietnamization, 1969," 7.

4. Harris, "Vietnamization, 1969," 7–9.

5. "Beginning of the End," *Newsweek*, July 21, 1969, 14.

6. Harris, "Vietnamization, 1969," A 2.

7. Moss, *Vietnam: An American Ordeal*, 462; Col. C. R. Carlson, USAF/PIO, "MACV Monthly Summary, Chronology of Significant Events," Entry for September 4, 1969.

8. "Report of 5th VC Region Announcing Ho Chi Minh's Death, and Review of Events of Summer 69," Captured Document, Vietnam Virtual Archives, *http://archive.vietnam.ttu.edu/cgi-bin/starfetch.exe?5TaZzXqx9M.xCKKP7G9-bfvBkpG4yzb@gqMcus7Gru49FcpVVj0ZumeppKFzcKEBKn.QX90oHHb-w2uSoK7N7P6kV3@TPpGmamzpP5wYE6BA8/2310309010.pdf1*.

9. "Report of 5th VC Region Announcing Ho Chi Minh's Death, and Review of Events of Summer 69," 2.

10. "Operation Report, First Battalion, 22nd Regiment, Fourth Infantry Division, August 1 to October 31, 1969," 1. This and the other military reports cited in this chapter are found in the National Archives and Records Center II unless otherwise noted.

11. "Gook" was one of a number of racist dehumanizing terms used to describe the enemy in Vietnam.

12. "Second Brigade, Fourth Infantry Division, After Action Report, Operation *Putnam Tiger*, April 16 to September 22, 1969," 6. Hereafter cited as "Second Brigade, Operation *Putnam Tiger*."

13. "Second Brigade, Operation *Putnam Tiger*," 7.

14. "Operation Report, Lessons Learned, General Intelligence Report for Fourth Division, August 1 to October 31, 1969," 3, 9.

15. "Operations Report, Lessons Learned, 2nd Brigade Highlanders, August 1 to October 31, 1969," 7.

16. "Operations Report, 4th Infantry Division, First Battalion, 22nd Regiment, August 1 to October 31, 1969," 1–3; Kelley, *Where We Were*, 5-43, 5-450, and 5-213 for the locations of the firebases.

17. "Operations Report, 4th Infantry Division, First Battalion, 22nd Regiment, August 1 to October 31, 1969," 4.

18. "Operation *Putnam Tiger*, Operations Report, Lessons Learned, April to July, 1969, Pleiku and Bin Dinh Provinces," 6.

19. "MACV Monthly Summary, News Releases, September 1969, Binh Dinh Province, September 20 and 23, 1969," 14.

20. "MACV Monthly Summary, News Releases, September 27, 1969," 16.

21. "Operation *Putnam Cougar*, Operation Report, After Action Report," 3–4.

22. Ibid.

23. "Operation *Putnam Cougar*, After Action Report, Chronological Summary," 6.

24. Ralph Blumenthal, "Maps of Infiltration Trails Guide GIs Stalking Foe," *New York Times*, December 15, 1969.

25. Ibid.

26. John Prados, *The Blood Road: The Ho Chi Minh Trail and the Vietnam War* (New York: John Wiley & Sons, 1998). Hereafter cited as Prados, *The Blood Road*.

27. John Prados, *The Blood Road*, 3; Blumenthal, "Stalking Foe."

28. Kelley, *Where We Were*, 5-213, 5-538.

29. "Operations Report, Lessons Learned, 22nd Regiment, Fourth Infantry Division, August 1 to October 31, 1969," 9–12.

30. "Operations Report, First Battalion, 22nd Regiment, August 1 to October 31, 1969," 1, 7.

31. James Olson and Randy Roberts, *My Lai: A Brief History with Documents* (Boston: Bedford Books, 1997), 146, 203.

32. C. D. B. Bryan, *Friendly Fire* (Boston: Putnam, 1976), and Peg Mullen, *Unfriendly Fire: A Mother's Memoir* (Iowa City: University of Iowa Press, 1995). Hereafter cited as Bryan, *Friendly Fire,* and Mullen, *Unfriendly Fire.*

33. Bryan, *Friendly Fire*, 341–79, and Peg Mullen, letter to Marie Gillam, November 6, 1970.

34. Bryan, *Friendly Fire*, 341–79, and Peg Mullen, letter to Marie Gillam, November 6, 1970.

End Notes for Chapter 4

1. Kelley, *Where We Were*, 5-47.

2. Lieutenant Harold G. Moore and Joseph Galloway, *We Were Soldiers Once, and Young* (New York: Random House, 1992), xxi.

3. "Operation *Putnam Wildcat*, November 1, 1969, to January 18, 1970, After Action Report, Concept and Execution of Operation," 1-5, and "Operation *Putnam Wildcat*, After Action Report, General Intelligence," 1-4. Both found in the National Archives and Records Center II.

4. "Operation *Putnam Wildcat*, Operations Report, Lessons Learned, First Battalion, 22nd Regiment, Nov. 1, 1969, to Jan 31, 1970, Enemy Strength, Tactics, and Losses," 2. This and the other operation reports cited in this chapter are found in the National Archives and Records Center II.

5. "Operation *Putnam Wildcat*, After Action Report, General Intelligence," 1.

6. "Duty Officer's Log, 1st Battalion, 22nd Regiment, 4th Infantry Division, November 1, 1969," entries for 0225, and 0530.

7. "Duty Officer's Log, 1st Battalion, 22nd Regiment, 4th Infantry Division, November 2, 1969." Entry for 0959, reads B Co, 2nd Platoon road security reports civilians who want to go past them to the river.

8. The Battalion Duty Officer's Radio Log is where the content of all radio traffic is recorded. These logs serve as an *aide memoir* for the officer assigned to write the "Chronology of Significant Events" attached to "After Action Reports" which are submitted at the end of major operations. All these documents are found in the National Archives and Records Center II in College Park, Maryland.

9. "Duty Officer's Log, First Battalion, 22nd Regiment, Fourth Infantry Division, November 3, 1969." The entry for 0735 said, "0735 C Co, 1st platoon had an ambush. 5 Dinks walk up on their position. The initial man in ambush tried to fire but weapon failed. He then knocked Dink to the ground, pulled back his charging handle and got a double feed. At this time another US fired at Dinks who were fleeing to west. They captured 1 pith helmet and 1 RPG and launcher. C Co found blood trail and are tracking. Found one pair of Ho Chi sandals. 0820 found another trail with tracks from 35–40 people on it."

10. "Duty Officer's Log, First Battalion, 22nd Regiment, Fourth Infantry Division, November 11, 1969," 1-4.

11. "Duty Officer's Log, First Battalion, 22nd Regiment, Fourth Infantry Division, November 16, 1969," entry for 0245.

12. Ibid.

13. "Duty Officer's Log, First Battalion, 22nd Regiment, Fourth Infantry Division, November 17, 1969," entry for 1815, Plan Summary.

14. "Duty Officer's Log, First Battalion, 22nd Regiment, Fourth Infantry Division, November 17, 1969," entries for 1920, 1921, and 1925.

15. "Duty Officer's Log, First Battalion, 22nd Regiment, Fourth Infantry Division, November 19, 1969," entry for 0945.

16. "Duty Officer's Log, First Battalion, 22nd Regiment, Fourth Infantry Division, November 19, 1969," entry for 0921.

17. "Duty Officer's Log, First Battalion, 22nd Regiment, Fourth Infantry Division, November 19, 1969," entry for 1425.

18. "Duty Officer's Log, First Battalion, 22nd Regiment, Fourth Infantry Division, November 20, 1969," entries for 1839, 1835, 1856, 1905, 1906, 1930, 1940, and 1945.

19. "Personnel Information for Operation *Putnam Wildcat*, Operations Report, Lessons Learned, First Battalion, 22nd Regiment, November 1, 1969, to January 31, 1970," 1 shows that at that time, the First Battalion, 22nd Infantry Regiment had 39 officers and 807 enlisted men.

20. This medic was promoted to sergeant, and moved to the battalion surgeon's staff because of the quality of his work. His initiative and care of my hands saved me from amputation of one or more fingers. Years later, this man's daughter was one of my students at Spelman College. She was one of several people who motivated me to write this book.

21. Brig. Gen. William Potts, MACV, "Medical Causes of Non-Effectiveness Among VC/NVA Troops (Third Update)." This document is available through both the University of California, Indo China Archive's History of the Vietnam War on Microfilm Series, and the Vietnam Virtual Archives Project at Texas Tech University. The URL for the Virtual Archives version is *http:/www.vietnam.ttu.edu*. Accessed December 15, 2009. Hereafter cited as Gen. Potts, "Medical Causes of Non-Effectiveness."

22. Gen. Potts, "Medical Causes of Non-Effectiveness," Introduction, i.

23. Gen. Potts, "Medical Causes of Non-Effectiveness," 2, and Annex C-1.

24. Gen. Potts, "Medical Causes of Non-Effectiveness," 2-5, and Annex E

25. Gen. Potts, "Medical Causes of Non-Effectiveness," 2, 12, 8.

26. "Operations Report, Lessons Learned, First Battalion, 22nd Regiment, Fourth Infantry Division, August 1 to October 31, 1969," 9–12.

27. "Copy of Public Papers of the Presidents of the U.S., Richard Nixon, 1969," 901–9, Vietnam Virtual Archives, *http:/www.vietnam.ttu.edu*. Accessed December 16, 2009.

28. "The Beginning of the End," *Newsweek*, July 21, 1969, 14.

29. "Duty Officer's Log, First Battalion, 22nd Regiment, Fourth Infantry Division, November 29, 1969," entry for 1650, Plan Summary for B Company, November 29–30.

30. "Duty Officer's Log, First Battalion, 22nd Regiment, Fourth Infantry Division, December 5, 1969," entry for 1100; December 6, entry for 1135; December 10, entry for 1042, 1420, and 1700; December 11, entry for 1230. Also see "Operation *Putnam Wildcat*, November 1, 1969 to January 18, 1970, "After Action Report, Chronological Summary of Events," 18–26. All found in National Archives and Records Center II in College Park, Maryland.

31. Douglas Pike, *The VC Strategy of Terror* (Washington D.C.: Indo China Archive, 1970), 43–52 for the four-point strategy against American forces, and 1-2 for the rationale for executing Captain Versace and Sergeant Roarback.

32. "Operation *Putnam Wildcat*, Operations Report, Lessons Learned, November 1, 1969, to January 31, 1970, Enemy Strength, Tactics, and Losses," 3, and, "Operation *Putnam Wildcat* November 1, 1969 to January 18, 1970, After Action Report, Results," 5.

33. "Duty Officer's Log, First Battalion, 22nd Regiment, Dec 25, 1969, LZ Beaver/Stinger," entry for 0751 shows that the B Co ambush from night before closed. The entry for 1321 noted that B Co 2nd platoon had a short-range patrol that returned to the Company Command Post at 1420. At 1710 a plan summary for December 26, 1969, was entered. B Co was ordered to continue search-and-clear operations in this Area of Operations. 1st and 2nd platoons got two coordinates to check, and 3rd platoon got three places to check.

34. "Operation *Putnam Wildcat* November 1, 1969 to January 18, 1970," and "After Action Report, Results," 5–6.

35. "Operation *Putnam Wildcat*, Operations Report, Lessons Learned, First Battalion 22nd Nov. 1, 1969 to Jan 31, 1970, Personnel Information," 4.

Endnotes for Chapter 5

1. Kelley, *Where We Were*, 5-213.

2. 1st Lt Leslie B. Hardy Infantry Adjutant, "After Action Report, Operation *Putnam* in Base Area 226, January 18–Feb 7, 1970, " 1. Found in National Archives and Records Center II. Hereafter cited as Hardy, "After Action Report."

3. William P. Head, *War from Above the Clouds: B-52 Operations During the Second Indochina War and the Effects of the Air War on Theory and Doctrine* (Maxwell Air Force Base, AL: Air University Press, 2002), 18–20. Hereafter cited as Head, *War from Above.*

4. Head, *War from Above*, 21.

5. E. W. Pheiffer and Arthur Westig, "Environmental Impact of Modern Weapons Technology in S. E. Asia," *Environment* 13, no. 9, 1. Hereafter cited as Pheiffer and Westig, "Environmental Impact."

6. Pheiffer and Westig, "Environmental Impact," 1, 10–11.

7. Moss, *Vietnam: An American Ordeal*, 238–39; Bryce Nelson, "Studies Find Danger in Herbicides," *LA Times,* Oct. 10, 1969.

8. Liberation Press Agency (Clandestine) Dec 15, 1970, "Liberation Committee Denounces U.S. Chemical Warfare," 16–17, and L7–L8, Vietnam Virtual Archives, Texas Tech University.

9. Bryce Nelson, "Studies Find Danger in Herbicides," *LA Times* Oct. 10, 1969.

10. Liberation Press Agency (Clandestine) Dec 15, 1970, "Liberation Committee Denounces U.S. Chemical Warfare," 16-17, and L7-L8, Vietnam Virtual Archives, Texas Tech University.

11. Hardy, "After Action Report," 3-4.

12. "Operation *Putnam Power*, Chronology of Significant Events," entry for January 24, 1970. This and other operation reports cited in this chapter are found in the National Archives and Records Center II in College Park, Maryland.

13. "Operation *Putnam Power*, Chronology of Significant Events," entry for February 7, 1970.

14. Hardy, "After Action Report," 5–6.

15. Ibid.

Endnotes for Chapter 6

1. Kelley, *Where We Were*, 5-306.

2. "Duty Officer's Log, 1st Battalion, 22nd Regiment, February 16, 1970," entries for 10:02, 11:45, and 13:25. This and other logs cited in this chapter are found in the National Archives and Records Center II in College Park, Maryland.

3. "Duty Officer's Log, 1st Battalion, 22nd Regiment, February 16, 1970," entries for 17:00 and 17:35.

4. "Duty Officer's Log, 1st Battalion, 22nd Regiment, February 16, 1970," entry for 22:01.

5. "Duty Officer's Log, 1st Battalion, 22nd Regiment, February 17, 1970," entry for 09:25.

6. "Duty Officer's Log, First Battalion, 22nd Regiment, February 17, 1970," entry for 10:04.

7. "Duty Officer's Log, First Battalion, 22nd Regiment, February 17, 1970," entry for 14:04.

8. "Duty Officer's Log, First Battalion, 22nd Regiment, February 17, 1970," entries for 16:40 and 16:45.

9. Information for placement of NVA and VC Base Areas in II Corps Area on this map found at Ben's Phaster Online Encyclopedia, *www.phaster.com* (Accessed December 15, 2009) and *http://www.mapquest.com/maps?city+An+Khe* (Accessed December 15, 2009).

10. "Duty Officer's Log, First Battalion, 22nd Regiment, February 18, 1970," entries for 10:23 and 10:24 recorded that Company A picked up a Chieu Hoi and B Company, Second Platoon, fired on one enemy with small-arms fire and found only a large blood trail.

11. "Duty Officer's Log, First Battalion, 22nd Regiment, February 18, 1970," entries for 14:00 and 17:10.

12. "Duty Officer's Log, First Battalion, 22nd Regiment, February 18, 1970," entries for 11:15 and 16:10.

13. "Duty Officer's Log, First Battalion, 22nd Regiment, February 18, 1970," entries for 22:25 and 22:50.

14. "Duty Officer's Log, First Battalion, 22nd Regiment, February 19, 1970," entries for 09:34 and 10:45.

15. "Duty Officer's Log, First Battalion, 22nd Regiment, February 19, 1970," entry for 11:06.

16. "Duty Officer's Log First Battalion, 22nd Regiment, February 19, 1970," entry for 12:25 records the capture of a female prisoner who claimed the unit she was traveling with contained children.

17. "Duty Officer's Log, First Battalion, 22nd Regiment, February 19, 1970," entries for 12:25 p.m., 13:35 and 14:00.

18. "Duty Officer's Log, First Battalion, 22nd Regiment, February 19, 1970," entry for 14:00.

19. "Duty Officer's Log, First Battalion, 22nd Regiment, February 19, 1970," entries for 12:25 p.m. and 17:00.

20. "Duty Officer's Log, First Battalion, 22nd Regiment, February 19, 1970," entry for 11:45.

21. Punji stakes were foot-long pieces of sharpened bamboo planted along likely avenues of enemy approach. The tips were usually dipped in feces. They could kill you outright if you fell on one in the middle of a firefight, or at minimum, they could give you gangrene or hepatitis if they hit a non-vital spot.

22. "Duty Officer's Log, First Battalion, 22nd Regiment, February 22, 1970," entry for 10:12 reported that B Company, Second Platoon, put out two ambushes and took a Chieu Hoi who was wounded in a running firefight as he fled in direction of LZ Louis. The man was Medevaced within the hour and turned over to the ARVN K-75 Rangers for interrogation.

23. "Duty Officer's Log, First Battalion, 22nd Regiment, February 22, 1970," entry for 11:55 was a request for Dustoff for two men. Advised use of a jungle penetrator and litter basket at grid reference 490016.

24. "Duty Officer's Log, First Battalion, 22nd Regiment, February 22, 1970," entry for 12:20 notes the Dustoff and gunship on station. Entry for 12:40 notes that the Medevac was completed by Dustoff Helicopter # 47 and its escort.
25. "Duty Officer's Log, First Battalion, 22nd Regiment, February 22, 1970," entry for 13:20.
26. "Duty Officer's Log, First Battalion, 22nd Regiment, February 22, 1970," entries for 23:00 and 24:00 of February 23, 1970.
27. Death Notice for Robert D. Frost, *http://22inf.bravepages.com/frostpers.htm*. Accessed December 16, 2009. This site is no longer active. Obituary printed in *The Lawton Constitution*, February 25, 1970, p. 7.
28. "Duty Officer's Log, First Battalion, 22nd Regiment, February 22, 1970," entries for 11:54 and "First Battalion, Daily Summary, February 22, 1970," and "Daily Staff Journal, First Battalion, 22nd Regiment," also indicate that Company A captured a man on February 22 who escaped, and that they killed him in a firefight three days later. He was identified by the fact he was missing his big toe, which had been shot off during the first encounter.
29. "Duty Officer's Log, First Battalion, 22nd Regiment, February 19, 1970," entries for 09:34 and 10:45, record the discovery of women's underwear and children's toys in the area. Entry for 13:25 that day records the capture of a female prisoner who claimed the unit she was traveling with contained children. "Duty Officer's Log, First Battalion, 22nd Regiment, March 1, 1970," entries for 11:30 and 11:54 record the discovery of the grave and a child's body inside by B Company, First Platoon.
30. Kelley, *Where We Were*, 5-499; "Duty Officer's Log, First Battalion, 22nd Regiment, March 10, 1970," entry for 14:30, and "First Battalion, 22nd Regiment Daily Staff Journal, March 10, 1970."
31. "Duty Officer's Log, First Battalion, 22nd Regiment, March 31, 1970," entry for 08:00, and "First Battalion, 22nd Regiment Daily Staff Journal March 31, 1970." Also, "Duty Officer's Log, First Battalion, 22nd Regiment April 1, 1970," entry for 22:04 and "First Battalion, 22nd Regiment, Daily Staff Journal, April 1, 1970."
32. Kelley, *Where We Were*, 5-99.
33. "Duty Log Officer's Log, First Battalion, 22nd Regiment, April 14, 1970," entry for 16:50; "First Battalion, 22nd Regiment, Daily Staff Journal, April 14, 1970."
34. "Duty Officer's Log, First Battalion, 22nd Regiment, April 17, 1970," entry for 12:40.
35. Xuan Phuong, "Actively Spreading a Wide Net to Down U.S. Helicopters" in *Quon Doi Nhan Dan*, March 13, 1970, 11–13.

36. "Duty Officer's Log, First Battalion, 22nd Infantry," April 17, 1970. Entry for 12:40 notes the battalion commander's aircraft was forced to land at LZ Niagara due to small arms damage and the pursuit of the individual by B Company's 1st and 3rd platoons. The entries for 15:53 and 16:16 note a brief firefight with 3rd platoon and the negative results of their sweep of the area.

37. Ibid., entry for 17:35.

Endnotes for Chapter Seven

1. D.R. SarDesai, *Vietnam, Past and Present*, 3rd ed. (Boulder: Westview Press, 1998), 7.

2. Seymour Hersh, *The Price of Power: Kissinger in the Nixon White House* (Orangeville: Simon and Schuster, 1983), 175.

3. James Lowenstein and Richard Moose, *Cambodia: May 1970, A Staff Report Prepared for the Use of the Committee on Foreign Relations, United States Senate, June 7, 1970, Part I, Events Since the Fall of Sihanouk* (Washington, D.C.:U.S. Government Printing Office, 2003), 1–3. Hereafter cited as Lowenstein and Moose, *Cambodia: Senate Foreign Relations Committee, Part I.*

4. Ibid.; Arnold Isaacs, *Without Honor: Defeat in Vietnam and Cambodia* (Baltimore: Johns Hopkins University Press, 1983), Chapter 8, "The Fall of the Khmer Republic," 242–89, and Wilfred Deac, *The Road to the Killing Fields, the Cambodian War of 1970–1975* (College Station: Texas A&M University Press, 1997), 57–58, 60–61.

5. George Webb, Colonel, Acting Chief of Staff, "II Field FORCEV (II FFORCEV), Commander's Evaluation Report—Cambodian Operations," Douglas Pike Collection, Vietnam Virtual Archives, 7. Hereafter cited as Webb, "II FFORCEV, Commander's Evaluation Report—Cambodian Operations."

6. Lowenstein and Moose, *Cambodia: Senate Foreign Relations Committee Part I,* 2, 4, and *Part IV Military Benefits,* 7–8. Also, Webb, "II FFORCEV, Commander's Evaluation Report—Cambodian Operations," 1–3.

7. Webb, "II FFORCEV, Commander's Evaluation Report—Cambodian Operations, Objectives," p. 2, Pike Collection, Vietnam Project, 9; David L. Anderson, *The Columbia Guide to the Vietnam War* (New York: Columbia University Press, 2002), 103–104.

8. Lowenstein and Moose, *Cambodia: Senate Foreign Relations Committee Staff Report, Part IV Military Benefits,* 4.

9. Lowenstein and Moose, *Cambodia: Senate Foreign Relations Committee Staff Report, Part IV Military Benefits*, 3–4 and "White House Briefing Report," April 30, 1970, .2.

10. Webb, "II FFORCEV, Commander's Evaluation Report—Cambodian Operations," 5.

11. Ibid.

12. Kelley, *Where We Were*, 5-260, and 5-410; Major Malcom Dixon, Adjutant, III Corps Mobile Task Force, "Operation *Binh Tay I*, Execution," 3, found in the National Archives and Records Center II in College Park, Maryland.

13. Kelley, *Where We Were*, 5-43; Dixon, "Operation *Binh Tay I*, Execution," 3.

14. Webb, "II FFORCEV, Commander's Evaluation Report—Cambodian Operations," 8–9, and, "General Intelligence: Enemy Strength," 1–2.

Endnotes for Chapter Eight

1. Col. George Webb, Acting Chief of Staff, II FFORCEV Vietnam (II FFORCEV), "Commander's Evaluation Report—Cambodian Operations, Execution," 3. This report and the others cited in this chapter can be found in the National Archives and Records Center II, College Park, Maryland.

2. Col. George Webb, Acting chief of Staff, II FFORCEV *Vietnam* (II FFORCEV), "Commander's Evaluation Report—Cambodian Operations, Chronological Summary," entries for 1600 May 7, and 07:24 May 8, 1970, 1–3.

3. Ibid.

4. Col. George Webb, Acting Chief of Staff, II FFORCEV Vietnam (II FFORCEV), "Commander's Evaluation Report—US Operations," 8-9.

5. Col. George Webb, Acting Chief of Staff, II FFORCEV Vietnam (II FFORCEV), "Commander's Evaluation Report—Cambodian Operations, Annex B: Intelligence," 3.

6. Col. George Webb, Acting Chief of Staff, II FFORCEV Vietnam (II FFORCEV), "Commander's Evaluation Report—Cambodian Operations, Appendix 12 (US and GVN Operational Area), Annex A (Summary of Operations) to Commander's Evaluation Report—Cambodian Operations."

7. Col. George Webb, Acting Chief of Staff, II FFORCEV Vietnam (II FFORCEV), "Commander's Evaluation Report—Cambodian Operations, Enemy Losses," 5.

8. Ibid.

9. Col. George Webb, Acting Chief of Staff, II FFORCEV Vietnam (II FFORCEV), "Commander's Evaluation Report—Cambodian Operations, U.S. Operations," 8.

10. Col. George Webb, Acting Chief of Staff, II FFORCEV Vietnam (II FFORCEV), "Commander's Evaluation Report—Cambodian Operations, Annex B: Intelligence," 3.

11. Ibid.

12. Major Malcom Dixon, Adjutant, III Corps Mobile Task Force, "*Operation Binh Tay I*, Chronological Summary of Important Events," 1. Found in the National Archives and Records Center II in College Park, Maryland.

13. Ibid., 4.

14. Col. George Webb, Acting Chief of Staff, II FFORCEV Vietnam (II FFORCEV), "Annex C to II FORCEV Commander's Evaluation, Report—Commander's Evaluation, Friendly Losses," 9.

15. Ibid., 2.

16. The Senate Foreign Relations Committee suspected that President Nixon was not truthful about cross-border operations in the winter and spring of 1970, so they sent James Lowenstein and Richard Moose, two Department of State investigators, to gather information independent of the president and MACV.

17. Lowenstein and Moose, *Cambodia: Senate Foreign Relations Committee Staff Report Part IV, Military Benefits* (Washington, D.C.: U.S. Government Printing Office, 2003), 7.

18. Col. George Webb, Acting Chief of Staff, II FFORCEV Vietnam (II FFORCEV), "Commander's Evaluation Report—Cambodian Operations," 4.

19. Julie Morgan, interview of Donald McBane conducted for the Vietnam Archive Oral History Project, Lubbock, Texas, February 19 and 21, 1990, 2, 7, and 22–24. Available on website: *www.vietnam.ttu.edu.*

Endnotes for Chapter Nine

1. Kelley, *Where We Were*, 5-42.

2. The 1st Battalion, 12th Regiment, the 2nd Battalion, 35th Regiment, and of course, my unit, the 1st Battalion, 22nd Regiment.

3. "Operation *Putnam Paragon*, Operations Report/After Action, General Intelligence," 4. This and the other military reports cited in this chapter were found in the National Archives and Records Center II in College Park, Maryland.

4. "Operation *Putnam Paragon*, Operations Report, Execution," 1-5.

5. Kelley, *Where We Were*, 5-99 for the location of LZ Challenge, and "Operation *Putnam Paragon*, Chronological Summary of Significant Events," entry for May 20, 1970, 10:45.

6. "Operation *Putnam Paragon*, Operations Report, Execution," 1–5.

7. Kelly, *Where We Were*, 5-279, 5-544, 5-36.

8. "Operation *Putnam Paragon*, Operations Report, Execution," 5.

9. "Operation *Putnam Paragon*, After Action Report," 5.

10. "First Battalion, 22nd Infantry, Fourth Infantry Division, Duty Officer's Log," entry for June 5, 1970, 12:30.

11. "Operation *Putnam Paragon*, After Action Report, General Intelligence," 5–6.

12. "First Battalion, 22nd Infantry, Fourth Infantry Division, Duty Officer's Log," entry for June 14, 1970, 11:30.

13. This man's daughter enrolled in Spelman College, in Atlanta, Georgia. During a World History class in her first year, we discussed the Vietnam War for awhile. After class, she told me her father died there when she was a child. Two days before she graduated, she and her fiancé came to my office to show me her father's Vietnam photos. She asked me to tell her about her father, and I did. I told her I wanted to put his story in this book, and she asked me to respect the privacy of her family and omit his name.

Glossary of Terms

Base Camp Commando—A derisive term used by infantrymen to describe men who lived in the safety of a base camp.

Battalion—The basic maneuver unit in the army. In the infantry, about 400 fighting men and their support network.

Bunker—A large foxhole with a log and dirt roof.

B-40 Rocket—A single shot, shoulder-fired anti-tank and anti-bunker rocket.

Claymore Mine—An electrically fired directional anti-personnel mine.

Combat Assault—A helicopter assault on an unsecured landing site.

CIB, Combat Infantry Badge—An award given in acknowledgement of skilled service as an infantry soldier.

Company—In the infantry, a unit of one-hundred-forty fighting men, officers, non-commissioned officers, and enlisted men.

Dustoff—A Medical Evacuation helicopter or the process of medical evacuation.

Fire Base or Fire Support Base—Usually a hilltop base in Vietnam where artillery support units and battalion commanders were stationed to support and direct the activities of the individual companies in a battalion.

Fish Hook Region —The border area of Cambodia and southern flank of the Cambodian invasion of 1970.

Gook—A racist term Americans used to describe the enemy in Vietnam.

Grunt—An American infantryman.

High Speed Trail—A broad trail frequently used by large numbers of people.

KIA—Killed in Action.

LZ—Landing Zone.

M-60—The standard light machinegun of the U.S. Army in Vietnam.

Medevac—A medical evacuation helicopter, or the process of evacuating wounded.

MOS—Military Occupational Specialty. Your job in the Army.

Mortar—A man-portable, crew-served short range artillery piece.

NCO—A non-commissioned officer. A corporal or any one of the ranks of sergeant.

Parrot's Beak Region—The border area of Cambodia on the northern flank of the invasion of 1970.

Platoon—In the infantry, a unit of 46 men: one junior officer, one senior NCO, four NCOs, and 40 enlisted men.

Point—The scout at the front of an infantry patrol.

REMF—A "Rear Echelon Motherfucker." A man who lived in a safe area and took advantage of those who did not.

Regiment—A military unit usually composed of four battalions and commanded by either a lieutenant colonel or a colonel.

Slack—The man behind the point man on a patrol.

Slick—A troop carrier helicopter. In Vietnam, the UH-1 "Huey" helicopter.

Squad—In the infantry, a group of ten enlisted men, led by a sergeant.

TOC—Tactical Operations Center. The nerve center of a battalion or regiment.

Trip Flare—An early warning device that ignites a flare when one trips over a wire attached to it.

WIA—Wounded in action.

Bibliography

Archives Consulted

National Archives and Records Center II, College Park, Maryland

Vietnam Virtual Archives at Texas Tech University, *http://www.vietnam.ttu.edu*

Websites Consulted

Ben's Phaster Online Encyclopedia, *www.phaster.com*. Accessed December 15, 2009.

Biography and Death notice for Robert Dean Frost. *http://c22inf.bravepages.com/frostpers.htm*. This valuable website is no longer active. *The Lawton Constitution* ran Robert Frost's obituary on February 25, 1970, p. 7.

Descriptions of Military Occupational Specialties. *http://about.comusmilitary*. Accessed December 15, 2009.

Map of "First Battalion, 22nd Infantry Area of Operations," derived from *http://freewebs.vietmap*. Accessed December 3, 2009.

Map of Major Attacks of Tet Offensive. *Commons.wikimedia.org/wiki/File:Tet-Offensive.*

Placement of NVA and VC Base Areas in II Corps Area and map of An Khe. *http://www.mapquest.com/maps.* Accessed December 15, 2009.

Powers, Rod. "Army Enlisted Job Descriptions and Qualifications," *USMilitary. about.com.* Accessed November 25, 2009.

United States Geological Survey Map, Lower (Song) An Lao River Valley. *usgs-store@usgs.gov.* Accessed November 10, 2009.

Primary Sources

"History of the PLAF-PAVN Sapper Unit," The History of the Vietnam War on Microfilm. Ann Arbor, Michigan.

Investigating Subcommittee of the Committee on Armed Services of the U.S. Senate, 19th Congress, First Session, April 5, 1967. Washington, D.C.: U.S. Government Printing Office, 1968.

Lowenstein, James, and Richard Moose. *Cambodia: May 1970, A Staff Report, Prepared for the Use of the Committee on Foreign Relations, United States Senate, June 7, 1970, Part I, Events Since the Fall of Sihanouk.* Washington, D.C.:U.S. Government Printing Office, 2003.

———. *Cambodia: Senate Foreign Relations Committee Staff Report, Part III, The View from Cambodia.* Washington, D.C.:U.S. Government Printing Office, 2003.

———. *Cambodia: Senate Foreign Relations Committee Staff Report, Part IV, Military Benefits.* Washington, D.C.: U.S. Government Printing Office, 2003.

"The M-16: What Went Wrong?" Transcript from ABC Television Program, broadcast January 6, 1968.

Mullen, Mrs. Peg, Letter to Mrs. Marie Gillam, November 6, 1970.

Potts, Brig. Gen. William, MACV. Seminar Notes, Ministry of Education, Ho Chi Minh City, January 16, 1991.

Tran Van Tra, interview with author, Ho Chi Minh City, January 16, 1991, with translation assistance provided by Professor Keith Taylor of Princeton University.

United States Military Assistance Command Vietnam. *Vietcong Base Campus and Supply Caches: Counterinsurgency Lessons Learned No. 68.* Saigon, Republic of South Vietnam, 1969.

Books and Book Chapters

Anderson, David L. *The Columbia Guide to the Vietnam War.* New York: Columbia University Press, 2002.

Bryan, C. D. B. *Friendly Fire.* Boston: Putnam Publishers, 1976.

Deac, Wilfred. *The Road to the Killing Fields: The Cambodian War of 1970–75.* College Station: Texas A&M University Press, 1997.

Head, William P. *War from Above the Cloud: B-52 Operations During the Second Indochina War and the Effects of the Air War on Theory and Doctrine.* Maxwell Air Force Base, AL: Air University Press, 2002.

Hersh, Seymour. *The Price of Power: Kissinger in the Nixon White House.* Orangeville, ON: Simon and Schuster, 1983.

Isaacs, Arnold. *Without Honor: Defeat in Vietnam and Cambodia.* Baltimore: Johns Hopkins University Press, 1983.

Kelley, Michael, P. *Where We Were in Vietnam.* Central Point, OR: Hellgate Press, 2002.

McMahon, Robert, J. *Major Problems in the History of the Vietnam War*. New York: Houghton Miflin College Division, 1992.

Military Encyclopedia, 1984. London: Orbis Publishers, 1984.

Moore, Harold G., and Joseph Galloway. *We Were Soldiers Once, and Young*. New York: Random House, 1992

Moss, George D. *Vietnam: An American Ordeal*. Upper Saddle River, NJ: Prentice Hall, 2002.

———. *A Vietnam Reader: Sources and Essays*. Englewood Cliffs, NJ: Prentice Hall, 1991.

Mullen, Peg. *Unfriendly Fire: A Mother's Memoir*. Iowa City: University of Iowa Press, 1995.

Olson, James, and Randy Roberts. *Where the Domino Fell: America and Vietnam, 1945–1995*. New York: St. Martin's Press, 1996.

———. *My Lai: A Brief History with Documents*. Boston: Bedford Books, 1997.

Pike, Douglas. *The VC Strategy of Terror*. Washington, D.C.: Indo China Archive, 1970.

———. "The Ho Chi Minh Trail," in *Military Encyclopedia, 1984*. London: Orbis Publishers, 1984.

Prados, John. *The Blood Road: The Ho Chi Minh Trail and the Vietnam War*. New York: John Wiley & Sons, 1998.

SarDesai, D. R. *Vietnam, Past and Present*. 3rd ed. Boulder, CO: Westview, 1998.

Spector, Ronald. *After Tet: Bloodiest Year in Vietnam*. New York: Free Press, 1992.

Tran, Van Tra. "Tet: The 1968 General Offensive and General Uprising." In *The Vietnam War: Vietnamese and American Perspectives*, edited by Jayne S. Werner and Luu Doan Huynh. New York: Armonk, 1993.

———. *Vietnam: A History of the Bulwark B2 Theatre*. Volume 5, *Concluding the 30 Years War*. Ho Chi Minh City, 1993.

Turley, William, S. "Tactical Defeat, Strategic Victory for Hanoi." In *Major Problems in the History of the Vietnam War*, edited by Robert J. McMahon. Lexington, MA: D.C. Heath, 1995.

Articles

Alsop, Joseph. "Khe Sanh, Major Turning Point." *The Washington Post*, January 31, 1968, Vietnam Roundup, page 1.

Associated Press Report, Saigon, March 26, 1969, "GIs Hurl Back Big Assault."

Baltimore Sun, "U.S. Recaptures Embassy in Saigon in 6 Hour Siege," January 31, 1968.

"Beginning of the End." *Newsweek*, July 21, 1969.

Blumenthal, Ralph. "Maps of Infiltration Trails Guide GIs Stalking Foe," *New York Times*, December 15, 1969.

Clifford, Clark M. "A Vietnam Reappraisal: the Personal History of One Man's View and How it Evolved." *Foreign Affairs*, July 1969, 609–625.

Huong Duy and Ngoc Doanh. "Practical Military Matters: Using the Weapon of the Enemy Against the Enemy, The M-16 Rifle." Translation of article originally published in Vietnamese. *Quan Doi Nhan Dan*, October 23, 1970, 13–14. Also found in Vietnam Virtual Archives. *http://ttu.edu*. Accessed December 16, 2009.

Johnson, Major Thomas. "The AK-47." *Army*, June 1970.

Lawton Constitution, "Robert Dean Frost Killed in Action in Vietnam." Obituaries. Feb. 25, 1970, p. 7.

Liberation Press Agency (Clandestine), "Liberation Committee Denounces RVN Chemical Warfare," Dec. 15, 1970. Vietnam Virtual Archives. *http.//ttu.edu* Accessed April 26, 2010.

Mohr, Charles. "Departure of Westmoreland May Spur Shift in Strategy." *New York Times*, March 24, 1968, p. 1.

Nelson, Bryce. "Studies Find Danger in Herbicides." *LA Times,* Oct. 10, 1969, World/Asia subsection, p. 1.

New York Times, "Army Rejects M-16 Rifles," August 28, 1968.

Pheiffer, E. W., and Arthur Westing. "Environmental Impact of Modern Weapons Technology in S. E. Asia." *Environment* 13, no. 9 (November 1971): 32–49.

Smith, Captain William. "The M-16 is a Good Rifle Says a Veteran of 82 Patrols." *American Rifleman*, January 1969, 24.

Xuan Phuong. "Actively Spreading a Wide Net to Down U.S. Helicopters." *Quon Doi Nhan Dan*, March 13, 1970, pp. 23–31.

Index